The Social Sciences: A Semiotic View

The Social Sciences: A Semiotic View

Algirdas Julien Greimas

Foreword by Paolo Fabbri and Paul Perron

Translation by Paul Perron and Frank H. Collins

University of Minnesota Press, Minneapolis

The University of Minnesota Press gratefully acknowledges translation assistance provided for this book by the French Ministry of Culture.

Chapter 1, "The Meaning of Meaning," was first published under the title "Du sens," in *Du sens* (Paris: Le Seuil, 1970); chapter 2, "On Scientific Discourse in the Social Sciences," was first published under the title "Du discours scientifique en sciences sociales," in *Sémiotique et sciences sociales*, (Paris: Le Seuil, 1976), pp. 9–42; chapter 3, "The Pathways of Knowledge," was first published under the title "Les parcours du savoir" in *Introduction à l'analyse du discours en sciences sociales* (Paris: Hachette, 1979), pp. 5–27; chapter 4, "On Chance Occurrences in What We Call the Social Sciences," was first published under the title "Des accidents dans les sciences dites humaines," in *Introduction à l'analyse du discours en sciences sociales* (Paris: Hachette, 1979), pp. 28–60; chapter 5, "Structure and History," was first published under the title "Structure et histoire," in *Les Temps modernes*, 246 (Nov. 1966), pp. 815–27; chapter 6, "The Semiotic Analysis of Legal Discourse: Commercial Laws That Govern Companies and Groups of Companies," was first published under the title "Analyse sémiotique d'un discours juridique: la loi commerciale sur les sociétés et les groupes de sociétés," in *Sémiotique et sciences sociales* (Paris: Le Seuil, 1976), pp. 79–128; chapter 7, "Toward a Topological Semiotics," was first published under the title "Pour une sémiotique topologique" as the introduction to *Notes méthodologiques en architecture et en urbanisme* (Centre MMI, Institut de l'Environnement) 3–4 (1974); chapter 8, "The Challenge," was first published under the title "Le défi," in *Actes-sémiotiques-Bulletin* (EHESS-CNRS), no. 23 (1982), pp. 39–48; chapter 9, "On Nostalgia: A Study in Lexical Semantics," was first published under the title "De la nostalgie. Etude de sémantique lexicale," in *Actes sémiotiques-Bulletin* (EHESS-CNRS), 39 (1986) pp. 5–11; chapter 10, "Ten Years Afterward," was first published under the title "Introduction" in *Du sens II* (Paris: Le Seuil, 1983), pp. 7–18.

Published by the University of Minnesota Press
2037 University Avenue Southeast, Minneapolis MN 55414
Printed in the United States of America.

Library of Congress Cataloging-in-Publication Data
Greimas, Algirdas Julien.
    The social sciences, a semiotic view / Algirdas Julien Greimas ; foreword by Paolo Fabbri and Paul Perron ; translation by Paul Perron and Frank H. Collins.
        p.   cm.
    Includes index.
    ISBN 0-8166-1818-6   ISBN 0-8166-1819-4 (pbk.)
    1. Social sciences—Language.   2. Semiotics.   I. Title.
H61.G686   1990
300'.14—dc20   89-34770
                                                                          CIP

The University of Minnesota
is an equal-opportunity
educator and employer.

Contents

Foreword
Paolo Fabbri and Paul Perron

Within the general field of semiotics, it could be said that there exists today a twofold movement regarding both the application of semiotic theory and its philosophical underpinnings. At one end of the spectrum the relationships between the philosophical and the semantic postulates of the theory are questioned (for example, by deconstruction and psychoanalysis) and, at the other, relationships between the object language and its instruments (for example, the large number of applications that are more or less well done). But the originality of semiotics is that while being situated between both of these extremes, which Algirdas Julien Greimas calls the epistemological level and the level of application, it maintains the articulation between them. For him, there exists here a methodological domain in which operational concepts and discovery procedures are interdefined and made explicit: "the concepts which are first posited as postulates must at least be integrated in a network of inter-definitions which guarantees the internal coherence of the system."[1] In other words, what is innovative in this semiotic enterprise is that it is at one and the same time speculative and empirical; the very raison d'être of methodology is to establish the missing link between epistemological and textual knowledge. From this perspective, methodology constitutes the meeting ground of the theory of signs and the human sciences. It is at this level that one finds a pertinent link between the Greimassian approach as represented in this volume and the human sciences, in particular linguistics, anthropology, history, sociology, comparative mythology, and folklore. This is why semiotics can be thought of not as a normative epistemology of signification but as a metalanguage of the human sciences, if the latter is defined as being made up of disciplines of signification, that is, the way humans organize the systems and articulate the processes of meaning.

It should not be forgotten that Greimas's original training was in philology and lexicology. In examining his writings on folklore and mythology (see *On Gods and Men*, forthcoming from Indiana University Press) one recognizes the tacit knowledge that stems from a long tradition of cooperation between linguistics and anthropology. This tradition, which has its roots in comparative mythology and grammar, encompasses, for example, Viggo Brøndal and Claude Lévi-Bruhl, Louis Hjelmslev and Jocelyn de Jong and finally, Roman Jakobson and Claude Lévi-Strauss. It should be stressed, however, that the methodological operationality of Greimas's work was totally reframed during the 1960s and 1970s thanks to his encounter with French phenomenology (Maurice Merleau-Ponty) and the consequences of the Saussurian epistemological break (Claude Lévi-Strauss, Jacques Lacan, Roland Barthes, Michel Foucault, etc.). It should also be noted that the epistemological field was already extremely articulated through the major renewal of models and methods in linguistics (Lucien Tesnière, André Martinet), history (Ernst Bloc, Fernand Braudel, and the Annales School etc.), art criticism (Henri Foçillon and Pierre Francastel), and sociology of literature and knowledge (Lucien Goldmann). Although the reframing in question bore essentially on the dimension of sense and its formal articulation in meaningful patterns, Greimas's long-term, consistent project, which has been worked out for over a quarter of a century, ranges from the interrogation of the discourse of science ("On Scientific Discourse in the Social Sciences," "The Pathways of Knowledge," and "On Chance Occurrences in What We Call the Social Sciences"), to the foundation of a French commercial company as a legal entity ("The Semiotic Analysis of Legal Discourse"), passing through considerations on historical discourse (cf. "Structure and History"), urban life ("Toward a Topological Discourse"), and intersubjective communication ("The Challenge" and "On Nostalgia").

Among all the important contributors to the structural reformulation of the epistemological domain, Hjelmslev and the Danish school of glossomatics had a decisive influence on Greimas. For Hjelmslev the role of a general semiotics was to describe the semantic universe in its totality, which in effect would correspond to describing the entire culture (in his own terms the substance of the content) of an ethnolinguistic community. While maintaining the fundamental theoretical framework, shared among others with the sociosemiotic project of Michael Halliday, Greimas took a certain distance from, if not a certain liberty with, Hjelmslev on this crucial point. To come to grips with the impossibility of describing the complete semantic universe of a given culture Greimas was led to introduce the concepts of semantic microuniverses and discourse(s), which represents a shift in methodological strategy implying a basic theoretical choice. The starting point was no longer language in general but the "discursive microuniverse" — in other words, the syntagmatic manifestation of the "microuniverse of meaning" that must be reconstituted by reestablishing isotopies and the basic axiologies. This is why the semanticist had to consider carefully how different human sciences take into account different types of social discourses (genres, legal discourse, ethnic literature, mass media languages, forms of the city, sociolinguistic variants, history) and the way in which they construct signification.

The relationship between the semantic microuniverse and the discovery procedures, or the formulation of the cognitive operations that permit its description and satisfy the conditions of "scientificness," needs to be elucidated. On this crucial point Greimas follows Hjelmslev's principle of empiricism by which the theory must fulfill three hierarchically organized conditions: coherence, exhaustibility, and simplicity. These criteria, which are interpreted by Greimas as a means of giving a strategic and operational orientation to research with the view to providing an adequate description of given significations, are considered more as conceptual formulations than as formal transpositions. It is important that a proper balance be maintained between induction and deduction, the strength of the models and the interest and complexity of the data. This is best illustrated by the example of Georges Dumézil, whose work Greimas highly respects. In his book *Naissance d'Archanges*, which Greimas studied, Dumézil analyzed the theonymes of the major epic religious and folklore texts in the European tradition. Starting from morphophonetic comparativism he ended up with semantic comparativism so that divinities were no longer analyzed simply at the surface level of their names but also at the level of the content features by which the names are primarily defined as intersecting points of the semantic networks. Through this major scientific discovery Dumézil was able to reconstitute the underlying semantic system articulated in three hierarchical functions thereby laying a foundation for describing the main aspects of the ideology of Indo-European peoples. From "Comparative Mythology"[2] to "On Chance Occurrences in What We Call the Human Sciences" (included in this volume) Greimas analyzed the narrative of Dumézil's findings in "ultrahistory" in order to reconstitute the mythologist's implicit discovery procedures.

Compared with other disciplines that limit themselves to examining the meaning structure of a single culture, Greimas insists on comparativism. Both comparative linguistics, applied to the expression plane, and comparative mythology (Lévi-Strauss and Dumézil), extended to the content plane, have, in large part, contributed to the methodological basis that is at the very source of French semiotics. The importance of comparative grammars from the viewpoint of the history of sciences is considered to be crucial, since, as Greimas and Courtés remark, it "is not merely as some people believe, an outmoded historical period marking one of the stages in the development of linguistics. It is rather a theory and an effective method which explore new linguistic fields and can be applied, after the necessary transpositions, to other semiotic domains."[3] The application to comparative literature of this effective theory and practice is still awaited: "It is not beyond the bounds of possibility that the notion of intertextuality, once it has been more rigorously elaborated, might bring comparativism into literary semiotics."[4]

It should be noted that Greimas found the inspiration and the sources of his work in two of the great twentieth-century scholars of anthropology and folklore: Claude Lévi-Strauss provided Greimas with the paradigmatic aspect of the theory and Vladimir Propp with the syntagmatic or syntactic one. This is exemplary of the way Greimas has always kept closely in touch with research being undertaken in the human sciences. After working out the necessary theoretical mediations he linked together two complementary models and constructed a generalizable theory in terms of a general narrative semantics. The next step in this construction project was to free the theory from Propp's formula of the tale as a means of analyzing narrative, and an elementary syntax that could organize any types of discourse was developed. Of course, for Greimas narrative is considered as a simulacrum, "a paper being" of all significant and culturally situated human behaviors. It was shown that Propp's model could be broken down into three successive sequences, which correspond to the syntagmantic unfolding of the actantial model (paradigmatically articulated in a quest sequence [subject → object] and a communication sequence [sender → object → receiver]), in which two sequences of communication frame an action sequence. The mandate sequence and the evaluation sequence bracket the action sequence that transforms the states. From this a semiotics of manipulation was worked out, how the sender manipulates the subject; then a semiotics of action, how competence is acquired to carry out performance; and finally a semiotics of evaluation or sanction, that is, the passing of judgments on self, on others, and on things.[5] Currently, an attempt is being made to give a semiotic interpretation to passions, a decisive step since what began as theory of action that basically attributed to subjects the ability to act, now considers subjects as acting beings with character and temperament. As Greimas himself has pointed out, "To analyze discourse in this way is to construct models that can account for the trajectory of the lives of subjects, of men."[6]

The foregoing follows in the main what has occurred in the human sciences from Max Weber to Alfred Schutz, from Talcott Parsons to ethnomethodology, through Irvin Goffmann, where attempts have been made to construct a model of meaningful actions in an intersubjective frame. Greimas first constructed a model of actions before introducing notions such as modalities and aspectualities that overdetermine the actants. Four fundamental modalities (two virtual ones, wanting-to and having-to and two actualizing ones, being-able-to and knowing), as well as three aspectualities (inchoativity, durativity, and terminativity), were posited and interdefined. Then, as folktales were considered as an intersection between two conflictual and contractual actions in progress, Greimas was able to transform the Proppian model into an interactional one. Instead of a subject, an object, and an opponent, two modally competent interacting subjects were posited. Each subject, with its own modal organization, was situated in a polemico-contractual relation with the other. Strategy became more important than rules. Moreover, in addition to the system of being-able, the actantial model could account for the construction and transmission of meaning. Thanks to the work of Marcel Mauss and Claude Lévi-Strauss, communication was rethought in terms of exchange and challenge, and the concept was extended from the circulation of objects and messages to the exchange of modal values within the framework of a fiduciary contract that must be actively maintained during interaction (cf. "Knowing and Believing: A Single Cognitive Universe").[7]

The main point to be made here is that starting from different realized discursive universes a constructed semantic simulacrum can be reconstituted (see "The Challenge" and "On Nostalgia") that can be realized differently, horizontally or vertically, according to spatial and temporal variants. This hypothesis seems to be oriented in the same general direction as in the sciences of culture. For example, in cognitive anthropology, concepts such as frame, script, and scenario, syntagmatically linked by inference, are used to describe actional representation in various cultures. Opposed to these strictly cognitive notions based on inference, Greimas provides us with a conceptual framework that accentuates isomorphism and analogy and that, in addition to the actional, takes into account knowledge as well as belief, the thymic and the passional dimensions, which are the uncircumventable and often forgotten components of signification.

Yet, at the risk of repeating ourselves, the opening of the fiduciary dimension introduces the subject matter of belief and adhesion in the cognitive dimension. This raises at least two orders of questions: first of all regarding the relevance of the figurative component and, second, that of the passional. Through the mediation of the enunciative instance the virtual structures of action are realized and figurativized differently according to the categories of the natural world employed as forms of expression. As far as the passional is concerned it is possible to give an operational characterization of emotional systems and processes, that is, the transformation of the *states* of souls (*états d'âme*) of the subject with respect to the actions that incite them and to which they lead (for a syntagmatic analysis of this pathemic component — modalities, aspects, time, etc. — see "On Anger" [in *On Meaning*, pp. 148–64] and, in this volume, "The Challenge" and "On Nostalgia"). When analyzing figurativity we encounter the problem of the typology of signs, especially nonlinguistic and nonarbitrary signs, and their efficacy. When studying passions we are basically concerned with the stringing of modalities, tensivity, thymism, and in general with the dimension of bodily propioceptivity. All of these questions are essential for the development of semiotics.

If, on the one hand, from an anthropological point of view, semiotics seems concerned with deep semantic structures (e.g., at the collective level the socio-lectal universe is characterized by use of the category *nature vs. culture* and, at the individual one, by the articulation of the category *life vs. death*), on the other, this is unsatisfactory, since from a sociosemiotic perspective one has to account "for the attitude that a sociocultural community adopts with respect to funda-mental issues that it faces."[8] At a more refined level it is also necessary to re-constitute the taxonomies underlying social discourse and practice, that is, the way in which the situated interaction generates the social connotations that make up their content plane (see, e.g., Dell Hymes and John Gumperz). This is where, for example, questions are raised regarding discourse of mass media communi-cation as opposed to ethnic literature and research carried out on the semiotic epistemologies, that is, the attitude that different cultures adopt with respect to their own signs. This perspective bears a striking analogy to the Tartu school's secondary modeling systems (Yuri Lotman) and Michel Foucault's concepts of discursive formation and episteme considered as languages with a general meta-semiotics of culture.

Furthermore, although it has always taken into consideration the social com-ponents of texts, contrary to widespread commonplaces, semiotics has never ig-nored historical relevance. Greimas has continually been involved in the histor-ical debate in an attempt to overcome the opposition between dialectical reason and analytic reason, dramatized by Jean-Paul Sartre and Claude Lévi-Strauss. In "Structure and History" (this volume) he demonstrates that one can constitute narrative structures beginning with the different structures of duration (struc-tural, conjunctural, and evenemential), economy, society, and mentality. In this text Greimas attempts to show how narrative events are generated from structures of long duration, whereas in another essay, "On Evenemential History," he sought to illustrate how these abstract syntagmatic utterances are realized in ty-pologies of variable discursive genres in different periods of time.[9] If today we see that vast historical frescoes are being abandoned for the biographical narra-tive, we also are aware of how Foucault's approach to discursive formations is in the process of renewing nonanecdotal historical approaches, for example, Paul Veyne's work. It is in this vein that Greimas as well as Michel de Certeau have insisted on the importance of historical microuniverses, which, like literature, can subsume any human signification.

It is at the same time a strength as well as a distinctive feature of semiotics to be able to describe texts of different types and conceptual levels, including philo-sophical and scientific ones. This implies once again that, contrary to what has often been stated, or, what we have not been led to believe, semiotics is neither a general philosophy of signification nor a metadiscipline of the human sciences, but is able to analyze the theoretical texts of the social sciences to lay bare their underlying episteme and make it possible to confront and evaluate them.[10] In the same way, it is important that semiotics itself not only be "the science of the science it is" but also carry out the description of its own discourse and its own concepts and methods. This reflexivity, which is at the heart of any practice of signification (metalanguages being only a level of natural language), is not a paradox but a fruitful option for understanding its own cognitive as well as social activity. Indeed, after having defined semiotics in a rigorously Hjelmslevian way (scientific sign system, the object of which is a nonscientific system of signs), Greimas has pointed out the dual possibility of "disloyalty," that of Barthes studying languages of connotations in a nonstructural way, and that of logicians using metasemiotic systems that have sign systems as their object. But, perhaps all progress in a discipline is as much at the price of loyalty as of disloyalty, and the question for semiotics should be to semioticize its own disloyalities. This is what Greimas seems to do when he deals with structural connotations within the framework of the social sciences. His text "On Theoretical Models in Sociolinguistics" could provide us with a definition of the discursive features of science for the reflexive treatment of semiotic discourse itself.[11]

Perhaps in its beginnings, like all signifying organizations and practices that attempt to unify meaning, semiotics dreamed of constructing an ultimate code of signification and, to quote Goethe, "Their chorus guides them toward a hidden law." This dream is no more, but semiotics as an open and unfinished project working toward the goal of scientificity can at least serve as a common methodological intercessor in the human sciences.

The Social Sciences: A Semiotic View

Chapter 1
The Meaning of Meaning

It is extremely difficult to speak about meaning and to say something meaningful about it. The only way to do this adequately would be to construct a language that signified nothing. In this way an objective distance could be established that would allow holding meaningless discourses on meaningful ones.

In fact, this is actually what the dreams and hopes of logicians are made of. They have even invented the expression "meaningless" to characterize a certain class of words that can be used to speak about other words. Unfortunately the expression "meaningless" is not meaningless: it is even at the origin of philosophies of the absurd. Neither are the words they cover. When we question the meaning of "and," of "or," or "if" and replace them with "conjunction," "disjunction," "condition," we simply begin the endless circular merry-go-round of synonyms and definitions that follow and cross one another in the pages of the dictionary.

Obviously one can always stop at one or other metalinguistic level; one can decide not to go any further and say that the concepts listed are undefinable, that we should get on with important considerations, that is, the establishment of an axiomatics. Proceeding from one level to another is the only thing that would enable us to get to the meaning of words and to the effects their combinations produce on us. Perhaps this is the wisest way to carry on, but it is also an expression of helplessness.

We can get rid of this cumbersome meaning for the time being by shifting its problematics. A painting and a poem are simply pretexts. The only meaning they have is the one — or those — we give them. Behold! The *we* has been raised to the ultimate instance of meaning. It commands the cultural filter of our perception of the world. It also selects and organizes the epistemes that "become implicit" in specific objects such as paintings, poems, and narratives, and are the result of the intertwinings of the signifier. The operation has succeeded; meaning has been evacuated from signifying objects; relativism has won the day: meaning is no longer there; all meanings are possible. In fact, nothing has changed, and the same problematics—with the same epistemic taxonomies and the same syntactic organizations—arise at a "deeper," or simply at another, level. Whether meaning is situated just behind words, in front of or after them, the question of meaning remains in its entirety.

In the past some have thought, and some still think today, that the difficulty could be skirted by affirming, after Saussure, that words have no meaning, that only oppositions and relations give some appearance of meaning to the words they jostle about. Unfortunately words that are deprived of meaning in this way simply transmit it to the relations that continue to signify. Yet, it is true that they do so in a less direct and especially flexible way that permits reintroducing the famous dynamism that most often can be equated to methodological license and wordy language. There remains a major obstacle: our inevitable insertion into the closed universe of discourse so that whenever we begin to speak about relations, they are transformed into substantives as though by magic, that is to say, into terms whose meaning has to be negated by positing new relations, and so on. Any metalanguage we can imagine in order to speak about meaning is not only a signifying language, it is also a language that substantivizes; it freezes all dynamism of intention into a conceptual terminology.

Consequently we end up by saying that our elders were perhaps not as naive as we think when, much like Bloomfield, for example, they professed that meaning exists as an obvious fact, like an immediate given, but we can say nothing more about it. At least they had the merit of reducing the problem to a more accessible level, in attempting to study the conditions of the manifestation of meaning, that is, in describing the sonorous or graphic cover that, while having nothing to do with meaning, lets it filter through and reach us. Their undertaking finally failed in part because, satisfied with the results obtained in the analysis of the signifier, they tackled morphemes, (i.e., signs), thinking that with the help of formal procedures they could, so to speak, trick meaning and imperceptibly go from one level to another, from an underside of meaning to the distribution of significations. In spite of all, however, they did leave us with the concept of "negative meaning," that possibility of saying that "peach" is not "beach," that there is a *gap* of meaning between them.

Suddenly the immense work undertaken to avoid coming to grips with meaning not only is justified in itself but takes on new meaning for us. The procedures of description and discovery at the level of the signifier in semantics become procedures of verification that must be used simultaneously with the description of signification.

We should not delude ourselves. These procedures teach us nothing about meaning; they simply establish a correlation of control between the two independent planes of language. Although the description of signification remains arbitrary, the procedures of control mainly guarantee its internal coherence. And we know that coherence is one of the rare truth criteria imagined by humans.

Let us suppose that to think more readily about this "differential gap" we use figurative imagery. Imagine a screen of smoke—the universe of meaning—and just in front of this screen a cobweb that can hardly be seen, made up of thousands of interwoven differential gaps: this is the Sausurrian vision of language. We can see that this articulated web does not correspond to what we actually perceive, the multicolored, weighty, frozen world of things. We can see, consequently, that these differential gaps are not immediately given in this "substance"; that, on the contrary, they are the consequences of the apprehension of the discontinuities in a world we know nothing about; that what constitutes this gap is the establishment of a relation, of a difference between comparable aspects of things. If one recognizes that this apprehension logically takes place before the identified gap and one draws the conclusions—saying, for example, that the substance of the signifier is simply a pretext that permits the apprehension of meaning, that it is "informed" by the said apprehension, that the form of the signifier (i.e. all the gaps) results, as an articulation, from the operations of apprehension—the problem of signification, which was sensibly situated at the level of the signifier, crops up again at the very core of the appearance of meaning. For the problem of the constitution of the signifier is already a problem of meaning. The concept of negative meaning that is so reassuring is no more founded than are all the procedures imagined by formalistic structuralism of old.

It is not this return to the origins of meaning that is bothersome in itself, but rather the observation that all reflection on the primary conditions of the apprehension of meaning—or, if you will, on the production of the generation of meaning—simply meets up with epistemological concepts as general as: the same and the other, negation and assertion, subject and object, and form and substance. Without actually wanting to, we are again immersed in "eternal philosophy." If we continue along this line, we run the risk of changing from linguist—with whose discipline we are more or less comfortable—into bad philosopher. When we think about the necessary conditions for the manifestation of meaning, we are first of all obliged to clarify and to manipulate all the concepts at the origin of different theories of knowledge, all the axiomatic categories used to construct formal languages: logics and mathematics.

There is a chance that semioticians will not be heard in this epistemological chorus. However, is this sufficient reason to leave the task of defining semantics to others?

The philosopher's first task at hand is to understand by establishing a discourse on meaning taken as an immense isotopic[1] metaphor of the world. It is essentially contemplative in nature. This is where the misunderstanding crops up. If semioticians are obliged to work in areas that are traditionally those of philosophy, they do so only in spite of themselves: they even prefer to hide behind the screen of technical terms and depersonalized discourse. In addition to this antiphrastic standard their attitude is also governed by the fundamental principle that thought must lead to scientific practice. Knowledge subtends a knowing-how-to-do, and leads up to it. Semioticians do not hesitate to borrow ideas from others and to use second-hand heuristic information. It is hard to imagine what one would come up with if an attempt were made to reconstitute Saussure's or Hjemlslev's philosophical sources. What is of greatest importance for semioticians is that these ideas conform to what they believe to be the actual state of the discipline and the fundamental requirement that they "have a grip on reality": so-called primitive peoples have philosophies of language that equal ours, but these philosophies do not give rise to linguistics.

Semioticians' attitude to formal languages is one of admiration tainted with suspicion. They feel attracted by symbolic logic because this is the form they would ultimately like to give to their operational concepts and relations that can be reduced to simple calculations. What is worrisome, however, is the tautological nature of logical calculation. Semioticians wonder if every transcoding, if every new articulation of meaning, does not indicate an increase or, at least, a differentiation that should be retained and noted. They are also embarrassed by the modalities of the true and the false, especially when referring to nonlinguistic reality. They are equally embarrassed because their conception of language will not allow them to consider such modalities before giving the language a semiotic status. They need a linguistic logic that would deal with, for example, the lie and the secret, ruse and sincerity, on the same plane as truth and falsehood. Instead of a logic of identities they need a logic of equivalences.

Semioticians are also attracted to logico-mathematical models both because of their former claims to fame and their recently acquired efficiency. Of course we are referring not to superficial applications of statistical computation, which have long gone out of fashion, but to the increasing number of formal models that are offered up as so many ready-made techniques and matrices that can be used to construct grammars and languages. It is not so much the number of these models that is disconcerting, but rather the pragmatic and apparently arbitrary attitude linked to their use. It is obvious that mathematicians have nothing to do with this: functioning at the level of formal languages they simply offer up a varied catalogue of possible models. It is the semioticians who chose them. In the exact sciences these choices are sanctioned by the efficiency of scientific practice and are situated within a network of restrictions made up of a mass of accumulated knowledge. Whereas in the young evolving disciplines the models selected not only threaten at any moment to change drastically the general economy of the scientific theory underpinning them, but also to mold and deform a fragile stock of knowledge in their own image. The state of advancement of a science, a criterion difficult to establish, is therefore decisive. The very models that are restrictive for an established science can be arbitrary for a discipline that has a scientific vocation. In both cases the problem of their adequation arises in a different way.

It is through the narrow gate, between the two undisputable competencies of philosophy and logico-mathematics, that semioticians must undertake their investigation on meaning. It is not a question of founding semantics the way philosophers would: many a science founded in this way had an ephemeral life. It is even less a question of developing a metadiscourse on meaning. The confusion maintained by works of philosophers and essayists on "structuralism" and the structural approach to the human sciences has caused widespread damage. To satisfy the real needs of semioticians it is necessary to have at hand a minimum number of explicit epistemological concepts that makes it possible to appreciate the adequacy of the models borrowed or constructed, when analyzing signification. Semioticians need epistemological control over their methods.

Human beings live in a signifying world. For them the problem of meaning does not arise; meaning is a given: it imposes itself as an obvious fact, as an entirely natural "feeling of understanding." In a "white" universe where language denoted only things and gestures, it would not be possible to question meaning, since all questioning is *metalinguistic*.

What does the word mean? What do we understand by it? From both ends of the communication channel anthropomorphic metaphors crop up by which humans attempt to question meaning naively, as though words actually wanted to say something, as though meaning could be heard by pricking up one's ears. However, the answers given are given only by proxy, maintaining the ambiguity: they are nothing but paraphrases, more or less inexact translations of words and utterances into other words and utterances.

Signification is simply this transposition of one level of language into a different language, and meaning is simply this possibility of *transcoding*.

Dramatizing somewhat, we end up by saying that human metalinguistic speech is simply a series of lies, and that communication is a series of misunderstandings. Obviously writing is a betrayal, whereas literary criticism is at best a free, metaphoric translation of semiotic activity that is not primary. There are so many literary variations on this theme, so many pretexts to writing about the impossibility, the impropriety, the absurdity of writing, and so on.

Curiously enough, while literature is busy denouncing itself, a parallel and synchronic activity that consists in translating unconscious social significations is valorized under the label of demystification. What is a lie and a source of misfortune at the individual level becomes truth and liberation at the social level.

For semioticians who are sometimes worried about the ideological use made of their research and sometimes satisfied in noting that it is nevertheless useful, lies and truth are one and the same thing. In their own jargon they will say that is not the point, that it is not pertinent. Whether metalinguistic activity of transcoding meaning happens to be moral or immoral, euphoric or dysphoric, is an observation that must be retained and incorporated into the problematics of contents and invested in metalinguistic operations that have an axiological mode of existence. At best, much like sociologists of advertising who promote the sale of soap, when describing and objectivizing the process of transcoding, semioticians can add that they may be creating a weapon of the future that, like all weapons, can fall into the hands of traitors as well as heroes. The following observations can be retained as their primary one: because natural language is never denotative but multiplanar, to live under the constant threat of metaphor is a normal state, a condition of the "human condition."

If therefore we reduce the problem of meaning to its minimal dimensions (i.e., to transcoding significations), and if we say that these transcodings take place naturally, we can ask if scientific activity in this domain should not consist in working out *techniques of transposition* that make it possible to carry out transcodings artificially, but properly. Consequently the semiotic description of signification consists in constructing an adequate artificial language. We do know more or less how to construct an artificial language, since hundreds of them are constructed every year; however, only the satisfactory solution to the problem of adequation, that is, the establishment of a system of equivalences between artificial language and natural language, can sanction the success of the enterprise. By a different route we have returned to the problem of the relations between the models of description and the elementary structure of signification, as it can be apprehended and clarified at its source.

To say that in order to account for meaning all we have to do is to construct a second language in an arbitrary fashion, can lead to establishing the arbitrary as a principle. To add that since the criteria of adequation are not solidly established, we can think of this construction as an activity that when carried out would be at the same time a reflection of its proper activity, would simply amount to giving oneself too easily a clear semiotic conscience. All discourse on meaning would therefore be transformed into a semiotic exercise, and semiotics would break up into innumerable eloquent pieces. The bothersome distance between individual praxis and collective praxis suddenly disappears.

Such a standpoint, however, infuses new life into literature, which justifies itself in a way. What was simply delusive writing that deceived people becomes a production, a constructive activity that assumes its condition and gets the most it can out of the situation. Semioticians are transformed into writers and writers become semioticians.

The misfortune—or the trick that meaning plays on its manipulators once again—consists in the following: what should be a dual, but global, activity under the pen of the practitioner separates into two distinct metalinguistic levels—a semiotic language that both blatantly implies its presence and authorizes a reflexive metalanguage of multiple questions and assertions. A metasemiotic discourse that implicitly and urgently postulates a nonexistent scientific semiotics appears as a new variant of the "terrorist" writing formerly identified and demystified by Roland Barthes.

Such an activity probably reflects a historical moment in the development of superstructures much in the same way as earlier attempts to denounce and to demystify meaning. All three constitute paradigmatic variations on meaning within the literary microuniverse of the time. Yet semiotic writing is not only the noble manifestation of history understood as a metamorphosis of forms. Since it is a historical praxis it is obliged to manipulate axiological and ideological contents. It even claims to transform these contents and considers their transformation as the ultimate meaning of its activity. History will be the judge of the efficacy of these procedures. What can be retained for the time being is this innovative ambiguity: the production of meaning is meaningful only if it is the transformation of a meaning already given; the production of meaning is consequently in itself a significant endowment with form, indifferent to whatever content it may be called on to transform. *Meaning, in the sense of the forming of meaning, can thus be defined as the possibility of the transformation of meaning.*

When one opens up the dictionary again looking for the meaning of the word meaning (*sens*), one finds a group of examples where *sens interdit* (one-way street) is found alongside expressions such as *le sens de la vie* (the meaning of life) or *sens de l'histoire* (the meaning of history). Meaning not only signifies what words want to tell us, it is also a direction, that is, in the language of philosophers, an intentionality and a finality. Translated into linguistic language, meaning is identified with the oriented process of actualization that, like every semiotic process, is presupposed by—and presupposes—a virtual or realized system or program.

This interpretation according to which meaning, in order to manifest itself, can sometimes take the form of a system, sometimes that of a process, while remaining whole—for the process presupposes the system, and conversely— opens up new possibilities in the operational field of semantics. This explains why there is only an apparent contradiction between systematic and syntagmatic grammars. It accounts for the fact that an activity can be transcribed both as a processual algorithm and transcoded as a systematic and virtual know-how. It establishes an equivalence between axiologies of a systematic order and ideologies that are recurring representations of the process of transformation.

Consequently, literary production is seen as a specific case of this process of actualization of virtual meaning, comparable to the production of automobiles, ending in the construction of a series of semiotic objects that are metonymic with respect to the virtual project of doing, with the following difference, however: writers are privileged compared to Renault factory workers, insofar as they themselves are virtual subjects of the programs they realize, whereas workers are undifferentiated operators of a desemantisized activity.

The desemantisization of the process of actualization is moreover an ambiguous axiological phenomenon. It transforms the artisan into an unskilled worker, but it also permits the constitution of great literatures without their author's raising the problems of language. It especially permits individuals to live by reducing thousands of their gestural or linguistic programmed behaviors into automatisms. What does it matter if pianists' gesticulations are absurd, as long as they end up playing Mozart sonatas?

We return to the semiotic plane of denotation where meaning seems to have been evacuated, where there subsists only an impoverished signifier, made up of automatisms of gesticulation and our familiarity with things. Seen from this angle, denotation is the locus of both the institution of meaning and its withdrawal. But if meaning can shift at any given moment, it is because there exist predictable metasemiotic trajectories of its transposition: procedures of vertical transcoding offering multiple possibilities for the explication and the implication of meaning; procedures of horizontal transcoding accounting for the dual implication of processes and systems.[2] If, in translations semantic effects occur on the axis of evidence and depth, oriented processes appear as loci of the transformations of meaning articulated into systems.

We can say that recent progress in semiotics has consisted essentially in the expansion of its field of action, in the more detailed exploration of the strategic possibilities of signification. Without knowing anything more about the nature of meaning, we have learned to understand better where it occurs and where it is transformed. Hence we consider it less and less as linear and uniplanar strings of significations in texts and discourses. We are beginning to understand what is illusory about the project of a systematic semantics that, much in the way of a phonology, would articulate the plane of the signified of a given language.

Along with an interpretive semantics whose right to exist is no longer questioned, the possibility of a *formal* semiotics, which would attempt to account only for the articulations and manipulations of contents, is opening up a little more each day. To determine the multiple forms of the presence of meaning and the modes of its existence, to interpret them as horizontal instances and vertical levels of signification, to describe the pathways of the transpositions and transformations of contents—all are tasks that no longer seem utopian. In the near future only such a semiotics of forms appears to be the language that makes it possible to talk about meaning. For, precisely, semiotic form is nothing more than the meaning of meaning.

Chapter 2
On Scientific Discourse in the Social Sciences

Introduction

Science: System and Process

It might appear naive or even misleading to use the word "science" when speaking about our knowledge of human beings, a knowledge that is uncertain and subject to controversy. This is all the more so that the idea that our knowledge of human beings is scientific has often been given great weight only so that its ultimate collapse, set up rhetorically, was all the more convincing. So it is that "austere scholars," while recognizing they have no choice but to continue to base their thinking on the as yet unfounded postulate that the world is intelligible, prefer to limit themselves to the claim that theirs is but a scientific attempt, and they are merely taking part in a collective development of scientific discourse.

Given this, if we want to think about the semiotic status of such discourse, we have to inquire into the specific modes in which it appears. We have to inquire into the conditions under which this discourse is produced and the criteria by which to distinguish it from other forms of knowledge. Thus we set aside the concept of science as system and instead represent it as a process, as scientific *doing*. This doing, which will always be incomplete and will often lead to mistakes, is manifested in the discourses it produces, discourses that are at first sight recognizable only because of their sociolinguistic connotations of "scientificity."

Semiotics now counts as one of its urgent tasks, the study of the discursive organizations of signification. Linguistics, for its part, being the most developed of semiotic disciplines, is recognized among the social sciences as having the greatest claim to the status of science. For these two reasons, both as subject and object of thought about scientific discourse, semiotics has taken up this project.

Discourse and its Subject

To go from a consideration of *system* to an examination of *processes* is not particularly revolutionary in semiotics. On the contrary, knowledge of processes is the only way we can cast some light on the operation and forms of organization of the system. However, use of the Saussurian *langue/parole* distinction does pose some problems, if only because it requires us to conceive of and put in place an *instance of mediation* that allows for the movement to and from these two forms of semiotic existence. So, if with Benveniste we believe that discourse is nothing more than "language as it is taken on by a person who is speaking," then we are not only postulating that these two linguistic forms are hypothetically identical, but we are also providing the pathway for movement between them, in that we grant that person the status of *syntactic actant*. He is not an ontological subject:

the *person* who is speaking

but rather a grammatical concept:

the *person who is speaking*

a concept that in linguistics has traditionally been called the "speaking subject."

This last observation, no matter how obvious it may appear, warrants emphasis. The introduction at this point of a psychological or transcendental subject—an attempt often made these days—puts into question the internal coherence of linguistics taken as a whole, not just one of its schools or particular thrusts. This it does because it brings into play a concept that is heterogeneous and incompatible with linguistics as a whole. Semiotically speaking, the subject of discourse is no more than a virtual instance, an instance constructed in linguistic theory in order to account for the transformation of language, from paradigmatic to syntagmatic form. Further, this mediating instance shows as a syntactic subject, an actant that—possessing linguistic categories that exist as differences "within language," as oppositions that demonstrate systematic organization—manipulates those categories in such a way as to construct a syntagmatic stringing, realized as a discursive program.

What occurs in this locus of mediation is more than just an *actualization* of language brought about by bringing into play some virtual terms from the syntagmatic chain, to the exclusion of other ones that are differential, set aside for the moment, although they are necessary for the process of signification. More

occurs because this locus of mediation also takes on certain semantic categories — such as assertion and denial, conjunction and disjunction, to mention
only the most obvious — that are necessary if the subject is to be able to assume
the role of an operator who manipulates and organizes the chosen terms, if only
to be able to construct elementary utterances using procedures that heretofore
have been subsumed under "predication." The subject of discourse is thus this
instance that, according to the Saussurian view of things, is not limited to just
allowing for the movement from a virtual state to an actualized state of language.
It appears to be the place where we find the whole array of mechanisms that have
to do with the *setting of language into discourse*. Situated where the *being of*
language is transformed into a *linguistic doing*, the subject of discourse can be
said to be, and this is not a poor metaphor, the producer of discourse.

All doing presupposes a knowing-how-to-do (or a not-knowing-how-to-do,
which amounts to the same thing). Thus, to discourse, which is a manifestation
of a doing, there corresponds the subject of discourse, a subject endowed with
discursive competence. The instance of the speaking subject, while being the locus for the *actualization of language*, is at the same time the locus for the *vir-*
tualization of discourse. It is here that the presupposed forms of discourse are
found and here that they have their semiotic existence. When actualized in discourse, such forms occur only in an imcomplete and partial mode.

Without pushing this kind of extrapolation too far, we can probably invert, and
likely should invert, this set of problems by revalorizing discursive performance.
We could note, for example, that at the level of the individual practice of language, locally concentrated competencies are acquired and added to, thanks to
discursive practice. We can also note that on the social level, syntactic structures
are susceptible of transformations and that as a result — within limits that have yet
to be set — the competent subject of discourse, while being an instance that is
presupposed by the functioning of discourse, can be considered as a *subject in the*
process of formation, constant formation. Indeed, it can be viewed as a subject to
be formed.

From another perspective, and at the level of that semiotic praxis that seeks to
apprehend linguistic doing as such, our knowledge of the subject of discourse or,
and it amounts to the same thing, our understanding of the procedures by which
that subject produces and organizes discourse, can be achieved by only two
means: either because the subject, by becoming explicitly identified within the
discourses it produces, itself brings us to a knowledge of it (and this in an always
incomplete and misrepresenting way), or because of logical presuppositions that
we can postulate about its manner of existing and that manner in which it is constructed. These presuppositions are based on already realized instances of discourse. Although they are not very reliable in themselves, the simulacra of the
activities of the subject of enunciation that we find in enunciated discourse can

nonetheless be interpreted through the process of presupposition and thereby give rise, as the case may be, to descriptions of semantico-syntactic representations of the organization of the instance of the subject of discourse.

These last two considerations tend to establish discourse—although only partially—as the locus for the creation of its own subject and as the sole source for our learning about that subject, and it is these considerations that are the perspective from which we can examine the specific status of scientific discourse.

Taxonomic Discourse

A Perfect Syntax and Semantics

As we have seen, even a brief description of the instance of the subject of discourse identifies a twofold activity taking place therein: on the one hand there are operations of selection that, with a view to ultimately using them, set in place bits of the semantic universe that are endowed with a systematic organization; on the other hand, there are manipulating operations that organize contents that are in the process of being actualized through hypotactic articulations and syntagmatic stringing.

This view of the production of discourse, although pretty rough and ready, will at least allow us separately to identify and examine the taxonomic and syntactic components of linguistic doing. It is only by basing itself more or less implicitly on this kind of distinction that logical language can lay claim to the status of *syntax* that organizes the discourse of rationality. It does this with a view to manipulating a *semantics* that is present in logical utterances only in the form of "proper nouns," empty spaces that can be invested with conceptual contents having to do with such and such a scientific universe whose taxonomic organization is presupposed.

We see that a logic that considers itself a perfect syntax that manipulates objects inscribed within established taxonomies results finally in a static, frozen notion of science. We also see how, by setting aside these legitimate fundamental considerations, a misrepresenting and sometimes ill-intentioned popularization ends up describing scientific discourse as the programming, so that it can be communicated, of an already constructed knowledge, and thus identifies it with didactic discourse.

Taxonomic Doing

If the hypothesis, according to which the "dictionary" of a given science encompasses a semantics that is organized as a system, is useful, then the temporary setting aside of its taxonomic component will greatly facilitate our examination and formalization of the mechanisms by which scientific universes function discursively. Such a hypothesis makes it almost impossible to apply formal syntaxes of this kind to the discourses of the human and social sciences.

This neutralization of "semantics" amounts to postulating that we have already resolved a problem that often is not even posed, and it delays our examination of the nature and status of the semiotic objects that the discourses of the social and human sciences manipulate.

If we examine certain discourses that consider themselves as scientific, such as discourses on the "earth sciences,"[1] we see on the contrary that a certain scientific practice is located midway between the two extreme cases we have just called up: an "average" science, in its daily activity, does not presuppose the taxonomic existence of the semiotic objects with which it deals. Neither does it confirm the taxonomic disorder that would render its taxonomic activity trivial. Instead, along with assumed taxonomic givens ("we know that . . . "), it demonstrates an ongoing effort to construct semiotic objects, a construction that is characterized by an unending acquisition of incidental and essential determinations (of the order of *having* and *being*). This construction is further characterized by inclusion and exclusion of qualities and potentialities of doing, by homologations that put a little order into these provisional conceptual constructs, and so forth. This sustained effort, present throughout the discourse in question, encompasses in a way an area of activities that are both semantic and syntactic, an area like that in which are applied the activities of class logic and set theory.

All of these activities, however, seem to be pursuing a twofold goal: (1) to assure oneself of the semiotic, not real, existence of objects, and to construct them as much by their determinations as by the taxonomic network in which they can be inscribed, and (2) to represent the doing of a discoursing subject who is trying to establish the primary level of his discourse not through a language that is an object but rather through a "language of objects," and with this language the subject can manipulate those activities. Thus, although we can admit that daily discourse, beginning with language considered to be the result of an earlier and "naive" categorization of the world, programs certain parts of the world that it encompasses, we have to recognize that scientific discourse, as we are examining it, is defined as the *locus for a taxonomic doing*. We must further recognize that the organization of the specific semantic universe it explores, far from being a given, is the *intended scientific undertaking of this doing*. If only in terms of this characteristic, scientific discourse is thus distinguished from other possible discourses on the world.

Taxonomic Doing in Linguistics

Without completely adopting Chomsky's optimistic certitudes and without claiming that the organization of the taxonomic level in linguistics has already been completed and that we have gone beyond it, we can at least take into consideration the experience of linguistics in that area, if only to see how it is that linguistics conceives of that organization and also to see if the results obtained justify the privileged status we sometimes want to accord that discipline.

Manifestation What seems to be specific to linguistics is the locus of its thought, a locus that situates it midway between the sciences of content (semantics) and the sciences of formal languages (logical languages and mathematics). At the same time linguistics is able to adopt the two roles discussed in the preceding section and thereby operate within the two registers at the same time. Thus, for example, if its taxonomic doing can be likened—and to a large extent even assimilated—to operations within class logic, and if in a general way the search for universals always haunts linguistics—because it would like to be a deductive theory of language—there is nothing in the way of an application of its doing to any given natural language. Linguistic doing can be applied to contents that are particular linguistic forms. Even more, linguistics can be called to account for the level of manifestation of the language in question—as opposed to what happens in logic, a language without content, in which all semantic investment is considered to be something that happens at an earlier stage and is no longer part of its concerns.

At this level of manifestation of a given language, linguistics inductively identifies "entities," the as yet unidentified objects of its future manipulations. It observes their recurrences, seeks to identify what is variable and invariable about them and finally organizes their occurrences into classes, classes that alone can lay claim to the status of the semiotic objects that constitute the taxonomic level. Its linguistic doing, both deductive and inductive, makes sense for it only if, although subordinated to a metalogic, it allows linguistics to account for its 'reality," for its linguistic manifestation. On the other hand, the complex grammatical mechanisms that this doing seems to strive to set up can be linguistically justified only if, in the final analysis, they can engender "surface structures."

This final and primary appeal to linguistic reality thus constitutes the unique and homogeneous reference—and referent—for the scientific doing of linguistics. This is the paradox we find at the level of deployment of signs that we call manifestation. It is a level that is not relevant to the activities of linguistics, yet it is necessary because it is its foundation and justification.

We can now understand why semiology, the "universal science of signs," when it seeks to establish any given specific semiotics, cannot avoid first postulating the level of manifestation for that semiotics, a level that will constitute the reference and controlling principles for the concepts it will develop.

A Hierarchy of Concepts What allowed Chomsky to declare that a linguistic taxonomy or, what amounts to the same thing, the taxonomic level of linguistic discourse, has already been developed, was largely the almost unanimous consensus among linguists as to how to interpret "entities" in terms of constructed units. This consensus was also the legitimizing principle, from the linguistic point of view, for the entire group of methodologies that we can call *procedures for description*. For, contrary to what happens in other social sciences, in which each theory offers its own group of concepts, present-day debates in linguistics, in the area that interests us here, never have to do with the definition of units (linguistic concepts), but rather with the choice, with analysis in mind, of these or those units—or, and this is simply another aspect of the same problem, the choice of this or that level of linguistic articulations.

In fact, in linguistics units are defined as "constituents"; that is, they are defined only in terms of the fact that they combine to construct other units that are hierarchically superior to them or can be broken down into units that are smaller than them. Given this, the idea of an "immediate" constituent cannot fail to further buttress this hierarchical view of the taxonomic level of language by making it appear to be a conceptual structure made up of isomorphic articulations and formal interdefinitions.

The taxonomic structure we have just represented briefly might appear to be of little importance in relation to problems of a different kind of complexity that linguistics is now confronting. Nonetheless it is the result of a taxonomic doing that can be traced throughout the history of linguistics since antiquity (the concept of "parts of speech"). It is still present when linguistics enters its scientific age in the nineteenth century (appearance of the concept of "morpheme"), and continues today with the semantics of distinctive features, the attempts to develop a discursive linguistics and, above all, with the problems posed by the attempt to adapt the fundamental principles of that doing to other semiotics that are in part nonlinguistic. Such as it is, the taxonomic structure, at least in large measure, assures linguistics a scientific status. The scientific discourse of linguistics shows itself to be able to manipulate a language that is already to a great extent formal. Its objects are concepts that are at the same time constructed and real.

Relevance Among concepts the other social sciences have borrowed from linguistics over the last ten years, the concept of relevance provokes the least flattering sentiments among linguists vis-à-vis its new adherents. This borrowing is sometimes used to identify the "importance" of a given phenomenon or of a given aspect of research. Sometimes it is used to underscore the "rigor" with which a given problem must be treated—both fairly fuzzy notions. The way this borrowed term has been used only illustrates the loss of direction that can result from the metaphoric game that so often today is what interdisciplinary work represents.

The concept of relevance that appears at the time of the taxonomic doing represented by the work of the Prague school is the result of the need to recognize, from among the many determinations (distinctive features) possible for a given object, those that are *at the same time necessary and sufficient* to fulfil all the conditions of its definition. It is a concept that can be understood only within the context of structural thinking. According to structuralism, the definition of any given object, no matter how incomplete it might be, is, in fact, an interdefinition of at least two objects. Identifying the distinctive features of an object means that the object cannot be confused with another object of the same level (same series). At the same time, however, its definition should not have so many determinations that, if they are to be discriminatingly identifying, come into play only at a lower level. Relevance is thus one of the main postulates of taxonomic doing because, while fulfilling the principle of reference to manifestation and also the principle of hierarchy, and especially in its justification of the concept of *level of analysis*, it allows linguistics to have the status of a formal language.

Indeed, linguistic description, while remaining linked to the level of manifestation, is, according to this perspective, nothing more than a corpus of "well-made" definitions. Because these definitions in turn are given names or denominations that are arbitrary, the problem of the metalinguistic status of semiotic objects, which constitutes the taxonomic level of linguistic discourse, is clarified: these denominations represent nothing in and of themselves. Their only function is to refer us to the definitions they subsume by naming them. As opposed to the concepts the other human sciences use in order to set up this level, concepts that are susceptible of a semantic analysis that can give rise to their being defined, denominations—which to a large extent make up linguistic terminology—are without any meaning other than those given to them by the definitions that logically precede them.

The concept of relevance is thus the basis for the procedures we call *reduction*. These require that nonnecessary elements be transferred from one level of the analysis to another, lower, one. The famous reductionism of which people love to accuse linguistics and, by extension, semiotics, appears thus to be not a fault but rather a claim to glory.

Veridictory Discourse

The Discursive Status of Truth

When we examined that taxonomic doing whose purpose is to construct semiotic objects, we carefully avoided talking about those objects in terms of "truth."[2] We granted them only a semiotic existence, that is, an existence that is revealed to us only through their manner of being present in discourse. At the very most, when speaking of linguistic discourse, we emphasized its uninterrupted link with the level of manifestation of natural languages. These are the "real" objects of its thought.

It must be said that even though we kept as close as possible to the level of manifestation and formulated one of its taxonomic utterances, of the type:

There exists an entity X,

far from immediately grasping one of the entities of which manifestation is supposed to be made up, all we really did was to make a judgment as to the existence of that entity. In so doing we produced a first utterance having to do with manifestation. The entities of manifestation are no more than pretexts from which linguistic objects are constructed, with the help of successive determinations.

Semiotic existence must not be confused with "true" existence, and the veridical character of our assertions must be identified separately from our competence to produce such assertions verbally. As for an assertion of existence, its truth appears necessarily as an overdetermination, that is, as a modalization of the assertion. Moreover, this consolidation of semiotic existence, if it appears to be an extra caution, can be no more than a positioning by the subject of enunciation vis-à-vis his utterance. Endowed with linguistic status, veridictory modalization thus is mainly concerned with the activity of the discoursing subject.

The Coherence of Discourse

If we are to speak of veridiction, it seems appropriate to first refer to the classical, twofold definition of truth. It identifies internal coherence while also basing truthfulness on the adequacy of language to describe the reality it does describe.

When we try to apply the concept of *coherence* to discourse, at first sight it seems much like the more general concept of *isotopy*. This concept is understood in terms of the unending recurrence, throughout a given discourse, of the same group of categories by which one might justify a given instance of paradigmatic organization. Thus, the definition of the logical coherence of discourse can be obtained through restrictions placed on the choice of those categories that, in their recurring, guarantee the permanence of a "common denominator" that will buttress the entire discourse. When "truth" is the common element of a given discourse, this categorical grouping would correspond to the system of truth-values responsible for the organization of the logic that articulates the discourse in question. The setting into discourse of a structure of modalities of veridiction would constitute its *rational isotopy*.

Although the preceding is helpful, it is not enough. From the syntactic point of view, modalities are no more than predicates of utterances whose object-actants are descriptive utterances. If we are to speak of the coherence of discourse, it is not therefore enough to see its rational isotopy set in place. The utterances that are thereby modalized must in turn be arranged in a parallel isotopy. In other words, a certain *semantic isotopy* must be postulated at the same time as the rational isotopy that modalizes it in terms of truth. Since all that is at play here is the form of the content and not the content itself, the semantic isotopy in question must correspond — as we have already seen in linguistics — to a unique *level of articulation and analysis* involving only a preselected type of semiotic unit. The tendency of scientific discourses to limit themselves to monosememe terminologies is an indirect consequence of this.

Finally we can see that the internal coherence of discourse, far from limiting its scope to the setting up of the isotopic level of veridiction (a level based solely on the underlying logic), on the contrary implies a prior knowing concerning taxonomic doing and its consequences. Coherence is of a paradigmatic nature, to the extent that it stems from a preliminary choice that the discoursing subject makes from among available veridictory modalities. It appears essentially to be an *implicit permanence of the subject's knowing* and has to do with scientific doing as a whole.

The Subject's Knowing

Indeed, it is as if "it is true that *p*" were not the objectivized form of the subject's knowing. It is the result of a twofold bit of camouflaging using procedures of actantial shifting out. With the aid of the impersonal "it" there is an attempt to screen out the subject of enunciation who is the guarantor of the truth of *p*. The predicate "is true" is just an indirect way of saying "I know." In other words, if the production of an assertive utterance such as:

$$p = \text{the Earth is round}$$

presupposes no more than the speech act that produces this utterance, which can be made explicit by saying:

(I say that) the Earth is round,

then the truth-value of this assertion can be based only on what the utterance in question and the explicated enunciation of that utterance contain. That is, that truth-value can be based only on a *knowing that logically precedes* the knowing that was necessary to produce the linguistic formulation. Thus this knowing can move from being a "personal conviction," based on the axiological universe taken on by the subject, to a "proven" knowing, through a prior experimental discourse.

Now we can say that if the knowing that finds its expression in our postulating such and such truth-values, assigned to manifested utterances, finds its source in the instance of the subject of discourse as that subject enacts its recurring "truth saying," then the subject itself plays no more than the role of mediating agent. The subject bases his knowing on something and somewhere else. The subject links his knowing to another discourse, another system of knowing, in the form of reference. This is an anaphorizing operation carried out by the subject. He takes what is known and transforms it into a causing-to-know that he brings about.

Referential Discourse

The mechanisms that set discourse into place—and the laying out of the subject's knowing, which produces his veridictory modalization, is one such mechanism—can, as we have already noted, be discovered only by using the procedures of logical presupposition or through our recognizing their partial identifications when they are manifested in discourse. These identifications, even if they do not correspond to the activities of the implied subject—performance always seems imperfect from the point of view of the competence one supposes is there—at least tell us a great deal. Once they are disambiguated and systematized, they can give a good approximation of the description of the instance of the subject of discourse. So, if we now come back to our "average" scientific discourse, we can find confirmed some of the things we have just proposed, and can make further observations.

Discursive Anaphorization

In order to make them less ambiguous, with the help of their contexts, we can easily classify expressions of the type:

> We know that . . .
> We realize that . . .
> We have seen that . . .
> It is obvious that . . . etc.

These are found in any would-be scientific discourse. Even discourse without scientific pretensions will contain such expressions. If we take as the criterion for this classification the typology of the loci to which the instance of the subject refers us in order to justify its knowing, we can immediately identify two areas of reference, according to whether they are located within the discourse itself or outside it.

In the case where discourse refers to itself, it is easy to recognize a normal anaphoric[3] activity on the part of the discoursing subject. Indeed, to the extent that all realized discourse is first an intended discourse, its linear unfolding requires frequent metalinguistic overviews. These give rise to repeated references to what "we have seen" and just as many promises as to what "we shall see."

Thus, while remaining within the context of discourse itself, we can attempt to disassemble the mechanism of its repeated assertions as to knowing. Discourse seems to function on two relatively autonomous levels. The first is made up of *cognitive expressions* that are recurringly manifested and that thereby establish the common element of the knowing that is enacted by the subject. Nonetheless each of these expressions modalizes and is the guarantor for a descriptive utterance introduced by "that . . . ," an utterance that is simply the *condensed* form of a sequence of discourse that is *undergoing expansion*, preceding or following the moment of its repetition. The relation between a segment of the veridictory level of discourse and a segment of its referential level is thus in the first instance a *semantic anaphora* postulating that the contents that have been articulated in the two different forms are identical. But this assertion that they are identical is made possible only by the introduction of a *cognitive anaphora* that modalizes the contents under its jurisdiction and causes them to shift from their status of "being" to a status of "knowing-to-be." It is as if the main preoccupation of any discourse were the laying out of a given knowing, one that is to be transformed into a causing-to-know. The contents that are the objects of this knowing are no more than variables that have been called on in order to constitute "discourse occurrences" that can undergo explanatory or justificatory expansions. In the process of the production of discourse, the setting into place of the level of veridictory modalities would thus logically precede the setting into place of the semiotic objects that are its main concern. This at least seems to be the way a great many discourses on the world as well as didactic discourses deductively work.

If, however, as we have already done, we admit that scientific discourse is essentially a doing that constructs its own object, that it is a progression in knowing, not a preemptory assertion, then the cognitive anaphorization of discourse appears to be a segmentation of scientific doing having to do with a general strategy of "wanting-to-know." Partial scientific programs that are the results of a dynamic and aggressive doing are thus consolidated one after the other into instances of "knowing-to-be" or "knowing-that-such-is-the-case" that authorize new investigative offensives.

The Enunciative Contract

The role of strategist that we have now assigned to the subject of enunciation confirms the existence of an autonomous cognitive dimension of discourse. It is after having laid out its knowledge that the discoursing subject segments and referentializes the other, earlier discourse. The anaphoric doing that is thus manifested really is of a much more general character because, not content with simply organizing the discourse that is in the process of being realized, it brings into its purview all of the earlier discursive programs that had simply been implicit or presupposed. Indeed, if we can view a discourse that has a particular discipline as its object as being the syntagmatic stringing together of all of the partial discourses of a single given isotopy, we can see that substantial sequences of this entire discourse, while remaining implicit, can serve as reference points for the discourse that is at that given moment being produced.

Establishing the line that separates what can be kept implicit and what should be made explicit does not have to do only with the good intentions of the discoursing subject, however. A given speech act implies the real or supposed presence of the receiver to whom the subject, as sender, addresses his discourse. Because discourse is both production and a product to be communicated, we have the problem of the transmissibility of knowing and of the objects of that knowing.

A strategy for communication, which raises among other things the problem of transmissibility, thus seems to accompany the strategy for organizing discourse. This strategy for communication generally is evident in the form of the initial choice that the sending subject must make as to the *level of intelligibility* of his discourse, this level being defined as keeping implicit what is known and making explicit what is knowable. Since in theory, the known is of the domain of the receiver, and since its being kept implicit depends on a unilateral decision on the part of the sender, that decision must be based on an evaluation of the extent of the receiver's knowledge, and it can be seen as an overture, a proposed contract to be set up between the two participants in discourse and based on shared implicit knowledge.

This presupposed *enunciative contract*, to the extent that it is accepted by the receiver and adhered to by the sender, guarantees that conditions will be satisfactory for the transmissibility of discourse. Such a contract is fragile and can be broken at any moment, however. This is why the development of techniques to optimize transmission is one of the main preoccupations of the linguistics of didactic discourse. As to scientific communication itself, a subject we propose to deal with separately later, its practical exercise is located within concrete sociocultural contexts and thus poses the problem of the collective sender. We know that cultural differentiation in macrosocieties produces semiautonomous sociosemiotic groups that possess their own specific knowledge and discursive competence and within which closed communication circuits are set up. Thus, a "learned society" is a sociosemiotic phenomenon. What can derail scientific discourse from its destination and give it ideological overtones is the fact that, outside of these privileged clubs—and because such discourse inevitably includes assertions of a shared implicit, unspoken knowledge—it is received along with secondary social connotations that vary according to the receiver and end up having meaning effects. "Respect," "transcendence," and "deception" can all be read into such discourse. Although the responsibility of a given scientist might not be directly implicated, we can nonetheless see the possibilities for pseudoscientific discourses, possibilities offered by closed sociosemiotic groups that possess an esoteric knowledge and in which the specialized manipulation of terrorizing connotations often replaces references to any preceding scientific doing.

Communicative strategy, a characteristic common to all discourses, is thus, in the case of scientific discourse, dependent on a pragmatics and ethics that are specific to that discourse.

The Internal Referent

There is thus a veridical discourse whose justification is found within itself, that is, in its own segments that have been made explicit at an earlier stage. There is another discourse whose veridiction is based on discourses that have already taken place and that have been called on and brought into play by the subject of enunciation. In both cases we have an identical anaphorization structure, a structure whereby one level of discourse refers us to another level and the guarantor of that level's truth. At the same time, that latter level is a supporting structure for the former. It does not matter whether that second level is explicit or implicit. It always appears as a *referential discourse* and as the basis for *veridical discourse*. The anaphora that links them is no more than the semiotic interpretation of *adequation*, the second criterion of truth to which we have already made reference. There is this difference, however: instead of reaching out to a referent that is outside the discourse, an *external referent* (an extralinguistic reality), the anaphora identifies an *internal referent*, one the discourse itself has created.

These two foundations for truthful discourse—its coherence and its adequation vis-à-vis the source of its justification—can be interpreted semiotically.

It must be noted, however, that if we are to postulate two discursive levels that are at the same time autonomous and anaphorically linked, the very concept of scientific discourse must be expanded. Thus, the cognitive anaphoric phenomena we have identified cannot be interpreted as such unless we postulate that discourse in the act of being produced, realized discourse, as it is formed and articulated before our eyes, is accompanied by an anticipated discourse, a *present* discourse that holds the subject of enunciation and constitutes the locus from which that subject observes earlier enunciative programs and enunciative programs to follow (which are sometimes announced with repetitions of "as we shall see"). These enunciative programs precede and will follow the subject's immediate enunciative performance, and the subject calls on them as needed to consolidate its discursive production. More than the uncertain future of its discourse, whose actualized organization it nonetheless projects, it is the responsibility of the subject to subsume, in one way or another, an entire prior discourse that appears to be of capital importance if scientific discourse is to be understood.

This desire to recapitulate all earlier knowledge explains the convention, in force until quite recently, that referred everything to Aristotle. It was an unwritten rule of "scientific" discourse in the human sciences that said that the examination of any problem had to be preceded by its entire history. This consisted in affirming, perhaps naively, the continuity of knowledge and the unicity of discourse, a continuity that persisted despite various inconsequential substitutions of one discoursing subject-actor for another.

This is, in fact, what is going on: if a given subject, as actor and as one of the properties of its scientific competence, possesses a complete initial discursive program, that program can be understood only if a subject actant, an invariant, is postulated for it. Everything depends on knowing what metalinguistic representation should be given to this program.

Further, if the justification of the knowledge mentioned earlier appears somewhat naive, it is not because the historical background established for the knowledge is sometimes lacking in rigor. It is above all because what this justification is intended to do implies a temporal and casual process—in a word, a *genealogical interpretation* of scientific discourse. What this scientific doing presupposes and brings to the fore at the moment of its producing act is not the wanderings—the detours, backups, impasses, and restarts—that in fact occur during its historical evolution as it is undertaken by such and such a discipline that sees itself as a science. What is brought forth is a scientific discourse that is virtual and actualizable at any given moment and that is organized as a unique and finalized a posteriori algorithm. Starting with the subject of the discourse, considered as an instance producing a new knowledge (that is, starting with the present state of a given science), the scientific program that precedes it is a doing that is reconstituted in reverse, as a group of utterances and subprograms that presuppose each other and go back not to the historical origins of a given knowledge but rather to its very first postulates and presuppositions. Given this, it does not matter if the representation of such a discourse is a little sketchy at the level of the producing instance taken on by a given actor. Nor does it matter if a given instance of such discourse is by chance situated within a historical impasse that will at a later stage be recognized as such. These are but the misadventures of performance. Scientific competence is founded on scientific discourse considered as a logical syntagmatic form that alone can serve as a basic *referent* for scientific doing seen as a producing act. In other words, the genealogical trajectory of a given science can be justified only if it has been possible to produce—and establish as referential discourse—a generative algorithm of that science, thereby giving it its birth certificate.

The Referent as Object of Science

The idea that scientific discourse, in order to validate its assertions, must construct its own internal referent, continues to shock a whole school of positivist thinkers for whom the ultimate end of science is the exhaustive description of reality. These philosophical presuppositions, of so little consequence in the physical sciences where scientific doing is no longer troubled by metaphysical considerations (Newton and his angels), on the contrary have undeniable repercussions in the area of the human sciences. Confusion there is all the more great because the first scientific discourses on human beings can historically be confused with the discourses of humanism.

In effect, *philology*, as it developed starting with the Renaissance and containing as it does on the one hand the seeds of linguistic and literary research and on the other the seeds of historical study, appears essentially to be a *science of the referent* that seeks to establish and validate textual reality and thereby reach reality pure and simple.

The tremendous amount of work accomplished by philology and whose methodological contribution is obvious, consists, as we know, in the twofold process that seeks at the same time to "establish the text" and the factual conditions needed to *attest to it* as well as to establish "criticism of the text" whose task is to determine the degree of its *credibility*. We can see that *philological discourse*, as discourse on the text, scarcely differs from other discourses that claim to be scientific. Establishment of the text is in fact nothing more than the doing of the discoursing subject, a doing that consists in making judgments on the existence of "entities" (texts), and the criticism that accompanies those judgments consists in the production of secondary discursive subprograms that serve as a reference and allow us to make statements as to credibility, that is, on the truth-values of authentifying discourse. Thus philological discourse that, as referent, seeks to validate the manifested text, must itself construct its own internal referential discourse.

Things become complicated when we stop considering the text to be a purely semiotic entity and presuppose not only its legibility but, above all, the possibility of a reading based on a given cultural code. A small number of concepts, those of literariness, of human nature and its universality, and so on, are thus postulated a priori as constituting the level of content that underlies the text, transforming it into a "language of connotation" whose selective reading cannot fail to enrich, in a tautological way, the already posited conceptual framework. *Humanist ideological discourse* is constructed in this way.

Contrary to this humanist discourse that, thanks to the postulate of the universality of human nature, considers the contents of "ancient" texts to be at the same time present and achronic, in the manner of the myths of archaic societies, *historical discourse* posits that its contents are representations of the nonlinguistic referent of the past. As a continuation, from the genetic point of view, of philological discourse, whose principal givens it takes on in the form of "source criticism," historical discourse differs from philological discourse in its more ambitious aim to reconstruct, with the help of the linguistic referent offered by philological discourse, the extralinguistic referent—"historical reality."

We can see that such a process includes some apriorisms. Instead of postulating, as does humanist discourse, the simultaneously present and universal character of the semantic content of texts, historical discourse introduces two new presuppositions, first replacing the concept of achronicity with that of *temporality* and claiming at the same time that the present signifier of the text is endowed with a past signified. Historical discourse next objectifies this signified of a semantic nature and identifies it with the referent that is external to discourse.

From the point of view of discursive linguistics, the temporalization found in historical discourse is a frequent phenomenon and is explained by the setting in place of the mechanism that consists in stipulating that present utterances are situated in the past, thus creating a *temporal illusion*. The objectification of the signified, in turn, is also known to result from the production of *referential illusion*. Based on the discoursing subject's competence in producing temporal and referential illusions, historical discourse, because it is incapable of attaining the "real" referent, has to comply with the conditions of scientificity of all discourses that claim to be scientific.

This positivist illusion would perhaps not be troublesome if the construction of the historical simulacrum—all sciences construct simulacra, which they substitute for reality—that appears to be the true object of this type of discourse were not affected by it. For it results in another implicit *presupposition*, of the same nature, which allows the claim to be made that "words fit things," that is, that the lexemes and phrases of historical texts really represent the objects of the world and their interrelations. Such an assertion has the unfortunate effect of relieving historical discourse of its duty to construct its *taxonomic level*, a level that linguistics, as we have seen, found so difficult to construct. In these conditions, the best historical discourse (whose "referent" is a given society) can, through the lexicological interpretation of its sources, reproduce only the "categorization of the world" that is inherent to that society and manifested by the lexemes of its universe. While producing as faithful a representation as possible of a given social entity, but while also confusing the instruments of description with the objects to be described, it can no longer account for either the synchronic diversity or the diachronic transformations found in human societies.

It does not matter whether historical discourse stops there or whether it seeks, by setting aside the question of its taxonomy, to construct for itself a historical syntagmatics. The locus at which an *anthropological discourse* has to take its place is now identified. For only a structural comparatism can give the science of history a *taxonomic model* for human societies or, what amounts to the same thing, the methodological tools for a taxonomic doing that it can carry out by constructing semiotic objects, objects to be subsequently referred into the past.

Referential Illusions

This long aside, which has taken us back to the primary scientific operations of the humanities — characterized by the search for a referent that would be at the same time the point of departure for scientific discourse and its *ultima ratio* — has brought us to some apparently paradoxical conclusions.

First, sciences whose inspiration is philological and whose goal is to establish a referent that is external to the discourse that treats it, inevitably end up giving themselves an internal referent, a kind of secondary discourse that allows them to speak of the "real" referent and that is the main support for veridiction of the initial discourse. Thus something specific to scientific discourse, something that unfolds at two levels, is confirmed by this seemingly borderline case.

Second, after recognizing the textual referent and trying to give it a semantic interpretation, philological discourse developed in a way that ended up with two kinds of identification: humanist discourse, which postulates its achronic and universal nature, elevates the text to the level of myth, and historical discourse refers its interpretation to the past and identifies it with a readable "historical reality."

One might say that the referential illusion of historical discourse is an extreme case and is not applicable to the other social sciences whose referent is not temporalized but is rather in a way concomitant with the zero degree time of the discoursing subject. It seemed wise to stop there, even if only because of the extrapolations that some have made using this representation of historical reality as a starting point from which they strive to provide sociology and social ethics with interpretive models and archetypes of behavior. This is a play of mirrors by which historical discourse projects a present "reality" into the past in order to then bring it back into the present. But now it is enriched with an authority founded on truth. This game is just an "ideological machine" that can easily be dismantled, and which in fact discredits all of the social sciences.

Discourse and Syntax

The Actantial Structure of Scientific Discourse

Throughout all of the preceding discussion, we have been able to see that a certain number of important revisions bring themselves to bear if, for the conventional concept of science considered to be an established body of knowledge, we substitute the concept of science as being an undertaking that is progressively being realized by an uninterrupted scientific doing. Scientific discourse then becomes the starting point from which the science that is in the process of being formed can speak of itself. It is also a semantic locus, the analysis of which can be carried out by applying to it an actantial model of a syntactic nature.

Indeed, scientific discourse, from the moment that it is considered to be a *doing*, can be defined syntactically; that is, it can be inscribed within the framework of the canonical utterance that implicitly includes the subject and object of that doing. Now the object of that doing is nothing other than the doing itself, or rather the act of constituting that doing as a state of knowing-how-to-do, just as the "description" of a state. Earlier formulations, according to which science is defined in terms of its reproducibility (or, quite simply, knowing is being-able-to-do), are to be interpreted within this framework. But since this goal is not attained, since it is only aimed for, it is defined as an object of desire, and scientific discourse thereby becomes *a quest for a knowing-how-to-do*.

Given this, the subject of scientific doing finds itself endowed with a *wanting-to-do* that is its desire to be in conjunction with the object of value. At the most, and to the extent that the subject is defined by its attributions, the scientific subject will, at the end of the quest, be conjoined with and confused with its object. In other words, the establishment of a given science means the end of that particular scientific doing. In the meantime, the scientific subject is a vague subject, a subject in the process of being created and one that seeks to bring about a discursive "trail breaking" that will lead it to its object.

As we have seen, the subject that is producing scientific discourse is carrying out a twofold activity. On the one hand it represents the instance that sets in place the mechanism that organizes the proper unfolding of the discourse to be realized. It posits it as veridictory discourse by establishing a whole set of anaphoric workings that allow for the manipulation of the referential discourse that connects the actualized discourse with all preceding knowledge and knowing-how-to-do.

But on the other hand, it carries out a straight and simple discursive doing. We have very much emphasized one aspect of this doing, taxonomic doing, if only because right now this is the activity that seems to be lacking most in the social sciences. This taxonomic doing, although at first blush it seems to have a predicative nature and thereby seems to be carried out only within the framework of a phrastic syntax, is in fact more complex. Since it works through interdefinitions—and not only through definitions—and since it establishes relations of opposition (but also of homology and hyponomy), its syntactic activity, going beyond the boundaries of the utterance, is already transphrastic and organizes whole discursive sequences.

It is obvious, however, that discursive doing is not limited to the construction of taxonomic objects and that its activity also includes the development of syntactic simulacra that can account for the organization of all kinds of semiotic practices, verbalized discourses as well as somatic performative programs. That is, in theory, they can account for all of the organized processes that we can see in the area of the social sciences. In other words, discursive doing, situated within the framework of scientific discourse, constructs taxonomic objects as well as syntactic objects and seeks to account at the same time for both the specific "structures" and "grammars" of the human universe. This discursive doing obviously requires and implies a certain knowing-how-to-do that we tend too readily to identify with methodological knowledge. Experience, especially experience in training future researchers, shows us that knowledge of the principles of classification and of models for construction of grammars does not establish their competence to produce scientific discourses that inevitably come up against the problem posed by the first, naive question, Where do we begin?—a question so often left unanswered. For indeed the question is not one of knowledge of taxonomic or syntactic organizations (which are discursive objects); rather we are dealing with the question of knowledge of the syntactic processes carried out by the scientific discourse that conveys them.

Deontic Doing

It is wise to come back once more to our "average" scientific discourse. Here we find a curious redundancy, all the more surprising as it is totally unexpected—and yet one that we practice ourselves daily. This redundancy involves expressions of the type:

> We must . . .
> It is necessary, indispensable, that . . .
> We are obliged to recognize that . . .
> It is wise to . . . (as indeed the above sentence began), etc.

A superficial examination of this class of expressions allows us to interpret them as being occasional and sometimes rhetorical explications of an autonomous level of discourse where we find the discursive subject's reasoning concerning its own doing, concerning the principles and requirements of its organizing activity. Whether it be partially explicated or whether it remains implicit, underlying the whole of the discourse as a permanent presupposition, the deontic level of discourse must be postulated as the locus at which the subject of enunciation organizes its own performances, foresees obstacles, and passes tests. It must also be seen as the place where the subject develops—or believes itself to be developing—its own rules of discursive organization.

It is a doing that we can also call methodological, as long as it is not confused with established, explicated methodologies. For example, the history of linguistics shows us the enormous gap between simplistic methodology preached by the neogrammarians and their implicit methodological doing, which is the foundation for modern linguistics. The value of the work of someone such as Dumézil certainly, to a great extent, is in the ingenious complexity of his implicit doing, and it is not just because of a simple taste for metaphors that Claude Lévi-Strauss

found that it suited him to refer to the broad outlines of the processes that organize his discourse using terms that designate musical movements.

This does not mean that expressions that come to the surface of discourse, to
manifest the presence of this methodological syntax, are any less consistently formulated in terms of *necessity*, as if one syntactic organization, and not another,
were indispensable, as if only one trajectory could be adopted, being the only
one that could successfully allow the task to be completed. If we take into account the fact that *necessity* ("It is necessary that . . . ") is no more than the
neutralized form of *duty* ("I must . . . "), a form that is obtained by an actantial
disengagement that objectifies and impersonalizes discourse—just as *truth* ("It is
true that . . . ") appeared to us to be the depersonalized form of *knowing* ("I
know that . . . ")—we see that, from the point of view of the discoursing subject, the metasyntactic doing formulated by that subject is regulated by a set of
rules it imposes on itself in terms of having-to-do. The term "deontic," which
we propose to give to this particular doing, is thus justified.

A new element of the actantial structure appears here. The subject of enunciation that, as we have seen, is already endowed with a *wanting-to-do* of a discursive nature, is now also given a new modality, a *having-to-do*, which concerns
the regulation of the discursive doing subordinated to the subject. At this point
we can either go no further or we can seek to interpret this *having-to-do* as being
the counterpart of the imperative contract the receiving subject concluded with its
sender, which in this way had transmitted its own original *wanting-to-do*. This
implicit sender would finally be, in its actantial form (i.e., having to do with the
anthropomorphic imaginary), no more than the affirmation of the presence of a
metalogic, of a universal reasoning that regulates the production of scientific discourses. Hence we see reappearing the old picture of a scientific sender who is
holding the disciplinarian's rod in his hand—a sadistic, or rather masochistic image of a scientific doing that is able to obtain pleasure and even enjoyment, despite what some might think.

Scientific Communication

Along with the deontic doing that we have just identified and the practice of
which presupposes the establishment of new mechanisms at the level of the discursive competence of the subject of enunciation, scientific discourse includes,
willingly or not, a communicative dimension and thereby a communicative doing
whose role, in the development of the modes of presentation of this discourse, is
far from negligible. Although we can claim that the object of scientific discourse
is to construct knowledge, not to transmit it, because its transmission can be carried out under other, more optimal conditions having to do with all nonfigurative
discourse, scientific discourse has its own set of problems: the universal communication of its knowledge.

As we know, the structure for communication includes a sender and a receiver who are interchangeable and each of which is thereby endowed with a sending and receiving competence. Given, however, that the syntactic roles of sender and receiver are assumed by two distinct semantic subjects, each having its own semantic universe and editing and reading code, interindividual communicability is neither obvious nor easy. It is therefore normal that, to the extent communication is founded on a bilateral wanting-to-communicate, a *persuasive doing* develops on the part of the sender and an *interpretive doing*, parallel to it, takes place at the other end of the communication chain. Thus we have two major categories of communication, taking two forms, which scientific discourse can and does assume in its need to be communicated.

As the point where these two opposite practices meet, communication is naturally where misinterpretations, lies, and secrets occur. To eliminate misunderstanding, and to make the knowledge under formulation transmissible, scientific discourse appropriates all those linguistic procedures that allow for guaranteeing as complete and veridical a communication as possible, procedures that have to do with a *knowing-how-to-do* concerned with *causing-to-know*.

It is obvious that the most certain way of eliminating the persuasion and interpretation that follow is by adjusting the scientifico-semantic universe of sender and receiver, in an attempt to establish their equivalence. We have seen that by its very nature scientific doing contributes to this. Taxonomic doing, which defines ''entities'' and substitutes arbitrary names for them, excludes figurativity and polysemy in favor of symbolic formulations based on monosememes. Cognitive anaphorical factors, while picking up earlier scientific *doing* contained in the referential discourse, brings it to the fore as a *knowledge about doing* thus integrating it within a single veridictory isotopy. The enunciative contract is thus struck under maximum conditions of intelligibility.

It is this illusory identification of sender and receiver initially explaining the appearance of a ''we'' that subsumes both of the preceding instances of communication (sender and receiver). This ''we'' readily becomes a ''they'' or ''people,'' labels that are supposed to identify just any subject of the discourse in order finally to shade out the subject with various ''it is true,'' ''it is necessary'' expressions that regulate the utterances of communicative doing. The subjects of those expressions become part of the inventory of names: algorithmic discourse is, finally, a discourse without a specific subject.

These are the actantial disengagement procedures that we know about. They in fact merely camouflage the subject of enunciation, and they are mechanisms we can easily dismantle. What is important in the final analysis is not their manner of linguistic existence, but rather the undertaking they reveal, an undertaking that is nothing else but the setting into place of the *subject, whatever subject, of scientific discourse, a subject that guarantees the generalized transmissibility of that discourse*. Everyone can speak the language of science, which, in theory, is understandable by all.

This is the way one can measure the gap between scientific discourse and what it undertakes to do. Just as with scientific doing, whose goal, as we have seen, is to eliminate the distance between the subject and object of its doing, communicative doing seeks to abolish the difference between sender and receiver. The scientific enterprise thus seems to be self-destructive, seeking to abolish the conditions under which it is practiced and to install a universal subject of knowledge whose doing would no longer have any meaning. Although the actantial structure that gives life to the subject by dividing it into distinct instances and positions and by being the foundation for its quest for knowledge and its desire to transmit, appears as a model having an ideological nature, the final undertaking inscribed within that actantial model seeks, on the contrary, to shade out ideological tensions.

Science and Ideology

The Ideological Model of Science

If we take into account not only the methodological uncertainties that today characterize the social sciences—some of which do not seem to have gone beyond a doxological state—but also the fallout from a generalized crisis in our culture, it is quite natural for the scientific status of those sciences to be called into question, quite natural for them to be considered ideologies. Both accusations are often unfounded. What is less acceptable is that these judgments are made, not by people who can claim to be engaged in a science, but rather by those who speak in the name of other ideologies, thus bringing scientific debate into the framework of ideological battles.

The social sciences are aware of their weaknesses and can be identified not by their scientific status but rather by their undertaking, and a certain scientific doing that they carry out in the name of that project. This undertaking, like any human enterprise, cannot fail to be ideological. We explicitly accepted this when we undertook to give an actantial structure to the subject of scientific enunciation. As soon as we begin to examine more closely the components of this model, however, we see them as having characteristics that distinguish them from other ideological models. We will not raise this point again. Given the present state of our knowledge concerning the conditions for production of discourse and our knowledge of the typology of discourses, it is perhaps premature for us to try to identify the specific traits of scientific discourse, and this is all the more so because any given instance of scientific discourse that is in fact realized is likely to show only tendencies toward those traits and therefore the criteria we might establish run the risk of being relative and noncategorical. Remember, scientific discourse is supposed to exhaust its own ideological enterprise.

Philosophical Discourse and Scientific Discourse

Nevertheless the debate within the social sciences concerning the interferences between science and ideology remains open today, and the problems thereby raised are significant. It appears that the comparison of scientific discourse with other doxological discourses (the name under which we bring together discourses of an epistemological nature, such as mythologies or philosophies of knowledge, but also prescientific theories and even certain aspects of scientific theories) can, even if it cannot solve those problems, cast some light on them. Let us take an extreme case as an example, one that involves a theory that claims to be scientific. At first blush, things seem relatively simple.

If, in order to define them, we were to examine all of the constituent concepts of a given field of knowledge and if we succeeded in establishing, through their interdefinitions, a stringing together of those concepts that was both hierarchical and logical, thinking that is founded on the fact that these concepts presuppose each other, we would end up finally being able to account for only a small number of the presupposed concepts. Further, these few concepts would remain undefined and indefinable even though we could say that they represent the epistemological level, a level that is at the same time unfounded and the foundation of this field of knowledge. It is possible then, starting from this inventory of epistemic concepts, to give an axiomatic form to the scientific theory concerned with this field and which justifies, using deductive procedures, the setting into place of its operative concepts. Under these conditions, the epistemic level could be seen as being the foundation for both the proper carrying out of scientific doing and as the locus for the examination of the consistency and value of the theory itself.

Thus, we take an example that concerns us closely from among those of us who have agreed to see in the Saussurian theory of the sign the foundational kernel of our theory of language. Philosophers who have become interested in it— from Merleau-Ponty to Foucault—have all put the sign at the center of their considerations. Yet, if we look at this from a semiotic point of view, we see that the theory of the sign is not a point of juncture but rather, on the contrary, the place where philosophical and scientific discourses diverge. Epistemologists, starting there, try to widen the debate by posing the general problem of semiosis; linguists, on the contrary, even if they are curious to know how signs are constituted, can focus only on the moment when they are dissolved, which opens for them the possibility of analyzing linguistic forms situated beyond the sign. Just as, in the seventeenth century, theories of representation did not allow linguistics to become a science, so too in the nineteenth century "false" interpretations of the sign did not prevent linguistics from making substantial progress. Scientific practice today remains independent of the theory of sign and its repercussions on philosophical thought. It is as if the theory of the sign were *presupposed* by semiotic practice while being nonetheless not *necessary* for its exercise.

This does not mean denying any relation between philosophical and scientific discourse—quite the contrary, we want to identify scientific theory as the mediating instance between the two. If, however, we can show the complexity of those relations, we can refute the simplistic explanation according to which epistemes are generative and, at the same time, regulate both ideologies and sciences. A scientist is a product of his or her time and must participate in the episteme of the time. But what the scientist draws from that episteme seems to require being integrated into something quite different, in a doing, which has its own logic.

The Diachronic Dimension

If we examine the status of the internal referent constituted by scientific discourse, we find it necessary to consider this discourse, taken as a whole, as being endowed with an algorithmic form, as a program whose end point becomes clear only after the fact, following the reconstruction of an earlier scientific doing. It is within the framework of such a discourse that *scientific progress* should be placed. This would be defined as the syntagmatic unfolding of a productive and transformative doing that, in the form of referent, is transmissible and reintegratable vis-à-vis discourses yet to follow. We can see that such a concept of progress is opposed to traditional myth and ideology concerning progress. These latter concepts appeared in certain historical circumstances that are epistemically identifiable. Likewise, the idea of progress, as it applies to science, cannot be applied to ideologies. It would be absurd to speak of ideological progress. Ideologies can be compared to each other, can confront each other and negate each other. They do not connect with each other to form a progression and negate each other. When he identifies epistemic discontinuities, Michel Foucault is simply drawing conclusions from that observation.

The problem of the segmentation of social history, seen as a catalogue of discontinuities or as an identification of changes, can be transposed in such a way as to give rise to questions concerning the nature of those transformations that affect scientific discourse. Yet it seems impossible ultimately to synchronize the two types of discourse because the only real problem arising when we examine the diachronic transformations of a scientific discipline concerns its nonconcomitance, or the ways it does not meet up with the prescientific theories covering the same area of interest. This problem arises when a practice that wants to lay claim to being a science begins to be effective, to "get a real handle on reality." The movement from a doxological to a scientific state, while confirming the attenuated nature of the links between the two modes of thought, appears no less to be a decisive break.

The advent of linguistics as a science can, as we know, be placed in the first decades of the nineteenth century. This scientific "revolution," however, shows up as being neither a discontinuity nor even a sudden change. It rather takes the form of an *event*. To interpret it, indeed, we have to appeal to many causes—of which none, taken separately, is enough. These causes represent references to heterogeneous semantic loci. The epistemic horizon that is the background for this event was, for a century and a half, made up of a linguistic debate having to do first with the origin of languages. Then came the debate as to their interconnectedness and sources, all problems which are a mark of the last century's great questions about history. Yet what was practiced, and was carried out within the framework of this debate, but independently of it, ends up in the constructing of a comparative grammar whose models are, at the very least, ahistoric.

If we now try to analyze the event itself, we see that it, to a large extent, presupposes taxonomic doing (recognition of units that were called morphemes), but that it also is part of the episteme of the eighteenth century ("love of system") and that of the nineteenth century (a positivism that led to dealing only with a closed corpus of identified morphemes). We can also see that the *event* cannot be explained without allusion to historical contingencies that are just as numerous (presupposing that people knew Sanskrit, for example, but also taking German because of its heavy morphological composition, and considering it as the place where the event can be seen, etc.).

Of course this was an event, and a historical event at that. The evenemential history of a social science—linguistics in this case—will continue as in the past and be filled, in its way, with "sound and fury." But at the same time this event will have produced something that goes beyond; it will have made a qualitative leap, by engendering, in the strong sense of the term, an embryo that will hereafter develop its own scientific undertaking, unbeknownst to those who participate in its practice. And things will not be as before. Linguistics, having escaped from ideological interplay, will be neither mechanistic nor positivistic nor historicizing, and, despite appearances, doxological discourses about it will no longer influence it. Something will have changed.

Chapter 3
The Pathways of Knowledge

A. J. Greimas and E. Landowski

Preliminary Remarks

Born of structural linguistics and the study of folklore and mythology and starting in the decade of the 1960s, semiotics began to assert its claim to autonomy, both as a way of thinking about the conditions under which meaning is produced and grasped and as group of procedures that can be applied in the concrete analysis of signifying objects. The relatively rapid development of its theoretical and methodological tools allowed it to multiply its forays into areas outside mythology and folklore, which had been its original fields of operations. Although this widening of its area of activity was at first done in the domain of literature and poetics, research (without neglecting the study of nonlinguistic meaning systems) soon encompassed many nonliterary discourses. These included religious, philosophical, legal, and sociopolitical discourses. In thus widening its investigation to include very heterogeneous textual and cultural realities semiotics was implicitly claiming the status of a theory (and a methodology) that, within the limits of its own principles of relevance, would be able to account for the widest range of the forms in which society produces meaning. Today, as we take up the study of a discourse that claims the status of *scientific*—particularly in the *social sciences*—we reach an important stage in the evolutionary path that, beginning with relatively simple forms (which at least were figurative), led semioticians to become more and more interested in signifying organizations, especially as they include greater and greater degrees of complexity and abstraction.

Toward a Semiotics of Cognitive Discourse

If, by way of preliminary remarks, we sought to set out this little "history of semiotics," we should have also described, along with the process of diversification of areas of research, the succession of revisions of tools of analysis that accompanied and, at the same time, made possible, the study of new semiotic objects. We would then see that, if semiotic theory became bit by bit richer and more complex, it was in large measure under the impulse and control of practical analysis. Conversely, one of the raisons d'être of any attempt at analysis is the hope that at least a modicum of reward will be reaped on the *theoretical* level. This is particularly true for the *readings* brought together in this collection.[1] But our historical retrospective should also show how, at a third level, the progressive taking on of bodies of knowledge that were very foreign to one another and that, generally speaking, had to do with "established" disciplines, periodically brought about the need to reformulate the overall goal of semiotics and above all define the place of its various enterprises in relation to its sister disciplines.

Thus, in this case, we have to ask to what extent semiotic metalanguage is based on principles and has goals that are distinct from those of other extant metalanguages — such as logic, epistemology, or philosophy of knowledge — which, from various perspectives, also take scientific discourse to be their object of study. Since we are not undertaking epistemologically to examine what constitutes the specificity of each of these disciplines, we will limit ourselves to emphasizing, with regard to the objectives of the semiotic approach, that we will not be formulating evaluations of the validity of the content of scientific discourses taken as objects, and we will not be defining rules for the production of true knowledge. Our task is limited to *identifying and explaining* discursive forms and their *typology*. This typological goal should not be confused with any kind of regulating activity concerning discourse in the human sciences. Semiotics makes judgments about "being," that is, about the manner of existence of semiotic objects; it does not try to set up any "having-to-be" or "having-to-do." It posits no necessity and establishes no norms (which does not at all exclude the possibility of examining the way in which discourse-objects do so). Just as analysis of literary texts allowed us to identify and explain the logical and grammatical regularities of narrative forms in terms that are not to be confused either with the formalizations of logic itself or with models for the grammar of a language, so too the identification of the discursive forms that organize texts of a scientific nature should lead to a *semiotic theory of cognitive discourse* that should be situated at a level other than a strictly epistemological one.

This collection represents an initial contribution to the development of this theory. Yet, true to an attitude known to most semioticians, we cannot conceive of the construction of models without a concomitant process whereby those models confront the concrete reality for which they are supposed to account. That is why our approach to scientific discourse will consist of a series of *analyses of texts*, an approach that of course does not prevent any later effort to systematize. This is borne out by the generalizations that several of the participants in this joint enterprise make throughout their analyses. It is also borne out by the theoretical model that we ourselves will later propose. Given this, and given the methodological advantages of concrete analysis, the choice of texts to be taken as our objects of study becomes very important. Two kinds of criteria of selection governed the definition of our "corpus." Some concern the degree to which given texts are representative; others concern the semiotic status of the texts.

On the Representativity of the Texts Analyzed

Bringing together and studying a small number of discourses that might be considered to be representative of some of the main orientations of research in the human and social sciences in France since the beginning of the century—this is the spirit in which, and the almost limitless framework within which, our participants were asked to make their choices of texts. Rather than utopistically trying to cover all of social science, we wanted to confront a limited number of procedures, as diverse and historically significant as possible. Taking into account the personal preferences and preoccupations of the participants, three or four areas of research, or kinds of approaches, were selected: anthropology (represented by extracts from the works of Georges Dumézil and Claude Lévi-Strauss), sociology and history (Marcel Mauss, André Siegfried, Pierre Francastel, Lucien Febvre), philosophy (Gaston Bachelard, Maurice Merleau-Ponty, Paul Ricoeur), and semiology (Roland Barthes). This is a pleiades in which the Collège de France is so abundantly represented that we have to block immediately the suspicion that we have confused our own criteria of selection with those of eligibility to the prestigious institution—a confusion that, in any event, would not have sufficed to justify all the lacunae in our "sample."

In addition to the complete omission of certain main disciplines, first and foremost linguistics and economics, one might wonder about the absence of any reference to some of the more important works, in those areas that we *did* choose, of such people as Jean-Paul Sartre or Raymond Aron, Michel Foucault, Jacques Lacan, or Louis Althusser. These exclusions—except for the last three— are arbitrary. They are dictated only by the preferences of the members of a team whose limited number prevented us from covering everything. This cannot alone explain why none of our analyses concerns the research of the great representatives of "structuralism" that we just mentioned (although this sometimes too facile label has often been refused by those to whom it has been applied). We did in fact begin to study them, then stopped. Whether it was an Althusserian reading of Marx or a Lacanian return to Freud, on the surface we found we were dealing with "authoritative discourses" organized around the rather prophetic relationship linking the interpreter's discourse with that of the original thinker. But even more importantly, these are procedures that are both related to and rival semiotics, implying the problematics of the Subject (Lacan), a concept of Ideology (Althusser), general thoughts on the "order of discourse" (Foucault), which could not be handled in only a few pages. Rather than being the object of individual analyses, they undoubtedly represent material for a truly theoretical debate that would be so extensive that it could not be undertaken here. That debate will surely find its occasion elsewhere.

Comparatively speaking, however, it seemed useful to us to add to our sample two kinds of very different texts that, while belonging to the humanities, are found on the margins of strictly scientific activity and seek only to identify certain forms of "comprehension." These are literary criticism on the one hand, and religious commentary on the other. Analyzing them allows us negatively to identify some of the requirements for a discourse that would be scientific, in particular as concerns the problem of metalanguage. It should be noted, for example, in literary criticism, how the status of the metaterms used—sometimes considered to be commonly used by both "critic" and reader—allow Sorin Alexandrescu to specify the nature of the interpretive discourse that takes place within this area. It is a discourse based on the use of an implicit metalanguage that allows interpretations to be superimposed on one another without the logical connection between them being all that obvious. Thus we see posited the problem of the *hierarchy* of interpretations. With the discourse of "commentary," analyzed by Louis Panier, we are, on the other hand, faced with the problem of a *typology* of interpretation that, transposed to the level of scientific discourse, is at the very heart of our inquiry into the social sciences.

If there is representativity, it is, in the final analysis, defined not so much in relation to the range of disciplines we might have undertaken to study, as it is in relation to observable kinds of *procedures*. From this point of view, the authors we are considering seem to us to be, albeit summarily, distributed according to three great families of approaches to research to which the main divisions of this collection correspond:

1. discourse in search of scientific certitudes;
2. questions as to the very meaning of research;
3. discourse of interpretation.

The first attitude somewhat reflects the optimism of a generation of builders (Mauss, Siegfried, Dumézil, Febvre, Lévi-Strauss). The second on the contrary expresses, through a much more "philosophical" kind of thought, a state of "crisis" in the social sciences. This is why we include texts that for us have to do either with a "philosophy of signs" (Merleau-Ponty), or with a "philosophy of language" (Ricoeur). This is also why we include texts that demonstrate a wavering between pure epistemological inquiry and true scientific practice (Bachelard, Francastel, Barthes). On the one hand, as a quest for scientific certitudes, the discourse of the social sciences is necessarily required to set out the conditions for the truthfulness of its own utterances. The problem of "truth saying" (veridiction) in this case constitutes its end goal. Conversely, once research starts inquiring into its own ultimate goals, the problem of veridiction is displaced. It is no longer a matter of *sanctioning* after the fact a knowledge acquired earlier, but rather of guaranteeing, in advance, the epistemic foundations of a discourse yet to come. As opposed to these two attitudes, there is finally the tendency to do away with all preoccupation concerning what constitutes the foundation, or what sanctions, discourse. This preoccupation characterizes all purely interpretive approaches.

The Semiotic Status of the Corpus

In order to put the procedures of semiotic analysis into practice and avoid having our reading take the form of a more or less loose and uncontrolled interpretation, it seemed prudent, if not necessary, to limit ourselves to relatively short texts, extracts even (at the same time it was convenient that they be short enough to be reproduced here, for reading as part of the analyses devoted to them). Thus, above and beyond the somewhat arbitrary choices of our authors, a new group of restrictions, this time having to do with the length and status of our text objectives, led us to opt for, using the very definition of the corpus, a *level* of grasping of scientific discourse that, alone might determine the general problematics of this work.

If we were to justify ourselves completely, we would probably have to go back to the "conditions of production" for scientific discourse and note, in a completely elementary way, that all research activity, before it can live up to its promise and *produce* knowledge, will have a certain number of requirements and will engage in *consuming* certain resources. These may be money, intellectual energy, and—as concerns what directly interests us, albeit seemingly trivial—unlimited amounts of paper that synthesized material from each stage of the research, from the simple initial undertaking to the final presentation of results, with all kinds of documents along the way (working notes, sketched-out plans, rough drafts, etc.). At an extreme, each one of these "traces" would warrant analysis itself. Since the semiotic perspective moved purely genetic preoccupations into a position of secondary importance, however, it should not be surprising that we concentrated our analyses exclusively on what was the *end product* of the research, or at least on what, in published form, presents itself as being, at least for the moment, its "final and finished" expression. Scientific discourse is probably not exclusively found in works or articles whose editorial status might make for this sole rightful claim to "scientificity" ("specialized" journals, "university" editions, "research" libraries). But it is on these texts that we in fact concentrated our efforts.

But another problem, to us more real, then came along. Given that we were going to take on only short extracts, what should dictate our choice of such extracts? We could see two different solutions. We could isolate sequences that directly represented *scientific doing* in process, the idea being to grasp the activity of the authors at the very moment when it was being carried out (although no reading can give direct access to the concrete steps of research because the discourse of the human sciences always conveys a reconstruction of the practice that is its foundation). Or, we could call on the metadiscourses with which the authors, in their desire to justify their methods, express — in the form of theoretical prefaces and conclusions — the results, strictly speaking, of their research. The participants adopted one of these solutions, although it was the second that clearly was preferred. In the first case, the choice as to what is "representative" is largely intuitive, but as Jean-Claude Coquet himself says, the relevance of this choice has to do with a hypothesis concerning the coherence of the discourse to be analyzed. In the second case, the perspective is quite different. It is not a study of the "real" procedures practiced by the scholar (if indeed such are ever accessible to us), but rather "secondary elaborations," simulacra of procedures that have been observed by a scientific subject who can stand back as if he had twinned himself.

The privileged status accorded by most of the participants to the study of discursive segments is not without consequences. First, it allows us to reconcile the shortness of the extracts chosen with as global as possible a perspective of the organization of the procedures of each of the authors chosen. Of course that organization is seen mainly in terms of the way those authors themselves conceive of it, or wish to have us conceive of it. At the same time, the typological ambitions that inspire this enterprise are undertaken less through a grasping of scientific discourse as we might find it uttered "in the first degree," and more in terms of a problematics of the "second degree" having to do with discourses that "stage for us the drama" of the quest for knowledge. This shift produces a reading that is less attentive to the *technologies of discovery* than it is to what we might call the *"scenography" of research*. In relation to what we set as our first intention, our activity has been a little skewed. Instead of analyzing the *functioning* (i.e., the manner of existence and production) of the discourses of the social sciences, the choice of metasequences leads us to ask questions about the *foundations* of scientific practice. This is why there is a perhaps excessive weight given to epistemological considerations in this volume. Nevertheless it is possible that the responsibility for this "deviation" does not rest entirely with the analysts and their *partis pris*. Perhaps the relatively arbitrary nature of the choice as to corpus also corresponds to certain properties that are intrinsic to the field of study. If in *logic*, for example, we think of the way in which shakiness of foundations (based on still-debatable axioms) contrasts with the solid validity of its calculation procedures (wherein we find the technological aspect of scientific practice), then can we not say that, conversely, it is the mark and in a sense the "weakness" of discourse in the *social sciences* that such discourse seemingly is constantly required to reformulate its "beginning" (through constant questioning of its foundations and conditions under which it can exist), before it can "function" and "produce" algorithmically?

The Problematics of Cognitive Discourse as Story

In a rough-and-ready way, we can see each of the fragments studied in this collection as a little *story*. We must, however, find a minimum definition for this term, one that will include the notion of a simple *transformation of state*. Beginning with an initial state of lack (which, in the cognitive dimension, is generally characterized by a /not-knowing/) and following the main outlines of the Proppian schema, there is progress toward a final state of conjunction with an object of value (in this case a certain /knowing/), the initial state of lack is corrected by a performing subject who, at an earlier stage, had been endowed with cognitive competence. Despite the schematic and, by definition, reductive, nature of the preceding, such a model for reading in fact includes several levels of function — and therefore of grasped meaning — for the cognitive discourses that it takes as an object of study.

Semantic Organization and Surface Syntax

The narrative schema we have just laid out first requires, from its *deep level*, the identification of the logico-semantic operations that account for the movement between two forms of organization of content (/inverted content/ → / posited content/), where the one, in relation to the central kernel of the quest for knowledge, includes a "before" of the story, and the other an "after" (a transformation that, for example, in Bachelard, is seen as a movement from a "dated story" to a "validated story"). This substitution at the level of content finds a homology in the modal transformation of the type: /knowing/ → /not-knowing/, which, in the interval between a "question" and its "answer" (cf. Dumézil, Siegfried), implicitly contains a complete program of acquisition (of knowledge) and thereby subtends the organization of the *surface level*, that is, of the narrative syntax itself. As we shall see, it is mainly this level that the analyses to follow study. In one sense, this orientation was predictable as soon as we decided that our goal was to identify and explain the procedures (the real ones or the "staged" ones, at this point it matters little) of research and not to analyze — even less evaluate — the contents research handles or produces. We must note, however, that the semantic component was not completely neglected because at least one of the contributors (Joseph Courtés), undertakes to clarify the interplay of isotopies (figurative and thematic ones) in the discourse of Lévi-Strauss. Courtés is able to demonstrate the fundamental role of transcoding phenomena (wherein one isotopy serves to describe another) in the development of scientific metalanguage. Following a different slant, the same problems are raised by Sorin Alexandrescu and Louis Panier in their discussion of the discourse of interpretation—which are metalinguistic but not scientific—upon which "criticism" superimposes itself and alongside which "commentary" juxtaposes itself.

In relation to the preceding semantic analyses whose objective was to describe the *systematic* organization of knowledge at the level of *discourse objects* that represent established theories (or, to use Anglo-Saxon terminology, at the level of the great scientific "paradigms"), the syntactic analysis carried out by most of the participants is on the contrary concentrated on a more "superficial" level, the level at which we can see the *cognitive doing* that represents the *process* of producing knowledge—it being understood that because of the metadiscursive status of the corpus chosen for study, we are dealing with a "reconstructed" activity. In the first case (with cognitive discourse being considered from the point of view of the system), the analysis was carried out on *uttered discourses* that, through actantial "disengagement," had acquired an autonomy vis-à-vis the instance of enunciation, an instance that thereby becomes irrelevant for that analysis. On the other hand, once we move away from process (i.e., where the procedures for the *narrativization* of cognitive discourse are taken as an object of study), the problematics of *enunciation* impose themselves as being one of the main dimensions of the analysis. Cognitive activity, being a narrativized doing, is in effect necessarily the responsibility of a semiotic "subject" (which is either directly set into the discourse, or is presupposed by that discourse) whose interventions will explicitly, or otherwise, manifest the presence of the actants of communication (and, according to the type of "engagement" so effected, we will speak sometimes of a relationship of narrator/narratee, and sometimes of a relationship of presupposed enunciator/implicit enunciatee).

The introductory metadiscourses we have seen are not articulated only as quest or construction stories whose goal is the setting up of *objects* (of knowledge). They are at the same time, and perhaps above all, stories that we might even call initiation stories that tell of the bringing into being of *subjects* (knowing subjects). One might probably wonder—from the point of view of "genre" typology—what writing *topos* our authors are implicitly conforming to by introducing their works using such highly narrativized discourse. (It will perhaps be noted that this very opening exposition itself has not escaped this tendency to "dramatize" the first steps of research.) If for the moment we leave aside the question of the function of such an arrangement, we can, with the help of semiotic tools that are already available to us, go a little further in our observation and description by specifying the nature of its syntactic constants.

Two Principles Concerning the Structuring of Narrative

If we keep to the general characteristics of the functioning of the surface level of discourse, we can schematically say that narrativity is manifested there according to two main principles of syntactic articulation: "polemicization" of discourse, and "programmation" of story.

A *polemical* structure (here, of course, the term is not accompanied by any value judgment) itself takes two forms (ultimately to be combined). Sometimes it represents a *syntagmatic doubling* of the cognitive discourse, presenting, in succession, the story of a failure, then the story of a success. Such is the case with Barthes, Febvre, and Dumézil. With Francastel, the first sequence can be further broken down into /virtual failure/ ("dangerous" or "risky" directions that might be taken) vs. /realized failure/. Sometimes we have the *paradigmatic projection* of an antisubject who might take on a figurative form (for example, the "first analysts of the story" that are recalled by Barthes. They might be, as in the case of Mauss, a group of anthropomorphic actors working in opposition to the narrator vis-à-vis the interpretation of a "difficult line of verse": "Some understand: . . . , others interpret: . . . I lean toward the second explanation"). In many cases, the antisubject will all the more "naturally" retain an abstract form for the fact that it generally appears less at the level of cognitive doing strictly speaking (or operative discourse), and more at the level of the epistemological preparatives for the modalization of the cognitive doing (or foundational discourse—these distinctions will be taken up and clarified in the next paragraph). Thus, for example, the presuppositions for ethnological description or for philological interpretation (for Mauss) or, even more generally, the presuppositions for "intuitionism" (for Francastel), will constitute a threat, since they are epistemological attitudes that represent the antisubject, against the very foundations of the enunciator-subject's scientific undertaking. If, in all of these examples, the dichotomy of the actantial positions (subject vs. antisubject) echoes the duality of the actors present (Mauss: "some" vs. "others"; Siegfried: "Many think . . . as for me, I am convinced that . . . "), nothing prevents us from conceiving of an "interiorization" of these contradictions at the level of just one actor. This syncretism is particularly obvious in Dumézil (the enunciator, led first into defeat, then success, himself takes on the two roles, each at the appropriate moment). It is equally obvious in Merleau-Ponty (where the epistemic subject appears both as subject and antisubject).

Even after we have noted these phenomena, they become especially interesting only if we can interpret them in terms of a more general model, a model into which will be integrated, among other observations, those that have to do both with sequential divisions and distribution of actantial roles. This theoretical model—or at least this hypothetical framework whose first purpose is to ensure the coherence of our own metadiscourse on our texts—represents the second principle mentioned previously (i.e., the organizing of cognitive discourse in the form of *narrative programs*), and it is this principle that will give us the means with which to conceive of the principal levels of articulation for those narrative programs.

Levels of Articulation and Types of Discourse

Two distinct formulations, which end up providing more or less equivalent representations of the same model, can be envisaged. There can be an actantial formulation (particularly in the analyses of Jean-Claude Coquet and Jean-Marie Floch), or there can be a functional formulation (which we will single out for discussion in the paragraphs to follow). The first is based on the specific identification of the semiotic status to be attributed to each of the *discoursing subjects* that, respectively, become responsible for the various logical sequences of the cognitive program. Thus, for example, the "epistemic subject" who inspires the quest for knowledge is, theoretically, distinct from the "scientific subject" who has to carry it out. The other formulation, on the contrary, directly highlights the narrative function of each of the sequences under study. It allows for the identification and putting into relation of the various *discursive levels* when we find ourselves faced with a group of texts representing the superimposition of all or several of the levels provided by the model. For instance, when we are dealing with texts that are, on the contrary, characterized by the dominance of one of the theoretically predictable levels, it allows us to posit the existence of *types of discourse*, each being defined according to the specific nature of the "disequilibrium" that it brings into the organization of the canonical model.

On the one hand this plurality of points of view does not seem troublesome to us, given that the different formulations with which we ultimately end up are, as we were saying, more or less equivalent. It does not matter if one and the same object-text is analyzed in terms of the status of its subjects (epistemic, scientific, etc.), or if it is described in terms of its hierarchical articulation into levels (foundational, operative, etc.). It does not matter if it is seen in terms of such and such a corresponding "type"—because all of the preceding different semiotic realities, and the terminologies designating them, are homologable. Yet on the one hand, vis-à-vis the orientation of our research, there is a source of possible ambiguity to the extent that hierarchical analysis—which *decomposes* the apparent unity of text-objects by identifying their various *levels* of internal articulation— can appear to be not immediately compatible with a typological focus that, for its part, in order to construct *types* or discursive classes, takes text-objects as being *unitary* components. This difficulty can be seen in the very organization of our collection. The distribution of the three main parts (making up the corpus of the work), which is determined by the grouping of our authors according to what we have called the three great families of attitudes, represents a "typologizing" perspective (the discourses of the "quest for certitudes" schematically having to do with the *operative type*, the "questions as to the meaning of the research" with the *foundational type*, the interpretations analyzed in the third part thus being able to be read as the negative version of a discourse of the *veridictory type*). On the other hand, it is the other "hierarchizing" perspective that, organizing here our view of the whole, will allow us to construct a hypothetical model with which to account for the *canonical architecture* of cognitive discourse. Specific instances of such discourses and the types noted earlier will thus appear after the fact as simple partial realizations of that model.

Hierarchy and Typology

The Operative Level: The Production of Knowledge

In various degrees, the group of texts analyzed here underline the logic of the constitutive *operations* of the research processes whose unfolding they are supposed to trace. Of course these operations can be interpreted only in terms of the actants they bring into play, that is, at a minimum, the subject that enacts them and the objects to which they are applied. Yet, independently of the actantial analysis that thus shows itself to be so necessary, it is possible, taking into account the recurrence of a series of predicates that lexicalize the cognitive activities of the operating subject (e.g., "noting," "observing," "examining," "clarifying," "grouping together," "comparing," "calculating") to identify and methodologically isolate, under the name of *operative discourse*, a first autonomous discursive level. Whether it is a simple informative doing, passive (e.g., "we see that . . . it appears that . . . ") or active ("if you look . . . carefully examining"), or whether, among other possible types of cognitive procedures, it is a taxonomic doing (based on such or such a principle of logical classification or semantic organization), or even a comparative doing whose aim is to clarify the relations between identified or constructed objects using the preceding operations), we have, at this level, a discourse composed of *utterances of doing* that reveal the performances that are productive of knowledge — as opposed to both modal utterances that, as we shall see in the following section, are the foundation for the competence of the performing subject, and as opposed also to utterances of state (see this chapter, "The Veridictory Level"), which are applied to the very objects of knowledge.

As we cannot fail to note, terminology will vary from one article in this collection to another — subject of scientific or methodological doing with some, performing or operating subject with others, or even cognitive subject *stricto sensu*: all are equally valid, and a coherence between the different approaches should be sought, more fundamentally, at the methodological level. That coherence is guaranteed by virtue of the fact that all proceed by breaking down cognitive discourse into /performance programs/ (operating level) vs. /competence programs/ (foundational level). Thus our own operative doing consists in first, very concretely, noting "significant formal disjunctions" (Ivan Darrault, in reference to the Roland Barthes text). These disjunctions, within the linguistic arrangement of the texts manifested here, convey the narrative programmation of discourse. At the level of performance (which presupposes an earlier phase at which competence is acquired—we will shortly be coming back to this point), it is the construction of the cognitive object that orients the *trajectory* to be followed by the subject—a term whose metaphorical value seems not to be misplaced, given the importance of spatializing and temporalizing images for the "placing of discourse" of the processes of research. However sophisticated in its procedures, however theoretical as to its purpose, the quest for knowledge remains, at the level of narrative imagination, a "road" to be traveled (Bachelard). Thus, in the analyses to follow, spatial or temporal disjunctions are frequently used among the various criteria for textual segmentation.

These figurative distributions represent no more than a metaphorical and simplified expression of the logic at work when access to scientific thought is sought. In this regard, the contrast is extreme between those forms—from the simplest to the most complex—which can take on the narrativization of cognitive doing within the discursive genres we are considering. On the one hand, as most simply expressed, the quest for knowledge can include minimal programs that are nothing more than the carrying out of a small number of individual acts at specific points in time (waiting→seeing; looking→discovering): this is the way things normally are done in the areas of mythological or folkloric literature. On the other hand, as it involves would-be scientific discourse, cognitive performance can be broken down into a multiplicity of acts that themselves are organized into subprograms (or use programs) that mediate in the process of acquiring access to knowledge. According to the logic that articulates any given article (i.e., according to whether that logic appears to be defined *ex ante* or whether it can be defined only *ex post*), we can theoretically identity two categories for the discourse of research. There is an *algorithmic* type, which is a succession of manipulations directly carried out on the object of the research and that unfolds "according to the rules" (Lévi-Strauss), that is, the more or less restrictive rules of a previously established method (which thus becomes representative of the subject's competence). The second type is *heuristic* discourse, which, on the contrary, accounts for the operations necessary if, however hesitatingly, there is to be acquisition of methodological tools and principles of organization (relative to the material that is taken as the object of research) that are needed if the main program is to be realized. So it is that, in the case of Georges Dumézil's comparatism, following an initial failure caused by the insufficiencies of an initial classificatory operation, his comparison of mythical figures was successfully realized only after the setting into place of a new taxonomic organization (substituting a qualitative logic of a semantic type for the logic of inclusion used in the first attempt).

No doubt greater emphasis could have been placed on an explanation and definition of these different "strategies" for scientific knowledge. From one article to another, the reader will find elements of some general thinking as to what constitutes both the common denominator and the raison d'être of those articles, that is, the construction of the object of the research, along with the inseparable correlated problem of setting up a principle of relevance—whether, among other examples, one is attempting to define a *sociology* of "art" (Francastel), a *geography* of "public opinion" (Siegfried), or the *evaluation* of a "text" (Barthes). Our comparative thrust is realized at this level with the description of the taxonomic doing, of which the main variants we have noted—typological with Mauss, comparative with Dumézil, homological with Lévi-Strauss—leave open the possibility of their confronting each other, a confrontation that would warrant being taken up and developed.

The Foundational Level: The Conditions for Knowing

However essential they might be (since they represent the very process of the production of knowledge), the utterances of the cognitive doing have a semiotic existence only in terms of the actantial arrangement according to which they are articulated. So it is that the discourse of research that has been identified can be conceived as an intermediary stage located between two other discursive levels with which it is linked according to a logic of presupposition. Thus we should first envisage a discursive level that is of an earlier stage and that reveals the *conditions* for cognitive performance, that is, the modal status—competence— of the subject. It can then, rather symmetrically vis-à-vis the core problematics represented by the performative discourse, provide for a subsequent level, this one reserved for the utterance that will convey the *results* of the cognitive doing and the validation of those results. It is indeed clear that the cognitive operations (taxonomic or comparative ones, for example), while conditioning the production of results, themselves presuppose, if they are to be carried out, the support of a modalizing subject. From the anthropomorphic point of view that regulates the surface syntax of discourse, we initially have "curiosity and the desire to understand" (Siegfried), desires born of the personal "experience" of the subject, or, what syntactically amounts to the same thing, some task that is assigned to the subject (such as the "collective" need that according to Lucien Febvre is what justifies "the social function of history")—these are figurative traits having to do, in terms of semiotic modalities, with /wanting-to-know/ and with /having-to-do/, respectively. This personal curiosity or externally assigned task "motivates" the potential researcher and thereby allows for the broad outline of a cognitive program in terms of a *virtuality* of doing. Then, possession of the tools for thought analysis—"theory" and "methods," which respectively represent /be-ing-able-to-do/ and /knowing-how-to-do/—"authorizes" the steps taken by the researcher and makes it possible to move to the stage of *actualization* (the phase of *realization* of the cognitive program having given way to the exercise itself of the cognitive /doing/).

We now have, superimposed on the utterances of doing, a second discursive level, composed of *modal utterances* and which is responsible for enabling the subject to undertake the quest for knowledge and bring it to a successful conclusion. This foundational discourse (in the sense that it founds the enunciative competence of the subject) corresponds, from the point of view of the organization of discourse into narrative sequences, to the qualifying test—as opposed to operative discourse, which, because it describes the scientific doing itself, conveys the sequence of the decisive test. Whereas the subject (as operator) had at an earlier stage come into contact with the object, here he is correlated with a *receiver* actant who at times will be manifested as an autonomous instance that (transitively) attributes to the researcher the means whereby to produce "true" utterances, and at times will appear on the contrary in syncretism with the enunciator. In this case, the latter (reflexively) gives to himself the elements that justify his own "right" to enunciation. In both cases, beyond the modalization of the "researcher" and his transformation into a true hero-subject (with, however, this difference that, as opposed to the subject of a popular story, his distant eponym, he carries out the main part of his quest within the cognitive, not pragmatic, dimension), in reality it is the epistemic conditions of "truth saying"—in other words, the conditions for theoretical possibility of knowledge—that are at play at this level.

Given this, the position and status assigned to the sender as *epistemic instance* will give us a further criterion by which to distinguish between two types (or subtypes) of discourse: the *discourse of discovery* on the one hand, in which the function of sender tends to become objectified into a figure that is distinct from that of the discoursing subject, and the reflexive *discourse of questioning* on the other hand, in which the enunciator subject makes himself his own receiver. To this first opposition, which can be seen in the narrative organization of actantial syntax, there corresponds at the same time, at the discursive and semantic level, a parallel difference that has to do with the relative manner of being present and degree of stability, different for each author, of the two great isotopies—epistemological versus methodological—which are characteristic of scientific discourse in general.

The Discourse of Discovery In terms of its being a narrative configuration, the mechanism for "discovery" constitutes one of the schemata that is common to all of the texts analyzed in the first part of this volume[2] (whereas it is concretely present with the other authors only in an accessory way, at the most). The way the epistemic instance appears on the scene is like the occurrence of an event, a more or less unexpected event—a "chance occurrence," to use Dumézil's term—that consists in, at a given moment in the knowing subject's movement toward discovery, meeting up with the object of knowledge. From this meeting there is born a certitude, an immediate obviousness. The sender, guarantor here of the "conviction" (Siegfried) thus attained, can, as is the case with Dumézil, be shaded out and maintain a kind of anonymous identity. As "something that seems to resemble order appears beyond chaos," it is the "human mind," which is both sender and object of knowledge, that allows us to see the principles according to which it functions. In both cases, the automatization of the *epistemic* instance (as narrative *actant*)—that is, its projection beyond the subject—is, at first sight paradoxically, accompanied by a near atrophying of the *epistemological* dimension (as discursive *isotopy*). When examined more closely, it is as if, faced with an object of knowledge that almost "of itself" proclaims its own "truth" (certain preconditions having, of course, been fulfilled, as we shall soon see), the subject finds himself freed of the need to provide his own account of the a priori proofs of his epistemic competence. This implies that there already exist models of intelligibility vis-à-vis the activity of the knowing subject. From this point of view, this same role of guarantor for scientific knowledge that, in Lévi-Strauss is assigned to the "real" (reality in his "guide"), is, in Mauss, given an "atmosphere." This "atmosphere," in Dumézil, is significant for the very organization of the mythical corpus of reference. In Siegfried it is significant in terms of the "intelligibility" of "laws" inherent in "politics."

Of course this preconception concerning the "objectivization" of the epistemic conditions for cognitive doing must not be confused with the epistemologically naive attitude that conceives of the production of knowledge in terms of an immediate apprehension and description of what is empirically given. The structures that guarantee the possibility for knowledge do not appear, with any author studied here, as immediately manifest.

On the contrary, for them to become obvious to the enunciator, they had to first be "discovered": whence Lévi-Strauss's "nebulous" metaphor and, more generally, the need, on the part of the subject, to, make it possible in his own activity for a meeting up with the epistemic sender. This, for example, with Francastel, happens because there has been an earlier break with the opposite and deceptive instance of the antisender (sometimes represented by "intuitionism"). It can happen, on the contrary, as with Lévi-Strauss, because there has been an initial enlightened and "intuitive" choice. In Mauss and Siegfried, it happens through attempts to take up a position at what might be called an "appropriate distance" from the object.

To the extent that here, despite all this, the subject remains the beneficiary of a competence that, in essence, he receives as a "gift" (or through an "initiation" carried out by some kind of "goddess of subtlety" [Siegfried]), it should not be surprising if that subject frequently displays—at least at this stage of the trajectory followed by his quest—the marks of a clearly *individuated* actor. For lack of a strictly defined spatiotemporal anchoring (which, however, must later be shaken off [Mauss, Siegfried, Febvre]), it is the uniqueness of an individual adventure, encountered alone (Bachelard, Barthes), sometimes anecdotal (the story, told by Marcel Mauss, of his friend Herz's manuscript), that is used to justify the subject's "predestination" to receive the "grace" of discovery. The elements of individuation are by nature, however, required eventually to disappear. Because the scientific process implies the reproducibility of the procedures followed and the communicability of the results obtained, the knowledge of the subject cannot for long maintain the status of a pure and simple "personal conviction." It must instead strive for the status of "demonstrated truth." This truth may indeed be relative since "in science there can exist no given truths" (Lévi-Strauss). This requires that the individual epistemic trajectory toward discovery be paralleled by a *methodological* trajectory that is of a more *impersonal* nature. It is this requirement that the distinction between discourse of discovery and discourse of research seeks to account for. As we said earlier, the discourse of research is sometimes called *operative discourse*, and now we see a new justification for that name in the sense that the discourse of research appears as the locus for an *operationalization*, by the cognitive subject (who can be assimilated to a collective syntagmatic actant), of the models for intelligibility that were "discovered" at an earlier stage by the individual actor (as a result of his meeting up with the epistemic instance).

The Discourse of Questioning The same "discourse of discovery" that, from the *syntagmatic* point of view is thus articulated with the discourse of "research" (as we have seen, what we have are two necessary stages in the unfolding of one and the same logic), is, from the *paradigmatic* point of view, opposed to what we suggested be called the discourse of "reflexive questioning." In order to situate the scope of this distinction concretely, it will be enough to recall the difficulties, diametrically opposed in terms of their principles, that some participants encountered when choosing what extract to analyze. On the one hand, some of those who were interested in texts that belong to the discursive type we have been examining (recounting the experience of one discovery), but who wanted no less to understand the theoretical basis of those experiences, came up against an extreme discretion on the part of their authors where "metascientific" preliminaries were concerned. This discretion, with different tones respectively, was maintained by researchers such as Lévi-Strauss and Dumézil, Mauss and Siegfried, for whom the possibility of attaining the knowledge sought is something to be hoped for as a result of an encounter with the object of knowledge—and is not guaranteed in advance through some theoretical and more or less peremptory proclamation on the part of the knowing subject. Others, faced with more "speculative" works, found it difficult to identify, from among all of the self-justifications of an *epistemological* nature, an extract that might be clearly representative of the use of an operative method or of an operative doing. This represents a constant flight in the direction of a meta-or prescientific dogmatism whose sociological discourse (Georges Gurvitch) might represent an excellent example.[3]

When taken to this extreme, the basic procedures analyzed in the second part of this work[4] surely offer another degree of complexity and open a new set of perspectives. If those perspectives stand out in terms of demonstrating a greatly increased importance of the epistemological level (to the detriment of the operative level), they cannot, however, be reduced to nothing but a search for pure ideal or principle. Instead of having a subject that manifests itself by announcing a /having-to-do/ that is at the same time theoretical and ineffectual (because it does not come out of the procedures that are indispensable for the setting into place of /doing/ strictly speaking), they, in a very global way, express a kind of philosophical expectation found at the moment when the quest for knowledge is about to begin. These procedures are neither prescriptive nor exclusive of all others. They simply reflect what we must accept as being a state of "crisis" in the social sciences. Far from claiming to impose rules, epistemological thinking engages in a *questioning* about the conditions of knowledge. Even more, this questioning becomes a "questioning about questioning" — an (epistemic) questioning about the identity of the (cognitive) subject conceived of as being the locus where questioning about the world originates: "to understand (this) initial questioning," Merleau-Ponty writes; "(to become") the subject who is conscious of the act of understanding," says Bachelard.

On the other hand, if we no longer relate this "philosophical" modality of foundational discourse to some "dogmatic" variable (about which we would have to wonder about the extent to which it can "found" anything substantial), but rather to the mechanism that articulates our "discourse of discovery," this change of perspective can, from a narrative point of view, be clarified as follows. We are dealing less with *qualification* (through meeting a sender that is responsible for actualizing the subject's /being-able/to-do/) than we are with the very *instituting* of the subject, and the thinking of the researcher concentrates on the virtualizing modality of /wanting-to-do/. Barthes writes, "Which text will I *accept* writing or rewriting?" On this distinction that has to do with the content of a transferred modal value, we find superimposed an opposition, mentioned earlier, between two principles of the organization of actantial structure: the autonomy of the epistemic sender vis-à-vis the cognitive subject, and therefore the *transitivity* of the process of attribution of competence in the discourse of discovery; and, on the contrary, in the discourse of "questioning," the *reflexivity* of the act of instituting the subject, with the fusion of the two actants (sender and subject) within the instance of an "I" that is in no way prevented from moving from one locus of enunciation to another (epistemic vs. cognitive).

The texts studied by Jean-François Bordron, Ivan Darrault, Pierre Geoltrain, Jean-Claude Coquet, and (although to a lesser degree, in connection with the discourse of Francastel), by Jean-Marie Floch are especially good examples of this. We find the following: uncertainty regarding the locus at which we will find "coexistence of contraries," the enunciating instance becoming a case of subject vs. antisubject in Merleau-Ponty (as indeed with Francastel); meaning, according to Bordron, resulting from the "tension" between subject and antisubject; in Ricoeur a dialectics of interactantial communication inscribed within the "I" who speaks; with Bachelard a superimposing of cognitive instances and a process of disambiguating; an instituting of the subject such as to imply a necessary surpassing of "psychologism" even though any "effort to construct" would still be based upon the individuated "I" of the researcher. The enunciator becomes his own epistemic sender. Thus, the introduction of methodological discourse—an impersonal discourse that is the responsibility of a collective syntagmatic actant—poses here, in a particularly sharp way, the problem of moving from a highly individualized discourse (in an extreme case it is the "body" that speaks [Barthes]), to a socialized discourse implied by the bringing into play of an operative doing. Finally it is Barthes's text (taken from *S/Z*) that most sharply expresses this duality of levels. We see the disappearance of the initial "I," replaced by a collective "we" or "they" or "people" and which marks a sudden return to a discourse on method, following on the foundational discourse.

The Veridictory Level: The Status of Knowledge

If utterances of doing (which make up operative discourse) on the one hand presuppose modal utterances that can be seen as the bases for the competence— in particular the epistemic competence—of the performing subject, the cognitive doing of the subject itself results in finally making possible a new category of utterances. At this third level we have judgments and conclusions that the cognitive subject makes as a result of his own investigations (informative doing) and manipulations (taxonomic doing, etc.) vis-à-vis the *manner of existence of the object* that inspired his quest for knowledge. Here is where we find announcements of what has been accomplished by the research in question. These take the form of *utterances of state* (involving verbs such as "being" and "seeming"), and they make up what we might call an *objective discourse*, or at least a discursive level that passes itself off as such. It should be made clear that the grammatical criterion on which we base identification of this level in no way prejudges the form—"static" or "dynamic"—of the scientific descriptions we are dealing with here. On the contrary, we can anticipate two subclasses of discourse according to whether the objective discourse's utterances of state take as object utterances that describe the /being/ of semiotic objects, or utterances that describe a referential /doing/. Both are systemic descriptions, distributional or taxonomic in the first case, functional, transformational, or generative formulations in the second.

All three kinds of utterances can be syntagmatically articulated within a single linguistic segment. Thus we can easily recognize in a short sentence from André Siegfried:

The lexical equivalent of a *modal utterance* that specifies an aspect of the competence of the cognitive subject (the conditions of his /being-able-to-do/):

(a) "With a little attention, and drawing back . . . "
    — a cognitive *utterance of doing* (in this case strictly informative):
(b) "we see that . . . "
    — a resulting *utterance of state* that speaks about the existence of the object (the mode of "being"):
(c) "there are political regions just as there are geological regions."
    In this same text, this threefold articulation is immediately followed by the following evaluation, one which we will have to account for:
(d) "This is so true that we instinctively use geographical vocabulary when speaking of political parties."

Subsegment (c), which, being an utterance of state, has to do with *objective discourse*, is anaphorically recalled here (by the demonstrative "this"), and is at the same time transformed into *referential discourse* from the point of view of (d). Once the objective utterance has been thus referentialized, the cognitive subject is no longer in a position to intervene directly concerning his object. He, however, now becomes able to evaluate his own formulations — for instance, here (c) — precisely by taking them as a reference. Now we are moving from a first level of modalizations, called alethic (necessity, contingency, impossibility, possibility) and which govern objective discourse's *predicates of existence* (e.g., "There are" /not-being-able-to-be/ /$\simeq$ necessity), to the hierarchically higher level of epistemic modalizations (certainty, uncertainty, improbability, probability) that overdetermine *utterances of knowledge* and speak to their validity (e.g. "This is so true that . . . " $\simeq$ certainty).

We suggested earlier in this chapter a possibility for an initial homologation of discursive levels and narrative sequences (foundational level: qualifying test; operative level: final test). This logically leads us to examine the extent to which the *veridictory level* (where validation of referentialized objective discourse takes place) can be placed in parallel with the glorifying test sequence that, in narrative terms, is the end point of the hero's evolution. The formal analogy between the structures of "veridiction" (which are discursive) and the structures of "glorification" (which are narrative) appears when we consider the actantial relationship that subtends both. In both cases the subject communicates an object of value acquired earlier (during the final test) and which is thereafter subject to the sanction of a *sender*. Within the framework of figurative discourse, this transfer can be seen as the transmission of a pragmatic value and in this case it ends up with recognition for the subject-hero through an instance that, although initially involving his receiving a mandate, appears at the end of the narrative trajectory as receiver and judge of the hero's somatic performances. In a parallel way, in the case of discourse with a claim to being scientific, the axis of communication is the support for the transfer of a knowledge object (constructed thanks to the cognitive doing of the enunciating subject): knowledge is thus transformed into a causing-to-know addressed to a receiver that is charged with evaluating its truth-value. Nothing prevents one and the same actor, who can move along the axis of communication, from alternately taking on the two actantial roles of sender and receiver. In our corpus, this is indeed the most frequent case. The subject of scientific discourse, a syncretic and continuously mobile figure, constantly varies the "locus from which he speaks." He might, as enunciator, be manifested as the subject of a *persuasive discourse* made up of objective utterances that are themselves modalized in alethic terms and have as guarantor the logic of the operative doing of which they are the end point. Conversely, now as enunciatee, he can become the subject of an *interpretive discourse* that evaluates and sanctions (through epistemic modalization) the objective discourse that it referentializes as soon as it is produced. Likewise, the procedure of referentialization appears to be the end point of research: it closes the subject's cognitive program.

If we remember, however, that the mechanisms for controlling narrative time are relative ones and that they are subordinate to the logical structures of narration, then what has to do with the "after" of a story here can, from another point of view, occupy the place of initial sequence. This is what happens when the discourse to be sanctioned is no longer a discourse resulting directly from operations carried out by the *enunciator* himself, but rather is a discourse that has been borrowed from (or attributed to) an *enunciatee* that is distinct from the discoursing subject. This brings into play a collective referential knowledge that is "disengaged" vis-à-vis the instance and the time of enunciation. This "discourse of the other" is not necessarily "true," in the sense that it is not *genetically* a reproduction of the story (the historical trajectory) of a science, but rather a reconstruction, through selections made by the enunciating subject, of an ideal discourse (which probably, in the most "powerful" sciences, would take the form of an operational algorithm), which is conceived in *generative* terms. As such, referential discourse can encompass discourses of very diverse provenance: earlier scientific discourses—from the most precise self-reference (Dumézil), to calling on the discourse of the social sciences considered in their totality (Francastel). It can also call on simple doxological discourses that occur in normal social communication (Febvre, Siegfried). Since these do not all share the same veridictory status, the enunciator's interpretation of them will sometimes take the form of negative epistemic modalizations and *rejections* (because arguments from earlier scientific practice might appear to be "sophistic" and unacceptable [Dumézil]), and sometimes they will take the form, positively, of *registered phenomena* (because they represent initial certainties from among the elements that make up the subject's competence). The veridictory level is thus defined as the dialectic locus for the consolidation of referentialized discourses, and this guarantees the transmission and "progress" of knowledge.

Discursive Grammar and the Social Nature of Discourse

Throughout this presentation, we have emphasized resemblances between the more or less abstract organization of discourse that claims to be scientific and the figurative forms of the narrative discourses of literature and myth. Our having recognized such formal parallels between discursive manifestations that are so far apart, and the precise identification of the levels of differentiation between them, in our eyes constitute our first result. A second result can be seen at the methodological level: the relative newness of the material studied led to a refinement in our manner of studying enunciative structures and modal articulations. Both, here, showed an unexpected richness and complexity. More generally, these efforts are now part of an enterprise whose goal is to construct a discursive grammar: this requires that we develop a theory that can account, in a homogeneous way, for the immense diversity in enunciative forms of knowledge, whatever their degree of scientificity.

With this new theory, we can expect to be able to take a more tranquil position within the debate that rages in the background with respect to all research in the human and social sciences. In that area, there is the never-ending question as to the subject of discourse—his position, his history, his legitimacy, not to mention his "desire." This "subject," as we call it, which we always study in terms of its being the social, political, and psychic instance that *produces knowledge*, could surely also be seen as a *product of discourse*, as a meaning effect—in other words, as a semiotic object. If contemporary epistemology, by introducing the idea of a "constructed" object, has slowly been doing away with the notion of a scientific practice that is carried out directly on an empirical "given," then maybe it is somewhat up to semiotics to show how scientific discourse also constructs another great artifact of language: a simulacrum of an object that, even if it seems to efface itself as incidental actor, never completely gives up the right to speak in its own name, if only to be able to give "meaning" to the scientific doing that transcends it. Febvre identifies the social "need" answered by the quest for historical knowledge; Siegfried locates his political analysis in terms of the expectations of the political world and of the university; Bachelard links philosophical thought with the main function of the "School"; Mauss rates the value of sociological research in terms of its contribution to the definition of a "new social order." We might say that none of these great constructors of methodology is happy simply to develop the narrative program of some "pure knowledge." On the contrary, given that these cognitive trajectories find themselves reintegrated within ideological programs that have a social and historical focus, we find that the actor in any given case of research takes center stage and delivers his own ideology.

Chapter 4
On Chance Occurrences in What We Call the Human Sciences: Analysis of a Text by Georges Dumézil

When we consider the layout of this book, readers will think that it was written in order to answer the following question: What happened, in the religious thinking of Zoroaster, to the Indo-European system of three social and cosmic functions, with the corresponding gods? This indeed is the problem that is presented here, but it was in the course of my research that it came to be substituted for quite another theme.

Several times we had reminded ourselves that surrounding the couple made up of the great sovereign gods (Mitra and Varuna in India, Adhinn and Tyr in Scandinavia, etc.), there exist, in the various Indo-European mythologies, what we might call minor sovereign gods, that is, less important gods whose jurisdiction remains within the first function, in magico-political sovereignty. They are, for example, Aryaman, Bhaga, and the other Aditya in India, Heimdall, Bragi, and some others in Scandinavia. We undertook to study these minor sovereigns, starting with India where the group of seven Aditya is clearly identifiable. We also had to study, in Iran, the group of six Aməsha Spənta, "Archangels" who are immediately subordinate to Ahura Mazdâh, the only god in pure Zoroastroism and who, since Darmesteter, are considered to be what in Zoroastroism correspond to the Vedic Aditya. Following Bernhard Geiger and Herman Lommel, we tried to describe more precisely those relations between them that seemed to us to be the most likely (see Mitra-Varuna, pp. 130 on). But this attempt did not bear fruit because insurmountable difficulties got in the way. If the first two archangels (Vohu Manah and Asha Vahishta) and maybe the third (Khshathra Vairya) are of a domain that is in effect that of the Aditya, the same does not hold for the last three (Spəntâ Armaiti, Haurvatât and Aməratât). Geiger's arguments, so convincing in the case of Asha, are weaker in the case of Khshathra and become out and out sophistic in the case of Armaiti.

Thus another possible solution suggested itself to us. Recent studies have increased our knowledge about Indo-Iranian and Indo-European religion. Benveniste and I have shown that these religions were dominated and enclosed within the system of three functions (sovereignty, military prowess, and fecundity) and their subdivisions. Among the Arya princes of Mitani in the fourteenth century B.C., and in several Vedic myths and rituals, this system is buttressed by a hierarchical series of five or six gods of whom, naturally, the first two, the gods of the two halves of sovereignty, belong, in India, to the group of Aditya. These gods are, first, Mitra and Varuna, then Indra, then the twins Nâsatya. Now, a number of immediately observable traits, which can readily be interpreted, *bring together the hierarchical list of the ancient functional gods and the hierarchical list of the Aməsha Spənta* and, in certain respects, cause us to see in the latter the heirs of the first. This is the source of the working hypothesis formulated in Chapter 2 and the verifications of it carried out in the subsequent three chapters. The problem with which we began vanished, but the real fallout provided the elements for another problem, a more real one: a frequent chance occurrence in the sciences we call human sciences.

It is also by chance that this research, carried out, as with earlier research, in a course at the Ecole des Hautes Etudes, is now coming to the fore.

Georges Dumézil, *Naissance d'Archanges*

Introduction

Presentation

The great progress in our knowledge of the organization of *figurative discourses* (folklore, mythology, literature) has given rise to hopes concerning the possibility of drawing up a classification and ordering of narrative forms in such a way as to produce a narrative grammar or logic. Two kinds of difficulty arose as progress was being made. We first noted the complexity of those narrative discourses we call literary and the complexity of the role played in them by the cognitive dimension that hypertrophies and, in many "modern" texts, even ends up being substituted for the evenemential dimension. We then noted that it was impossible to construct a discursive grammar without its also accounting for *nonfigurative discourses*—or discourses that so appear—which are the discourses pertaining in the vast field of the "humanities." Inevitably this grammar would also cover the discourses we ourselves engage in within the human sciences.

In this last area, it was impossible to not first think of Georges Dumézil, whose contribution to our research was decisive and whose discourse, the apparent simplicity of which has as much to do with modesty as it does with conviction concerning the role of the researcher, includes procedures that are rigorous, complex, and demonstrative of the greatest intelligence.

From among all of his work, we had to choose a representative text, and we are grateful to the author for indicating to us the one whose makeup most pleased him. Then we had to choose between two possible approaches, between analysis of the totality of the text, which, while perhaps identifying a certain number of general characteristics, would be necessarily superficial, and a microanalysis of an extract of the text in which certain identified mechanisms, some incontestable phenomena, would run the risk of becoming lost in a maze of detail.

The Semiotic Status of the Preface

We finally chose the preface of the methodologically important text *Naissance d'Archanges*, a preface whose exceptional nature, external to the text, is emphasized by the fact that it is separately and redundantly credited to the author.

We did not fall into the trap that this choice represented for us. The preface is not part of the corpus of this book. Along the temporal axis, it is a postface and follows on the discourse of the research and its being put into writing. Its status is that of a *metadiscursive* thought concerning a discourse that has already been produced. Thus an initial segmentation of the book's discourse would separate the preface out from the rest of the text just as it would the title and the various subtitles. The question would thus be posed as to the relations maintained between these various textual segments.

This metadiscourse is supposed to reveal what the author himself thinks of his own discourse, its goal, and its organization. One might ask what this "second-instance argument" contributes, as much in terms of the discourse of which it is a reflection as in terms of the "textual truth" that the author inscribes without looking for it in his metadiscourse. For example, one cannot help being surprised when faced with the gap that separates the theoretical weaknesses of the nineteenth-century neogrammarians and the rigorous complexity of their methodological activity, an activity that seems to be carried out without their being aware of it.

If it is interesting to see how the author conceives of the process of production of the discourse conveying his research, it is also interesting to follow, step by step, the manner in which he recounts its unfolding. We note that the intentions declared therein seem to be submerged by waves of discursive procedures having to do with a practice and writing, said to be scientific, that go beyond them because they are of a sociolectal nature and/or because the author uses them in the name of an ethics of research.

While trying to make clear his personal conception of his research—and the scientific discovery that is its raison d'être—in our examination of the preface-discourse it is legitimate for us to hope to find certain regularities that are characteristic of any discourse that would be scientific.

Textual Organization

As a written and printed text, the preface is divided into six paragraphs that we can easily group into two symmetrical parts. This twofold structure is justified by the recurrence of the lexeme "chance occurrence" contained in the sentence that ends the third paragraph: "a frequent *chance occurrence* in the sciences we call human sciences, and which recurs at the beginning of the next paragraph: "It is also *by chance* that this research . . . is now coming to the fore."

If we can agree—as we will attempt to demonstrate—that "chance occurrence" is the key term of the text and that the word *also* emphasizes a certain equivalence between the two parts of the preface, then we can see that the preface is given over to the *account of two chance occurrences*, the first being a chance occurrence in the research and the second, in the life of the researcher.

Thus the organization of the text, viewed from its surface structures, shows as being a simple articulation of $6 = 2 \times 3$, that is, as a syntagmatic projection of the binary and ternary structures so dear to the author.

The object of our undertaking—the examination of the discourse of research—obliges us to limit the analysis to the first part of the preface, of which we will now reproduce in a progression, following its distribution into paragraphs:

> When they consider the layout of this book, readers will think that it was written in order to answer the following question: What happened in the religious thinking of Zoroaster, to the Indo-European system of three social and cosmic functions, with the corresponding gods? This indeed is the problem presented here, but it was in the course of my research that it came to be substituted for quite another theme.

The Discourse of Knowledge and the Discourse of Research

Discourse That Is Being Actualized and Realized Discourse

From the opening paragraph, an opposition, marked by an articulation of two sentences of different structures, appears: (a) between two phases of the production of discourse, that of discourse *realized* in the written form of a book and presented as an "observable" object, and another, earlier one, where discourse is grasped as being a *process*, as "research in progress," and is in a state of having been *actualized*; and (b) between two discursive forms, the first presenting the discourse as an object of knowledge offered to the "readers" who are set up as being the subject of the sentence, and a second, which, using a passive voice, shades out the subject of the scientific doing and thus gives a picture of discourse creating itself.

This seemingly innocent conception of discourse, first as the process of production and then as a produced object, is buttressed by an interplay of much more subtle syntactic and semantic constructions.

Realized Discourse and the Competence of the Narratee

The enunciator, by setting into his discourse an actant of communication, the "reader," whom we can designate as narratee,[1] then effects a *delegation* of his *parole*, which allows him to reveal his concept of research without directly attributing it to himself. The narratee-actant thus created is more than a rhetorical figure. He is, on the contrary, endowed by the enunciator with a certain number of *competencies*:

(a) a competence that can be attributed to any *enunciatee* and that allows him to carry out an:

informative doing (the readers "observe" the setting up of the book) and

interpretative doing (they can have "the feeling that . . . ");

(b) with *narrative competence*, that is, a knowledge and a knowing-how-to-do concerned with the syntagmatic organization of discourses and that serve as a buttress for the interpretive doing, which is manifested as:

a *general narrative competence* (which allows, starting with the "setting out" of the book, for an understanding of the ultimate purpose that organizes it); and

a *specific "scientific" competence* (which postulates that books are written as "answers" to "questions");

(c) a strictly speaking *linguistic competence* that renders the narratee able to formulate questions and, even more remarkably, formulate a question that he does not himself ask, but which is supposed to be asked by the enunciator in an internal discourse that he addresses to himself.

A very complex mechanism is thus set up within the discourse. It has the effect of creating a distance between the subject of enunciation and his utterance while at the same time linking the realized discourse to the instance of reading.

The Discourse of Research and the Absence of the Subject

The movement from one sentence to another ("This is indeed the problem . . . ") allows one to believe that the theme of the book, that is, the *object* of research, has not changed, regardless of the perspective from which one considers it. Nonetheless, a slight lexical deviation suggests a different perception or appreciation of the *form* to be taken by that research.

Thus when, in the first sentence, the goal of the work was seen as an answer to a *question*, in the second sentence the book appears to be the presentation of a *problem*: a "question to be answered" is replaced by a "question to be resolved" (which is the definition given for "problem" in the *Petit Robert*).

Likewise, while the term "setting out" (disposition) of the book, which was used first, led one to believe that it could be any work, as long as it was ordered according to the rules of *rhetoric*, the *problem* is defined as a "question to be resolved," which opens a discussion, within a *science*.

Moreover, while the setting out or disposition of the book immediately suggests the complementary term "invention" and also recalls the classical linear concept of discovery, the *problem* that appears is the result of a *substitution's* taking place, not of another problem, but of another non-problematic "utterance," and it suggests an entirely different conception of research.

Thus, standing in opposition to the concept of discourse as a classical literary genre, there is the concept of problematic scientific discourse.

This brief lexical examination we have just carried out is not just a game indulged in by a semanticist who is used to seeking out the meaning of words. The terms under study are *metaterms* dealing with the formal organization of discourse, even if in only an allusive and incomplete way, and they are references to ideological microuniverses whose shapes we can plot. The more or less implicit oppositions they reveal are consolidated and clarified by the setting into place of distinct grammatical apparatuses:

   (a) first, using the passive voice in the first clause: "the problem . . . presented (by . . .)" allows for a shading out of the *narrator*, even though his positioning is quite clearly indicated;
   (b) second, through the reflexive construction of the second clause: "the problem . . . came to be substituted for . . . " (the French uses *s'est substitué à*), in which "problem" occupies at the same time the positions of subject and object, leaving no place for the marks of enunciation.

If, as in the first sentence, what we have here is the procedure of actantial disengagement, the results are different. In the first case the utterance is linked and subordinated to the simulated interpretation of the narratee, whereas, in the second case, it is as separated as possible from the instance of enunciation so that it can appear to be the discourse of a nonperson, belonging to no one, that is, as an *objective discourse* whose subject would be self-creating science.

This first paragraph is thus able to receive two readings: syntagmatically it unfolds the two phases through which the discourse of research is realized; paradigmatically it sets into opposition two different concepts of that research. Further, these two kinds of "contents" are set into two different discursive forms. Paradoxically enough, the first discourse, which is "personalized," is a discourse without problems, whereas the second, a discourse with problems, shows as a depersonalized utterance.

The Question

To the extent that, according to our hypothesis, the discourse of the human sciences is supposed to obey the rules of narrative organization, it must take on the form of the quest for an object of value. Since this object is a certain *knowledge* that one seeks to obtain, scientific discourse thus shows as a *cognitive adventure*. Since the knowledge object is the goal of the discourse, it is obvious that the initial state from which the quest begins is a state of nonknowledge. The scientific account can thus be defined as the transformation of a /nonknowledge/ into a /knowledge/.

The knowledge in question, as a *modality*, necessarily regulates an *object* of knowledge that is situated on a hierarchically inferior *discursive level*. In the case under study, the biplanar structure of *question* vs. *answer* is just an anthropomorphic formulation of the narrative structure subtending the account. The question the subject of discourse is supposed to ask is an implicit or simulated admission of ignorance. The answer is supposed to fill this gap, offering the acquired knowledge as being the result of the quest. Thus the question contains the object of the knowledge, that is, the topic of the discourse, modalized by ignorance.

The question, in its surface formulation, has to do with the predicate *becoming* whose function is to link two specific historical states and that, from the narrative point of view, is the *object of knowledge*, which is the goal of the quest:

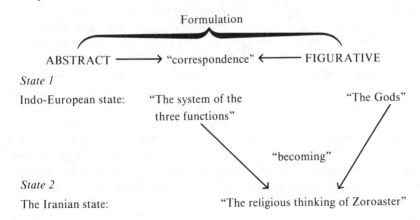

Formulation

ABSTRACT ⟶ "correspondence" ⟵ FIGURATIVE

State 1

Indo-European state: "The system of the   "The Gods"
                          three functions"

                                        "becoming"

State 2

The Iranian state: "The religious thinking of Zoroaster"

Because the preface is a metadiscourse produced after the text, at practically the same moment when the text is being given a title and subtitle, it is interesting to compare the problem posed in the preface with the titles' formulation.

Curiously, the title (*Naissance d'Archanges*) and the subtitle (*Essai sur la formulation de la théologie zoroastrienne*) mention only the second state, the Iranian state of religion, and present it in two forms—*abstract* ("Zoroastrian Theology") and *figurative* ("The Archangels")—which correspond to the twofold articulation of state 1 within the question posed in the preface, and which we can set in a parallel way:

	Abstract Formulation	Figurative
State 1	the system of the three functions	the gods
State 2	Zoroastrian theology	the Archangels

After noting that the sentence of *becoming* is state 1 and that of the other two predicates is state 2, the different lexicalizations of the *function* that links the two states can in turn be represented as follows:

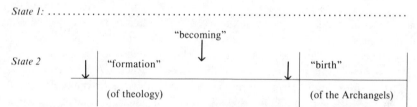

If we remember that the *function* that represents the object of knowledge of the scientific program can be interpreted, in another language, as being a "historical process," it has to be noted that this process is only partially referred to and that this is a process seen from the two perspectives of "upstream" and "downstream." We also have to add the curious fact that the lexemes that designate the process in question are verbs or nominalizations of the *intransitive* verbs "becoming," "being born," and "being created," and this is so despite the fact that they are supposed to express the *transition* from one state to another and that, since they are endowed with *durative* semes, the duration they express cannot fail to overdetermine the other aspects—*inchoate* and *terminative*—of the process. It is as if the process of *transformation*, which is the object of the desired knowledge, were in large measure emptied of its semantic contents to the benefit of the two clearly uttered historical states whose opposition is confirmed by the bringing together of the preface's questions with the answers furnished by what the titles allow us to anticipate.

The problem of how to grasp, to represent and define, *diachronic transformations* is thus implicitly posed.

The Story of Failure

Several times we had reminded ourselves that surrounding the couple made up of the great sovereign gods (Mitra and Varu*n*a in India, A*dh*inn and Tyr in Scandinavia, etc.), there exist, in the various Indo-European mythologies, what we might call minor sovereign gods, that is, less important gods whose jurisdiction remains within the first function, in magico-political sovereignty. They are, for example, Aryaman, Bhaga, and the other Aditya in India, Heimdall, Bragi, and some others in Scandinavia. We undertook to study these minor sovereigns, starting with India where the group of seven Aditya is clearly identifiable. We also had to study, in Iran, the group of six amǝsha Spǝnta, "Archangels" who are immediately subordinate to Ahura Mazdâh, the only god in pure Zoroastroism and who, since Darmesteter, are considered to be what in Zoroastroism correspond to the Vedic Aditya. Following B. Geiger and H. Lommel, we tried to describe more precisely those relations between them that seemed to us most likely (see Mitra-Varu*n*a, pp. 130 on). But this attempt did not bear fruit because insurmountable difficulties got in the way. If the first two archangels (Vohu Manah and A*sh*a Vahi*sh*ta) and maybe the third (K*hshath*ra Vairya) are of a domain that is in effect that of the Aditya, the same does not hold for the last three (Spǝntâ Armaiti, Haurvatât and Amǝrǝtât). Geiger's arguments, so convincing in the case of A*sh*a, are weaker in the case of K*hshath*ra and become out and out sophistic in the case of Armaiti.

Discursive and Narrative Organization

The substitution that replaces virtual "utterance" with the "problem," the theme of the book, a substitution that is cataphorically announced in the first paragraph, justifies the *discursive expansion* that covers all of the first part of the preface. From the narrative point of view, this substitution corresponds to the well-known syntagmatic schema made up of the repetition of tests and where ultimate success is valorized by the failure of the first attempt. Two stories—the story of a failure and the story of a victory—serve as the foundation for the discursive development of the text under study.

The story of the failure is readily articulated in two segments: the quest carried out by the *subject* is recounted by a "we"—a syncretic manifestation of the *narrator* and of the *subject* of doing—who maintains a discourse in the *past*. The defeat, marked by the appearance on the scene of the *antisubject*, is directly taken in hand by the *enunciator*, thus producing an objective discourse, given in the *present* tense appearing as an atemporal present of the truth.

The Story Told by the Subject

The surface isotopy of this story is as dependent on the repetition of the sentence subject, *we*, as it is on a succession of predicates that lexicalize, with some semantic variations, the *cognitive activities* of the subject:

"... we had *reminded* ourselves that ... "
"... we undertook to *study* ... "
"... we also had to study ... "
"... we tried to *describe more precisely* ... "

This succession of utterances, whose characteristics can be identified with precision, constitutes an autonomous discursive level that we can call "cognitive discourse."

This discourse in the first person—the *we* being, through some connotation, a substitute for *I*—includes, subordinated to each of its cognitive predicates, utterances of objects the stringing together of which constitutes a level of discourse that is hypotactic vis-à-vis the first level. Characterized as discursive having to do with the *objects* of knowledge, it at the same time presents itself, in terms of its syntactic form, as an *objective discourse* (or it passes itself off as such) because of its actantial depersonalization and the way in which its predicates are maintained in the atemporal present.

This objective discourse constantly refers to other discourses that are supposed to buttress it and that, being absent from the text becoming actualized, are represented therein only by allusions and references that are taken to be known as verifiable. A sequence of anaphorical utterances such as:

"... since Darmesteter ... "
"Following Bernhard Geiger and Herman Lommel ... "
"... (see Mitra-Varuna, pp. 130 on) ... "

to which we should add the initial "reminder" (which is just an *auto-reference*), constitute a third discursive level, which we call "referential discourse."

Instead of being the locus of a linear syntagmatic unfolding, the discourse we are examining appears to be a construction on several levels, each of which has its own formal characteristics and plays its own particular role.

Cognitive Discourse It will be noted that this discourse is in turn composed of *two levels*, the lower one being a sequence of lexicalizations of the different forms of cognitive activity:

"study" → "study" → "describe more precisely"

whereas the upper level is made up of *modalizations* of the cognitive predicates. Their stringing together constitutes a *narrative program* that organizes the whole of the discourse.

Except for the initial utterance, "we have reminded ourselves," which, as an autoreference to the preceding discourse, represents the situation that is the starting point for the story about to be told (and whose pluperfect tense is to be compared with the compound perfects of the rest of the story), the modal structure corresponds to the predictable schema of *acquisition of competence* on the part of the subject of the cognitive doing. Briefly:

(a) "We undertook to study . . . " represents the syncretism of the sender and of the subject of the doing who himself sets himself up as *subject of wanting-to-do*.

(b) "We also had to . . . " is the manifestation, in the form of a prescription, of the modality of *having-to-do* and of the identification of a new sender to whom the subject willingly submits. This new sender is that *metalogic* that requires the inclusion of the Archangels in the class of Indo-European "minor sovereigns." "We also had to . . . " is like a reference to "the nature of things" and manifests this logical prescription.

(c) " . . . we tried . . . " manifests the *being-able-to-do* that is thought to be possessed by the subject. It is a modality that is necessary if the move is to be made to *realization*, that is, conjunction of the subject with the desired object of value. This object, as defined by the question to which the book is responding, is knowledge concerning the function relation between two states of a religion. The cognitive subject is trying to make clear the relations between the two states.

The narrative program, conceived as the modalization of the subject, is carried out right up to the decisive test.

Objective Discourse Being subordinated to cognitive doing, the so-called objective discourse describes the objects of knowledge and the successive manipulations they undergo:

(a) *Taxonomic doing* consists *grosso modo* in consolidating the object of knowledge using operations of inclusion. Thus, the "minor" sovereigns" are placed "around" the two major sovereigns, and the two subsets are included in the "first function" set. The "minor sovereigns" are part of "Indo-European mythologies," however. We will return to this.

(b) *Pragmatic doing* establishes the syntagmatic order of the cognitive operations. The minor Indian sovereigns are the first to be "studied." The group of Iranian Archangels is "studied" next.

(c) *Comparative doing* has to do with the objects of partial knowledge that are identified through programmatic doing. Its task is to "clarify the relations" between them.

All of the preceding represent various kinds of cognitive manipulations—the list of which, of course, is not exhaustive—that characterize the subject's doing within the framework of cognitive discourse. The discursive objects thus manipulated show as *utterances of state*. Here are some examples:

". . . there *exist* . . . minor sovereign gods . . . They are . . . "
". . . the group of seven Aditya *is* clearly identifiable."
". . . of six Archangels who *are* . . . subordinate . . . *are* considered to be . . . "
". . . those relations between them that *seemed* to us the most likely . . . "

If there is no doubt as to their status as *utterances of state*, which distinguishes them from the cognitive *utterances of doing* that regulate them, we can readily note that the predicative relation establishing existence that constitutes them is in a way *modalized* each time by expressions such as "clearly identifiable," "considered to be," "seemed to us," and "likely." These expressions overdetermine the predicative relation establishing existence by indicating the degree of necessity or certitude to be attributed to it.

The objective discourse, just like the cognitive discourse we have just studied, thus includes *two distinct discursive levels*. One, a *modal level*, regulates the predication establishing existence, which constitutes the *descriptive level*. We will later have to come back to this new kind of modalization, which is no longer a modalization of *doing*, but rather of *being*.

Referential Discourse Referential discourse is referred to here only in terms of its being a discourse of authority, an authority later to be contested. That is why it is not yet possible for us to examine its formal organization. At the most we can identify a certain number of *convocation modes* pertaining to referential discourse. These we see when we consider referential relations as being *tropic structures* that serve as linking structures. Two procedures—*reference* and *autoreference*—must be distinguished from each other.

In the case of reference (a) the author's name serves as an anaphoric reference for his discourse, and (b) his name is considered to be setting off the sequence of discourses (" . . . since Darmesteter . . . " " . . . *Following* Bernhard Geiger and Herman Lommel . . . ") that sanction and depersonalize the discourse by making of it a *unique referential discourse*.

Autoreference, on the contrary, reestablishes continuity between the various discourses of a single author and brings them together within a single and coherent personalized discourse. It does this by making it appear to be inspired by a single, global goal (cf. the second subtitle of the book: "Jupiter, Mars, Quirinus''). It can even produce a new syncretism by which the "we" actor, which already fills the roles of *narrator* and *cognitive subject*, incarnates the *subject* of referential discourse.

In both cases, we recognize, in referentialization, the phenomenon of *semantic anaphora*. Within the discourse in the process of being created, "recalled" referential discourse, a form undergoing *expansion* but a form that is absent, is represented by its *condensed* and *present* form. Indeed, in the segment we are studying, referential discourse, which is actualized in its condensed form, is identified with objective discourse.

Now we know why the author, from the beginning, took care to name this form of discourse about research using the vague term "utterance," a term that took on some substance only because of its opposition to the "problem" discourse of the text. Indeed, research, as it is conceived of here, consists in the selective bringing together of a certain number of referential discourses whose condensed formulations are strung together according to an order that is dictated by what we have already termed "programmatic doing" and that is the only thing new about this discourse. This is a classical and not fully satisfactory form of discourse, summed up by the *question* versus *answer* formula, and the author dismisses it by attributing it to the imaginary narratee.

The Antisubject's Account

Discourse Surface and Narrative Mechanisms The appearance of the disjunctive "but," in the middle of the text under study, produces the effect of a break in the unfolding of the story. This is all the more so for the fact that this logic sign is accompanied by a change in the form of the discourse. The cognitive level seemingly disappears, leaving objective discourse.

This change in form is just a surface phenomenon. It is significant in and of itself because it conceals direct manifestation of the narrative account whose privileged locus, as we have seen, is cognitive discourse. It does not, however, thereby abolish that manifestation. Thus: (1) the "attempt" that "did not bear fruit" is just a semantic recurrence, in the form of a noun, of the verb "to try" and represents a cognitive doing that is seeking to move on to *realization*. Likewise, (2) the "difficulties" that "got in the way" signal the appearance of the opponent actant or, even better, of an antisubject that is introduced into the text by semifigurative procedures: "got in the way" personifies the "difficulties"; the adjective "insurmountable" brings up an anthropomorphic figure.

The only irregular factor we can observe is the syntagmatic permutation of the two narrative utterances: failure in the test ("did not bear fruit") precedes rather than follows the appearance of the antisubject and the setting up of the polemic structure of the story. Other than the fact that the irrelevance of the linear unfolding of the story vis-à-vis our ability to recognize its underlying narrative schema no longer has to be demonstrated, the reason, and it is a discursive reason, for this is very simple. "Difficulties" is a cataphoric phenomenon that anticipates the discourse to follow and, therefore, must be seen together with the expansion of that discourse.

The depersonalizing of the discourse does not succeed in hiding the fact that the adjective "insurmountable" refers to "difficulties" only as being the *object* actant, because the *subject* of this unrealizable process, "which *we* could not surmount," is none other than the subject of the cognitive discourse already manifested by a series of "we's." The /being-able/ modality that contains this lexeme is thus inscribed in the sequence of modalizations that mark the progressive acquisition, by the cognitive subject, of his competence. The /being-able-to-do/ that governs the "attempts" and "efforts" of the subject is incomplete and illusory in the face of the antisubject. It is replaced by a /not-being-able-to-do/ and accounts for the nonrealization of the narrative program whose schema shows as:

$$[/wanting/ \rightarrow /having-to/ \rightarrow /being-able/] \rightarrow [/not-being-able/ \rightarrow /doing/]$$

Failure of Cognitive Doing As we move from the modal level to the *strictly speaking* cognitive level, we note that the failure, caused by a /not-being-able/, has to do with a /doing/ that had sought to "make clear the relations," that is, to account for the relationships between the Indian Aditya and the Iranian Archangels. Consequently, on the cognitive level, the narrative failure signifies the failure of *comparative doing*.

Now comparative doing presupposes that the objects to be compared are inscribed within a *taxonomic framework* that alone will allow for the identification of a *tertium comparationis*, an axis common to the two objects. The logic called on is the logic of inclusion, and the key term of its operations is "situation." Thus, (a) the Aditya and the Archangels are figurative representations that are "situated" or located in a "domain" that is properly theirs; and (b) the "domains," loci at which they are situated, are in turn "situated" within "functions" and, in the case under study, within the first function.

If we can be sure that the Archangels' "domain" is identical to that of the Adityas, then we can establish their joint belonging to the first function. We can see that a cognitive doing whose ultimate goal is comparison necessarily has as a prerequisite a subprogram of taxonomic doing that seeks to "situate" the Archangels, taken one by one, within the "domain" they share with the Aidtya. We see further that the failure of this classificatory attempt brings about a nonconjunction of the cognitive subject with the desired object of value.

Modalization of Objective Discourse The failure is not abrupt but rather progressive. A series of cognitive operations allows us to account for this deterioration.

First, the Archangels, divided into three subsets—an operation that has to do with the *programmatic doing* to which we have already alluded—are "situated" in one and the same "domain"—an operation of inclusion that gives rise to the production of three *utterances of state*.

Second, each utterance of state is then *modalized* according to the degree of "solidity" that the relation of existence constituting it is supposed to include. Expressed in natural language, the modalities can be interpreted as follows:

(a) The first two Archangels, "maybe" ≃ /possibility/
(b) the third, "possibly" ≃ /small possibility/
(c) the last three, "not the same" ≃ /impossibility/.

We can see that the first and third of these modalizations correspond to easily recognized posts of the *alethic* square.

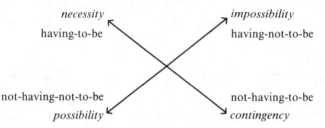

necessity
having-to-be

impossibility
having-not-to-be

not-having-not-to-be
possibility

not-having-to-be
contingency

Note: Modalization by /*small possibility*/ seems to be an element of *relativization* vis-à-vis categorical relations. This is a general tendency that we will see again several times.

Objective discourse, as it is seen here, emerges as being constructed on two levels: (a) the *descriptive level*, made up of a sequence of utterances of state, represents the results of *cognitive doing*; (b) the *modal level*, which overdetermines the first, is the locus at which *alethic modalities* are manifested, modalities that regulate the predicates that establish the existence of descriptive utterances.

It is these modalities, and especially the last one, *impossibility* (which is just the logical name for a /having-not-to-be/), that stand in "opposition" to the doing of the cognitive subject and disqualify that subject as /not-being-able-to-do/.

Modalization of Referential Discourse The passage dealing with the "difficulties" includes two sentences of which the first, which we have just analyzed, has to do with objective discourse and the second, with referential discourse. The latter, now using only the occurrence discourse of Geiger, is divided into sequences that are anaphorically designated as "arguments," so that to each argument sequence of referential discourse there corresponds an utterance of state pertaining to objective discourse.

The term "argument," which we have chosen to designate referential sequences, is, most likely, motivated, and it shows that we are dealing with a *persuasive doing*. (The question that remains is whether scientific persuasive doing has specific characteristics that distinguish it from the discourse of persuasion in general.) This persuasive doing is divided into narrative subprograms called "arguments," the results of which, when they are brought together and integrated within the objective discourse, create utterances of state in that discourse. That reference that can move from one discursive level to another can now be defined as a structural relation between a process and a state, between a narrative program and its results.

It will have been noted that the argument sequences (in our specific case: subprograms intended to include such and such an Archangel in the chosen domain) are one by one subjected to a kind of *modalizing evaluation*, the results of which are presented as constituting the "force" of the arguments. Thus, when choosing a representative for each of the subsets of Archangels previously identified, it might be said of the arguments' relation to:

the second Archangel, that they are "so convincing";
the third Archangel, that they are "weaker";
the fourth Archangel, that they are becoming "out and out sophistic."

In the same way as the descriptive utterances of objective discourse correspond to the "arguments" of referential discourse, the alethic modalizations depend on the "force of these arguments."

The Narrative Economy of the Story of the Failure A very important question now must be asked: what constitutes the authority by which legitimately to evaluate these arguments, and where is the subject of this new modalization situated? At first glance, it seems that the "force" of the arguments has to do with persuasive doing and, consequently, with the subject of referential discourse. Such is not at all the case, however, because, whereas the subject "Geiger," while engaging in his persuasive doing, believes himself to have won his tests, someone else examines his subprograms and their results and then evaluates them in terms of success ("so convincing") or failure ("out and out sophistic"). This person thus takes the referential discourse in hand and exercises his *interpretive doing* on it, the results of which constitute a new overmodalization of the discourse under study. We can see that this person can be none other than the *antisubject* who, through his modal judgments, throws up "insurmountable difficulties" that doom the *subject* to failure.

All this allows for a better understanding of the general economy of the narrative organization of the discourse under study. There is a subject who, being present in the text in the form of a "we," carries out his cognitive doing by appealing to a series of *helpers*, which are selected fragments of various referential discourses. But opposite that subject there appears an *antisubject* whose interpretive doing, concerning those arguments of the referential discourse that he has called on for the role of *opposers*, halts the subject's narrative progress and dooms his activity to failure. When it is organized as the story of the failure, the discourse of research presents its *polemical structure* as a combat engaged in, within the actor called the ''author,'' by the subject and the antisubject, two objectivized projections of the instance of enunciation.

Now we can understand the repercussions of this narrative arrangement on the surface discursive organization. The cognitive discourse, identified and personalized as such, is the locus at which the unlucky researcher is manifested, whereas the objective discourse that follows, by camouflaging the antisubject, makes it so that ''science'' appears to be the only winner in this test. (For the French word *science*, the best translation is *knowledge*.)

Epistemic Modalities Identification of the modalizing subject does not end the question posed by the nature of the modalities that appear at the surface of discourse as evaluations of the ''force of the arguments.''

They are, as we have seen, evaluations that are formulated after the interpretive doing that is carried out on the discourse that is called on for that purpose. The locus of their production therefore corresponds to the *instance of the enunciatee* and not that of the *enunciator*. They set up a *fiduciary distance* between the words of others and the credibility that should be assigned to them, and they thereby appear to regulate our knowledge about the world. Called ''epistemic modalities,'' they can be distributed along the square as follows:

$$certitude \longleftrightarrow improbability$$
$$probability \longleftrightarrow noncertitude$$

The ''so convincing'' and ''out and out sophistic'' lexicalizations would be identified with the /*probable*/ and /*improbable*/ positions, whereas ''weaker'' would be situated along the axis that links them.

Placing these modalities on the square could be misleading as to their categorical status, however. Contrary to alethic modalities where the opposition /*possible*/ vs. /*impossible*/ is present in the form of two *contradictories*, oppositions of epistemic terms are just *polarizations* of the continuum that allow a large number of intermediary positions to be manifested. For example, in certain contexts, the lexeme ''to believe'' can alone represent all of the positions between /*certitude*/ and /*noncertitude*/.

We can immediately see the unfortunate consequences this relative nature of epistemic modalizations can have on the rigor of so-called scientific discourse. For if, as everything would have us believe, the alethic modalities that regulate it are founded on epistemic modalizations that evaluate referential discourse, then the passing of judgment about categorical statements cannot be taken for granted.

The /*slight possibility*/ that we saw appearing in objective discourse is witness to the difficulties discourse comes up against in the human sciences.

Being and Seeming The confusion between epistemic and alethic modalities can be seen in the first part of our story where referential discursive selections were called on to play the role of helper. Do expressions such as "clearly definable" or "usually seen" have to do with epistemic or alethic modalization? Would they not instead be syncretisms caused by the problem of distinguishing the two levels of discourse, a difficulty caused by the fact that the subject of cognitive discourse is at the same time the subject, at least in part, of referential discourse?

The same does not hold with the third modalization where "most likely" comes through directly as an epistemic judgment. However, and this is troublesome, this /*strong possibility*/ is situated within an *isotopy of seeming* ("appeared to us to be the most likely"). It is as if the principal function of epistemic modalization—which is the foundation for alethic modalization of objective discourse, the latter, in turn, having the role of determining the modal status of the cognitive subject—were to facilitate movement, by abolishing the distance between them, between the *phenomenal isotopy of seeming* and the *noumenal isotopy of being* (in the semiotic, not the metaphysical, sense of these terms). Thus the basic articulation—as we discover it at the level of the deep structures of this story of a discovery that we are analyzing—shows, starting with the isotopy of *seeming* (which is the first to be set up), as being the *negation of seeming* (corresponding, on the surface, to the story of failure). In the second part, which tells of victory, this causes a bringing to the fore of the until then effaced term "being":

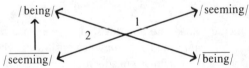

Note: Operation (1) is taken care of by the story of the failure. Operation (2) corresponds to the story of the victory.

At risk of anticipating the analysis that follows, in order to confirm the proposed interpretation we should recall the last, concluding sentence of the next paragraph of Dumézil's preface. Taking up again the theme of substitution, it observes that "the problem with which we began *vanished*," leaving instead "another problem, *a more real one*." We can identify these two lexicalizations with the negation of seeming and the assertion of being.

The discourse that recounts the discovery thus is like a revelation almost in the etymological sense of the word, of the realities that are hidden behind appearances.

The Account of the Victory

Thus another possible solution suggested itself to us. Recent studies
have increased our knowledge about Indo-Iranian and Indo-European
religion. Benveniste and I have shown that these religions were
dominated and enclosed within the system of three functions
(sovereignty, military prowess, and fecundity) and their subdivisions.
Among the Arya princes of Mitani in the fourteenth century B.C., and in
several Vedic myths and rituals, this system is buttressed by a
hierarchical series of five or six gods of whom, naturally, the first two,
the gods of the two halves of sovereignty, belong, in India, to the group
of Aditya. These gods are, first, Mitra and Varuna, then Indra, then the
twins Nâsatya. Now, a number of immediately observable traits, which
can readily be interpreted, *bring together the hierarchical list of the
ancient functional gods and the hierarchical list of the Amǝsha Spǝnta*
and, in certain respects, cause us to see in the latter the heirs of the
first. This is the source of the working hypothesis formulated in Chapter
2 and the verifications of it carried out in the subsequent three chapters.
The problem with which we began vanished, but the real fallout
provided the elements for another problem, a more real one: a frequent
chance occurrence in the sciences we call human sciences.

It is also by chance that this research, carried out, as with earlier
research, in a course at the Ecole de Hautes Etudes, is now coming to
the fore.

The Acquisition of Competence

The new paragraph begins with a sentence whose syntactic structure is rather
unexpected. Its formulation would make it appear to belong within objective discourse, but at the same time it includes a *we* that extends the preceding cognitive
discourse, conferring on the narrator the status of *passive subject*.

To bring back the active voice would require a different lexicalization in which
"seeming" would be replaced by "perceiving." The choice made by the enunciator is therefore significant: it attributes to the *we* the role of *passive receiver* on
whom an "appearance" is imposed.

Given the sudden "Thus another possibile solution" in the unfolding of the
discourse, we are obliged to note a break in the story or, more accurately, the
irruption on the scene of an *event* that allows for a reorientation of that story.
Even more: appearance, defined in the *Petit Robert* as the manifestation of an
invisible *being* that *suddenly shows itself* in visible form, includes, in its underlying syntactic structure, a subject that must seem implicit and is different from
the subject manifested by *we*.

Such an interpretation of the phenomenon of *appearance* is further confirmed
by the emphasis with which the author returns to it in the second part of his pref-

ace where, referring to the same narrative "Thus another," he speaks of a "surprise" that awaited him. Now *surprise*, according to the *Petit Robert*, is an emotion brought on by something unexpected. The receiving subject is thus characterized as receiving the "provocation" of another *sending subject*.

"Thus another possible solution" plays the role of subject in its sentence. If we remember that passive constructions represent an inversion of the roles of subject and object, we can readily see that the preceding sentence fragment that we identified as the subject of the whole sentence is semantically no more than the object "vision" experienced by the subject "we," whereas the sending subject from whom the vision originates is implicit and represents, on the narrative level, the actantial instance of *receiver X*.

Let us look more carefully at the content of this "appearance." As we remember, from the beginning, discourse about research was presented as being a *problem*. Its complementary term, "solution," appears now, and this allows us to represent the program of this research as being situated along the axis

$$problem \rightarrow solution$$

We thus can interpret the solution as being both the process that allows for the resolution of the problem and its *end term*, the acquisition of the desired knowledge.

The "possible solution" that appears thus shows itself to be a *virtual narrative program*. This program—or rather, the subject to whom this program is attributed—is furthermore *modalized*. The lexeme "possibility" (which normally would have to do with the alethic square if what we had were an utterance of state) is here an expression of enunciative modalization because it is concerned with *doing*, and not being, and must be seen as the attribution of a /being-able-to-do/.

What appears for the subject *we* is, lastly, both the modal and programmatic content of scientific doing, a content that constitutes the *competence of the cognitive subject*. The attitude of the subject who finds himself in the position of *receiver* shows him to be ready to welcome that competence, and his *passivity* shows us that he plays no role in its acquisition. We know that transfer is performed by another—in other words, that competence is a *gift* from sender *X*, a gift that is given suddenly and unexpectedly to the receiving subject. This subject, who had earlier been disqualified as /not-being-able-to-do/, is thus now endowed with the modality of /being-able-to-do/, and the actualization of the new program can now begin.

Dialectical Manipulation

Thanks to the detailed examination of the preceding paragraph, we find ourselves better equipped to understand the complex workings of scientific discourse and to recognize the tricks it can play. Thus, we can easily see in the lexeme "studies," occupying the position of subject in the new sentence, a condensed representation, in substantival form, of the *cognitive doing* whose verbal forms "study" and "make clear" were found here and there throughout the preceding story. "Studies" is not just a condensed form announcing the existence of the cognitive level of discourse. It is also a cataphoric element that announces the final production of that discourse through the process or expansion.

The function of cognitive discourse is clarified by the predicate "make known better." This is a doing that consists in quantitatively and qualitatively increasing knowledge ("*better* known"), but also in "*causing* to know," that is, in producing knowledge so that it can be *communicated* to an actant that is implicitly included, namely, the *enunciatee*. The same actantial structure of communication is taken up again in the next sentence in which two actors ("Benveniste and I") take on the task of "showing" something to someone. Cognitive discourse includes, as one might expect, a twofold function: it is both a *doing* and a *causing-to-know*, a cumulative process or production and transmission using the procedures by which semiotic objects are constructed as well as the procedure of persuasive doing.

We can now better understand the way dialectic manipulation works as it accounts for successive changes in the formal status of scientific discourse. As a cognitive doing, it is a process creative of knowledge. As a causing-to-know, it shows as an operation involving transfer of knowledge seen as a consolidated object. All this is because manipulation is the result of cognitive doing and takes the form of objective discourse. As an object acquired by the ultimate enunciatee, it changes status in order to appear as referential discourse, a discourse that, once it has been deciphered and evaluated, can become the buttress for a new cognitive discourse. In other words, one and the same discourse, having — setting aside the different modalizations that represent various systems for regulating and mediating between different instances — a more or less constant narrative and rhetorical organization, can change its formal status and acquire with each change a different *specific or localized signification*, a signification that, each time, is relative to its position within the framework of the global discourse.

Manipulation that consists in grasping *cognitive discourse* in order to transform it into a *referential discourse* that can engender a new *cognitive discourse* is one of the constitutive elements in the definition of scientific progress.

Without looking for symmetry at any cost, we can still clarify things by saying that cognitive discourse is situated in terms of the perspective of the *enunciator*, whereas referential discourse has to do with the enunciatee who takes it in hand. Thus just one actor can — and almost always does — take on the two actantial positions. This is so because the process of communication, of which global discourse is in so many ways a simulacrum, consists in a continuous exchanging of the two roles. Vis-à-vis these two mobile instances, the discourse object (a depersonalized and objectivized object) is more than just a fraudulent camouflage of persuasive doing and of interpretive doing, practices that are its foundation and supporting structure. As a locus of uncertain knowledge, it is, at the same time as the preceding, an enterprise seeking to discover true knowledge.

Cognitive Performances

A New Taxonomy Because the failure of the first quest was due to taxonomic insufficiencies, it is natural for the enterprise to start off again with the subject in place of a new taxonomic organization of semiotic objects.

This beginning consists of the presentation of what has been learned in the course of "recent" studies and this is done by reference to earlier research. This identifies both the object of knowledge in this case (i.e., the semantic universe to be explored) and the interpretation to be given of it:

semantic universe ⟵——————— relation ⟵——————— *interpretive model*

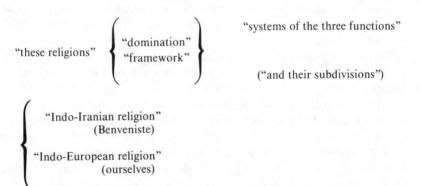

"these religions" { "domination" "framework" }   "systems of the three functions"

("and their subdivisions")

{ "Indo-Iranian religion" (Benveniste)

"Indo-European religion" (ourselves) }

What follows takes the form of setting up a parallel between the concept of *system* (which in an *abstract* manner articulates the semantic universe under study) and that of a *hierarchy of series* (which is supposed to reproduce the same articulations on the *figurative* level that is inhabited by gods). The parallelism thus obtained, however, is more than just the establishment of two superimposed levels of "religious reality"—which the term "inspired" (which lexicalizes their relation) might lead us to believe. It is true *homologation* of the gods, considered under the rubric of their names, and their functional definitions. It also is responsible for the figurative level's being established as the level at which the *signifier* is endowed with a *signified*.

Each name of a god is thus attached to a "function," and the new label of "functional gods" can only confirm their status as *signs*. Our taxonomic progress, compared with the first attempt, is here remarkable. Having started with a logic of inclusion that, "situated" each god within a "domain" without wondering about the semiotic nature of either, we have moved to a qualitative

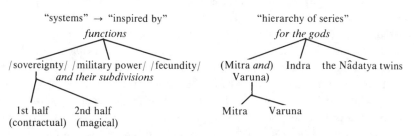

logic according to which divine figures, considered to be signifiers, can be compared according to their signifieds and can be identified by the semantic *features*—a timely term—that define them.

At the same time as the semiotic status of the objects under study is receiving this clarification, the interpretive model is also being improved on. When we move from the concept of system to one of a hierarchy of series, we note that, if the first is a *systematic organization* that projects a ternary structure onto a given semantic field, the second can be defined as a *hierarchical organization*, that is, as an ascending (or descending) arrangement according to the criteria of superiority (in ability? position?). Now the homologation of the names of the gods with their functional definitions shows that the hierarchical order, valid for the gods, is no less so for the functions. The "system of the three functions" is thus articulated in a twofold way and can be seen as a *hierarchy with a ternary structure.*

From the Conceptual to the Textual At first glance, the discursive unfolding of this paragraph seems to correspond to a deductive process. The taxonomic doing that takes place here first takes as its object the whole group of Indo-European religions and then considers only their individual manifestations, as found "among the Arya princess of Mitani" and "in several Vedic myths and rituals."

On closer examination, we see that we are dealing not with a conceptual limitation but rather with a change in attitude regarding the objects under study. What we have is a movement away from the *semantic universe* ("religious"), posited as an unanalyzed concept, to a *corpus* that, from a philological point of view, we see as a *manifest* reality and that, from a historical point of view, we see as an *attested* fact. Both of these conditions allow us to consider that corpus as a *referent* that is endowed with a certain materiality.

Note: This movement from concept to corpus is thus founded on a whole implicit tradition in scientific activity and in the human sciences, a "tradition" that is to be seen as a global *referential discourse* whose presence is presupposed in all sciences.

This change in referential level abandons conceptual manipulation in favor of the analysis of a corpus. The change is emphasized by the use of the expression "hierarchical *list*," which alerts us to the fact that the corpus itself is to be considered not as a simple collection of linguistic objects but rather as a *text* endowed with a syntagmatic organization. The hierarchical principle, which is the manner of articulating the model of the three functions, is now interpreted as being a property of the referential text with the ordinal arrangement of the names of the gods in the text being seen as signifying their hierarchical organization. It does not matter whether such a reading is legitimate or not. What is interesting about the procedure lies elsewhere, notably in the desire to *validate* models constructed with the aid of referent structures, which, in turn, have an objectivity about which the least we can say is that it is based on procedures of a different kind. The procedure whose aim is to circumscribe the object under study thus follows this route:

$$\text{/semantic universe/} \rightarrow \text{/corpus/} \rightarrow \text{/text/}$$

Comparative Doing Setting up the linguistic referent allows us better to understand the *comparative doing*, the last stage of the cognitive doing of the scientific program we are examining. In the first instance, it consists in adapting, to a new object, the methods of comparative grammar, which, in an approximate manner, we can give in the form of a small number of *operating rules*:

(a) establishing of two corpora, *presumed* to be comparable;
(b) determining the units to be compared and the manner of their syntagmatic distribution in the text;
(c) drawing up two exhaustive and closed inventories; and
(d) establishing, on the level of the signifier, correlations between the units thus placed in parallel.

The preceding is a phonetic *comparatism*, which, for example, once a text has been segmented and the morpheme units have been identified, allows us to establish a network of constant phonetic correlations between two Indo-European languages. This network of correlations, which is the guarantor of their "genetic relation," allows us, in turn, to establish a comparative morphology.

Note: This group of comparative procedures must again be considered to be an earlier scientific discourse that has been referentialized and has become implicit in the present discourse being examined.

In relation to the first cognitive discourse whose heuristic value lay only in the selection and judicious distribution of segments of an earlier discourse, we have made remarkable progress in terms of analogically transposing models for cognitive doing and thereby renewing *narrative competence*.

Note: It must remain understood, however, that this is not a psychological and historic study of the scientific personality of Georges Dumézil, but is rather an examination of the preface-discourse and is narrative and textual "truth."

The success of this comparative doing is, however, not the goal directly sought by the narrative program. Rather it seeks to determine the relation between the "functional gods" (state 1) and the Iranian Archangels (state 2). In relation to this main program, in this first step consisting of comparing and identifying the Vedic gods and the gods of the Mitani, all we have is a *usage* subprogram, or a *mediation* subprogram, which allows us to obtain a tool-helper with the aid of which to realize the global program (the stick a monkey might look for in order to knock down a banana that hangs beyond reach). Now the objective obtained by this subprogram is not an increase in knowledge of the object under study (by correlating another series of gods, the Mitani gods, with the series of functional gods already known) but rather the acquisition of a methodological tool that will allow undertaking the last phase of the program. Just as, in comparative linguistics, establishing phonetic correlations is useful only if it is part of a wider context, the context of morphemes that is established at an earlier stage, so too a comparison of divine figures considered in terms of their *signifiers* can be done only if their *signifieds* have already been mutually defined within the framework of a system of "functional" oppositions.

Now we can understand the nature of "another possible solution," that is, of a true scientific discovery. At the level of cognitive doing, it shows as a methodological change marked by *a movement from a phonetic comparatism to a semantic comparatism*. Since the gods are signs endowed with signifieds and since these latter can be analyzed in terms of *features*, identifying the features common to the "lists in hierarchy" can allow for establishing a network of semantic correlations, not only between the two series, but also between the two systems under study. It does not matter if the names of the gods, situated at the level of the signifier, cannot always be phonetically correlated—they can undergo semantic avatars (epithets can replace nouns, for example), or phonetic ones (given that the contradictory phonological tendencies can converge)—the "rapprochement" between the systems is a given. The quest's desired object is in sight and the hero's victory is close.

Discovery as Evidence

Mutation (a term we use to mark this methodological break) is inscribed within the global discursive context whose mechanism we must try to understand.

It at first appears as an explanation of the cognitive doing, and it integrates that into the narrative schema of discovery, a schema introduced at the beginning of the paragraph with "another possible solution." The competence of the cognitive subject ("possible") is a gift to him, and this is reaffirmed by "observable features," which are features we can see, an underlying definition that identifies the /being-able-to-do/ of the subject who acts on the "features" object. There is one difference and one aspect of progress to be noted, however: whereas in the first case the cognitive subject was situated in the position of passive receiver, here, thanks to an already acquired competence, he exercises an *active* receiving.[2]

In both cases, from the discursive point of view, the receiving cognitive subject is identified with the *enunciatee*. We can thus expect that the constative doing that he is called on to exercise will have to do with the discourse of another, that is , with the referential discourse called up for that purpose.

Now—and here is where we see a first deviation vis-à-vis "normal" discourse—the object of the constative doing is not referential discourse but rather the *linguistic referent* itself, which is present in the form of two "lists" that have been brought together so that their similarities have become identified. What at first was presented as a possible *solution* is now, after being integrated with the cognitive level, a *statement of what has been observed*, that is, the grasping, in the form of common *features*, of the relation of similarity between the two lists.

The *informative doing* we see at work here is, by definition, not modalized. It is normally followed by an *interpretive doing* that guarantees signification and solid validity for the statement about what has been observed. In the case under study, the instance of interpretation is well prepared, but the two successive activities are carried out under conditions that seek to *abolish any discursive distance between the knowing subject and the object to be known*. Thus, (1) the information is received *without mediation* (the features are "immediately observable"); and (2) the interpretation is carried out *without any previous preparation* ("they need no preparation in order to be understood"), that is, without the need for the earlier exercise of a *causing-to-know*.

If we take the current definition of *evidence*—"a characteristic of that which imposes itself on the mind with such force that there is no need for any proof for us to know its truth, its reality" (*Petit Robert*)—we can see that in our case we have a particular form of *epistemic modalization* that corresponds, when put on the square we set up earlier, to the position of /certitude/. But whereas certitude sanctions the interpretive doing being carried out on the referential discourse, *evidence* represents a statement of observed adequation between the referent and the discourse conveying it.

The attempts to express this adequation explain the inversion of the discursive form by which the attempt is made to carry out that expression. It is as if the referential text, being in the position of the subject, itself claims its own truth, thus rendering the researcher innocent of the discovery.

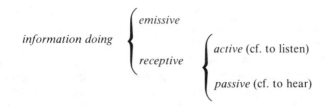

The epistemic modalization is the guarantor of the relation between the two "lists in hierarchy," and the comparative doing is thus closed out with the establishment of a partial identity between the semiotic objects inscribed in those lists. This is semantic comparatism, a procedure that allows us to correlate two (or more) syntagmatic phenomena on which an initial taxonomic doing has been carried out, one that establishes the loci and criteria for their comparability. What is basic about the "appearance" (i.e., the discovery) is all there. Yet the discovery does not entirely correspond to the stated goal of the discourse of research. Its goal was to determine a "historical process" situated somewhere between the two states of religion represented by the two parallel lists.

Thus a new interpretation of the acquired object of knowledge, a kind of secondary fleshing out of certain results, is immediately proposed. The "features," being the sentence subject of comparative doing, "lead us to see" in the Archangels the heirs of the functional gods. The cognitive subject is thus invited to cast his eye, that is, to *interpret* the structural and achronic correlation between the two texts and two series of discursive objects as being a *diachronic relation* between two states and the two kinds of divine figures representing them.

This is not the moment to inquire into semiotic status of the texts under study, or into the fact that those texts, present *hic et nunc*, are considered to be projecting their signifieds into the past and thereby establishing a "historical reality." Yet it is that very jump from textual reality to historical reality that the cognitive subject is "called on" to perform. We will soon see what precautions surround that moment and what *restrictions* limit it.

First of all, on several occasions the diachronic relation is lexicalized in terms of *heredity*. Whether we take this term in the genetic sense as "transmitting characteristics from one living being to another," or in the legal sense as "the one who inherits goods," the common denominator of both definitions is the concept of *transfer* of specified properties from one individual to another, *from one discrete state to another*. When we go from textual comparatism to historical comparatism, identifying features is a process that is interpreted as being a transfer of those features, which is not self-evident. This transfer is, however, partial (the Archangels inherit from the functional gods only in "certain respects"). It takes place against a background of differences, a background of a great divide between two states, which in any event, the very concept of transfer implies.

Second, contrary to the evidence that is the guarantor of semantic comparatism's becoming a cognitive procedure, modalization of historical comparatism does not seem to be of an epistemic nature. Whereas epistemic judgment is the result of interpretive doing (or of its suspension where there is clear evidence), the "being led to see," an invitation to exercise epistemic judgment, precedes interpretive doing. It thus appears to be the launching of a new program whose purpose is to make the cognitive subject competent to carry out the interpretation of data acquired in the course of the preceding program (recognition of common semantic features). Further, even if it is understood in this manner, the "*led* to see" does not seem to be a matter of deontic modalization, that is, /having-to-do/, but rather it is a matter of /wanting-to-do/, a /wanting-to-do/ that is transmitted by the text sender to the interpreting receiver-subject.

Discourse of Discovery and Discourse of Research

The surface discursive organization, as we find it announced in the third paragraph, is to be seen as the manifestation of *deductive reasoning*. Indeed, the paragraph is articulated in three propositions:

"Recent studies . . . "
"Now . . . "
"This is the source . . . "

of which the first two show as premises, followed by the third, a conclusion.

We have seen that, from the narrative point of view, its organization is something quite different. The first two sentences constitute the locus at which a narrative program of discovery is manifested. This is a complex program, composed of a usage subprogram (first sentence) and a detour that allows for the realization of the main program (second sentence). As for the third sentence, it serves to inscribe the movement from discovery to its manifestation in written form. If, in connection with this graphic activity, we can speak of a conclusion, it is not in the logical sense of the term but rather in the more general sense of "final disposition of a given affair."

The third sentence calls on a discourse that is entirely different from the preceding discourse, a written discourse whose organization in five chapters is announced by this sentence. If for the first discourse we keep the name of discourse of discovery, keeping for the second, the name of discourse of research *stricto sensu*, the parallelism between the two can perhaps be represented by the accompanying tables:

Story of Failure	Story of Victory	
	use NP	main NP
second paragraph	third paragraph	
	first sentence | second sentence	

Discourse of discovery

third sentence

	first chapter	second chapter	third chapter	fourth chapter	fifth chapter
Discourse of research	prelimin-aries	"working hypothesis"	first function	second function	third function
	hypotheses			*verification*	

Each of the two discourses, while having a common source, develops its own sequences. Thus the discourse of discovery has the story of the successful narrative program (NP) be preceded by a sequence that recounts the failure of the earlier NP. This discourse unfolds according to well-known rules of narrative organization that, while making use of an inversion of the discursive figures represented by the tests, make it possible to construct the story in terms of a quest for values, a quest engaged in by the *individual subject*.

Because the preface is a metadiscourse that recounts the story of our two discourses, we can better see the special role assigned to the third sentence of this paragraph. It accounts for the "formulation" of the working hypothesis described in the written discourse. The "formulation" is, however, more than just a change in the form of expression; it is more than just an indication of the movement from interior discourse to written discourse. The solution to the problem, seen as *evidence* in the first discourse, when "formulated" in the second, is presented as a "working *hypothesis*." That is, it is seen as an interpretive model whose epistemic value is no longer one of *certitude* but rather one of *probability*. Curiously, its mechanism is still obscure, even if its ultimate purpose is quite clear. In the move from the discourse of discovery, of the order of the *individual*, to the discourse of research, of a *social order*, modalization of the interpretive model undergoes a change. Considered as obvious on the personal level, the model can be integrated only as probable in the discourse of knowledge, where it is subject to procedures of verification.

The discourse of research that then develops shows as a *social discourse* (i.e., as a discourse carried out by a *collective subject*), not only because it makes a hypothesis of the individual discovery, but also because it modalizes the competence of this new subject differently. Whereas discovery has to do with an interpretive doing that does not require "any preparation," "verifications," on the contrary, presuppose a "preparation," that is, a *scientific knowing-how-to-do*. This knowing-how-to-do, in turn, is not of the order of the individual. The *spoken discourse* mentioned in the second part of the preface (and which we cannot discuss here) takes place within the framework of a seminar at the Ecole des Hautes Etudes and is presented as having as subject a plural *we* that "is in no way rhetorical." In that setting, the knowing-how-to-do of the small number of participants is carried out at the same time as that of the lecturer.

The discourse of research, articulated as /hypothesis → verification/, in a sense just parallels the discourse of discovery. The results of this latter, received as *proven* or evident, are once again questioned, made into hypotheses, so that, following on a new cognitive program, they might be verified and identified once again as being *certain*. As to the verification procedure itself, defined as an examination of "the value of something (that is, in this case, the interpretive model) by confronting it with facts" (*Petit Robert*), we can easily break it down into the already identified steps for cognitive doing: the bringing together of referential segments, their epistemic modalization, and finally, the transformation of epistemic judgments into alethic judgments, which are the basis for objective discourse.

A final point remains obscure in this procedure for converting one discourse into another, in this construction of a discourse of research. The source that is common to the two discourses shows not just one discursive segment that, after remodalization, is transformed into a statement of a working hypothesis. It also has a preliminary sequence that, covering all of the first chapter of the book, reproduces the discourse of discovery's usage program. What do the gods of the Mitani princes have to do with the "birth of the Archangels," we might naively ask.

Indeed, if the successful comparison of the Vedic and Mitanic gods can be identified as a *qualifying test* within the framework of the discovery, it is not necessarily transposed during construction of the discourse of research because the working hypothesis is formulated on the sole basis of the undisputed observability of semantic features. Given this we might wonder—it having seemed necessary to reproduce the entire *trajectory* of the discovery—if the discovery itself is as immediate and obvious as we are supposed to believe; if, on the contrary, it is not conditioned by the earlier choice of the *locus* of the problem and the setting up of a certain kind of *knowing-how-to-do*. Scientific discovery, although at a quick glance it seems to be a matter of sudden obviousness, would then be subject to its own logic and should be interpreted, in the same way as genetic processes, in terms of its being a coherent program whose end point is clear only a posteriori.

Epistemological Thoughts

The sentence that ends the first part of the preface constitutes both a reiteration of the problem of the substituted goal of research, articulated in the introductory paragraph, and the anaphora of the discursive sequences provided by paragraphs 2 and 3. This sentence is the topical locus for the discourse of the preface. Summing up the account of one given quest, it generalizes in aphoristic form:

". . . a frequent chance occurrence in the sciences we call human sciences."

This Demézil does with the simple procedure of positing that what is valid for the discourse entitled "Birth of the Archangels" is valid for all of the human sciences, that the unique chance occurrence that characterizes the unfolding of that discourse is a frequent occurrence in those sciences.

Such a generalization has nothing strictly scientific about it. It has more to do with epistemological thinking about the ways in which the mind works and the limits of human achievement.

Thus, as we have already noted, the term "vanished" is a suitable complement here for the term "appearance," which designates the discovery. Progress in the human sciences, when we consider them in terms of their phenomenal aspect, is regulated "phantomatically," according to repeated vanishings and appearances.

Nevertheless the scholar must try to go beyond this phenomenal level in order to reach a deeper level of reality ("another, more *real* problem"). We have already seen how the narrative progress, in the case of the quest for knowledge that is marked by the "substitution," could be interpreted as representing the negation of /seeming/ and the assertion of /being/.

Yet this new reality, a result of the discovery, is not absolute. The clarified problem is not "real"; it is "more real" than the first one. Because the first problem that "since Darmesteter" had been "generally considered" to be real "had vanished," nothing guarantees that the same will happen to the new solution. A fundamental doubt subtends all progress.

The relativism of the categories of /seeming/ and /being/, when that category is projected onto the evolutionary trajectory of the human sciences, and when that trajectory is seen as syntagmatic, explains its "chance occurrence" nature:

(a) Thus, the path of a human science is always marked by *chance occurrences*, that is, evenemential breaks that articulate that path into discontinuities.

(b) These breaks are *chance occurrences*, which means that they are also contingent. The discontinuity, responsible for creating meaning here, as well as non-necessary, which is an objectivized form of liberty, thus characterize this social discourse.

(c) But these frequent chance occurrences are, finally, not *accidents*, that is, superficial events that "add" something to what is essential without "altering its nature." These occurrences are modes in which knowledge is produced. They bring into question neither knowledge nor its search for intelligibility.

It is through the identification of the locus for his research—"the sciences we call human sciences"—that the enunciator completes his thoughts on the avatars of knowledge. It is an ambiguous label and he refuses to be solely responsible for the qualifier "human," letting some doubt remain as to what that means exactly. Does it qualify the very complex object or the exceedingly fragile subject of this quest?

By Way of Conclusion

The results of the microanalysis just undertaken seem interesting to us to the extent that they can be taken up again, by way of hypotheses that can be generalized to all discourses in the human sciences. They can, after verification, constitute a certain number of stable reference points that will allow for a better understanding of what is at work during the production and manipulation of scientific knowledge.

Discourse in the human sciences, far from being linear, appears to unfold on several levels at the same time, and these levels, while being recognizable as being endowed with a formal autonomy, interpenetrate each other, succeed each other, and are supporting structures of each other. They thereby guarantee a validity and progression—both obviously relative concepts—for a would-be scientific procedure. Each of the three principal levels we identified—cognitive discourse, objective discourse, and referential discourse—includes its own modal level, thus allowing for the sketching out of an initial typology of those modalities whose role in the discursive unfolding is capital. The modalizations of the process of enunciation are distinct from those of the utterances that record their results. Epistemic modalizations, which are linked to the instance of the enunciatee, have to do with already constituted discourse. They are its guarantor and, by referentializing it, allow for a redeployment of new programs for research.

The examination of Georges Dumézil's text has allowed us to get an idea of the complex relations contained within the discourse of research. It tries, using ruse and labels at the same time, to pass itself off as being an objective and sociolectal discourse whose subject is both collective and a specific individual. It passes itself off as a discourse in which the speaker-researcher is just an actor to whom has been delegated the discourse of discovery. That actor is necessarily personalized but is inscribed, as we have seen, in an underlying algorithm that regulates him. These are paradoxical relationships between a social discourse that cannot hide its links with the specific, individual enunciator who produces it, and an individual discourse that is controlled by a surpassing end goal.

Independently of these fundamental ambiguities, we see a certain kind of scientific practice identifying itself. It is made up of continuities of research and breaks produced by discoveries. The event in the case of each of these interruptions is absorbed by being integrated into social discourse; and, as we have seen, this is done by reformulating the certitudes of the discovery in terms of hypotheses, a remodalization that has the result of paralleling already actualized programs with validation procedures.

If it is in the nature of human discourse, whichever it might be, to finally be dependent on the enunciator-subject that produces it *hic et nunc* by subjectivizing and relativizing it, we have nonetheless seen what precautions, what complex procedures, encompass discourse that would be scientific, in its quest for true knowledge.

Chapter 5
Structure and History

The lack of a clear long-term focus in the human sciences, a sign of their weakness, is rather disturbing. Over the last few decades, in France at least, where philosophical and political thought have endeavored to delimit the concept of history and to work out methodological postulates likely to establish a science of society, linguistics, a social science if there exists one, has abandoned the historical dimension of its object of analysis and has attempted to exploit only the Saussurian notion of synchrony. For reasons that we shall not dwell on here, the heat has now been taken out of the great historical debate. In linguistics and within the structuralist epistemology in general, we are beginning to see the first symptoms of an increasing interest in diachrony, the first efforts to get beyond that dichotomy whose terms seemed irreconcilable. This chapter will therefore be dedicated to considerations that tackle the problem the other way around, starting from *the atemporal to the temporal*, from more or less justified extrapolations *beginning with the linguistic* and seeking to exploit both its discovery procedures and descriptive models, while keeping in mind their wider anthropological dimension.

History and Permanence

For a long time, and still today, the Saussurian dichotomy of *langue* and *parole* seemed to provide the explanatory framework that allowed us to account for the permanence of a structure underlying the totality of message-events that are both contingent and justified. This concept of system, which was immanent to a large number of linguistic activities, was rounded off by the recognition of the temporal linearity of discourse. Structure, which was timeless, could produce sequences of significations that were both evenemential and temporal. It generated historical events.

With respect to the problem of how temporality is produced from structures, difficulties almost always arise when the primary elements have to be exploited and integrated as explanatory elements in partial analyses. Hence the temporal nature of discourse becomes indistinct when describing the syntax of a natural language. We know that this type of description functions only with units of discourse that do not exceed the limits of the sentence, for it is a fact that syntactic structures do not organize the totality of discourse but only very limited segments of it. Discourse is therefore not the articulation of successive structures but the redundancy of the utterance, a single hierarchical structure. From this limited point of view, an author perceives signification not as being spread out over time but rather as the iteration of a certain number of *permanencies*.

Even if we set aside the grammatical manifestation of linguistic reality to analyze the transphrastic level of signification whose elements seem distributed along the continuum of time and constitute discourse as the temporal manifestation of meaning, we encounter the same conditions that transform temporality, considered as the means of transmission, into simultaneity, the extralinguistic conditions of the reception of messages strung together into discourse. Hence, every apprehension of signification transforms histories into permanencies; whether we happen to question the meaning of life (or of history), the interrogation (i.e., the fact that one assumes the role of receiver of messages when faced with a linguistic manifestation) has the following consequence: historical algorithms appear as states, in other words, as static structures.

We can reserve judgment as to the restricting value of the Brøndalian notion, according to which the synchronization of information, a necessary condition for its setting into structure and, consequently, for its capacity to signify, cannot exceed the simultaneous apprehension of more than six terms. It does seem impossible, however, not to take into account the fact that at the syntactic level, the utterance always appears as a minute spectacle with a very limited number of actors (subject, object, sender, receiver), and the fact that the fundamental signification of a story (narrative, myth, tale, etc.) can be reduced to a simple homologation. In the case of written discourse, temporality or spatiality at the level of expression is simply the means by which signification manifests itself, which is nonetheless neither temporal nor spatial.

Therefore, the problem must be formulated in a different way. We cannot infer their historicity from the obvious temporality of linguistic phenomena. Since linguistic description is directed only at structures, we must attempt to understand whether and how they are anchored in history.

Duration and Hierarchies

To ask oneself about the "meaning" of a film one has just seen consists, within the framework of one's own proper internal language, in organizing a limited number of elements making up the narrative, with a totalizing aperception in mind. Every subsequent step could only consist in choosing one of these elements and decomposing it. A new level of signification would be situated at a hierarchically inferior level and would correspond to the analysis of one of the terms already posited. All theories of language agree on this point: language is a hierarchy. It matters little, following one's acquired habits or the exercise of such and such a discipline, whether by process of visual symbolization one designates the elementary level of this permanence as analogical or substructural or, on the contrary, as situated at the level of the metalinguistic or superstructural pyramid. The elementary signification of any story, taken within the limits of its entire duration (which, in the historical sciences, would correspond to Braudel's "long durations"), can be posited as an invariant, "medium durations": being considered as variables, and "short durations", as stylistic and conjectural variations.

Such a correlation of *durations* and *structural levels* can appear tempting. A unique *hierarchical* model would therefore enable us to account for all sorts of diachronic transformations, interpreted as paradigmatic substitutions of variables situated at a specific structural level. Historical duration would not be completely abolished, however, but transcoded into a new descriptive language, and history itself would be integrated into a wider semantic universe. Finally, periodization, a procedure inherited from the nineteenth century, could be made more flexible and reinterpreted as an intermingling of manifestations belonging to different historical structures.

Unfortunately, such a conception does not bear up under examination. First of all, we cannot see how to found the equation that postulates that what lasts longer is more essential than what lasts for a short period of time. The misapprehensions of old are instructive on this very point. To explain the permanence of certain phonemes, one referred to the ease of their articulation, but in other cases, one claimed that the difficulty of their phonation, requiring an additional effort of concentration, guaranteed their stability. If this were so then the permanence of the round shape of bread would mitigate in favor of integrating "rotundity" into the fundamental structure of Mediterranean civilization. Without being false, such considerations could easily bring about "harrowing revisions" in history.

On the other hand, the articulation of duration into long, medium, and short underscores the operational and not the real nature of the conceptualization proposed. The three terms are semantically articulated according to the subjective category (that is to say, they refer to a speaker) of "relative measure." And if, after beginning with the example of the spectator interrogating the structure of the signification of a film narrative, we broadened the problem by seeking the possible correlation between collective corpora and social structures, the same holds true for the ideolectal history of a Mallarmé, where historical and stylistic levels correspond to the same relative durations.

The establishment of a correlation between durations and structures is undoubtedly valid at the level of procedures and facilitates the strategic choice of the homogeneous level of description. But duration understood in this way cannot serve as a bridge linking history to structure.

Synchrony and Diachrony

The difficulties encountered in integrating the temporal dimension in our reflection on the mode of existence of the structures of signification, for us, simply underscore the nonpertinence of the Saussurian dichotomy between synchrony and diachrony. Whether we take them etymologically or in the historical sense of their formulation still permeated with nineteenth-century historicism, both of these antonymic concepts are essentially conceived of as two complementary aspects of temporality, the "chronic" axis being logically prior to the opposition they are supposed to establish. This is not the case with post-Saussurian theories of language. For them the structure of any language contains no temporal reference and the term "synchrony" is simply maintained by tradition. The description of a structure basically corresponds to the construction of a metalinguistic model dependent on its internal coherence and within the manifestation, able to account for the functioning of the language it proposes to describe. For this type of model, the historical dimension is simply a backdrop on which linguistic behaviors are inscribed, the study of which does not appear to be pertinent at first glance.

Considering the distance that linguistics has taken in relation to diachrony, a real misunderstanding takes place when historians decide to incorporate synchrony into the main body of concepts they are used to manipulating. For historians synchrony signifies the assembly of a series of events taking place at the same time, and the description of a linguistic synchrony would ultimately signify the recording of all the words spoken at the same time by thousands of speaking subjects. Even if they are forced to acknowledge a certain staggering of messages in duration, nothing allows them to fix its limits. Do sentences, paragraphs, chapters constitute synchronic units? Will they attribute one or two years to the duration of a synchrony? Although this is what is commonly done, the exercise is rather pointless.

The relation between the functioning of a structure and the historical space it occupies is partially specified by Louis Hjelmslev through the use of the concept of *linguistic state*. A model that attempts to describe a linguistic state such as Old

French, for example, is generally constructed by means of a dual procedure. It appears sometimes as a *hierarchy of systems and categories*, and sometimes as a *set of rules of functions* (of derivation, production, conversion). But although this is commonly done, it is wrong to consider the latter as diachronic. Because a twenty-year-old Dane needs to do his military service, does that not mean that at a given moment Danes are transformed into soldiers. The organization of military service is a typically static rule. Consequently, regulations are part of the linguistic state. There is a difference in formulation and not in nature between categorical and statutory descriptions, and the transformation of one code into another is always possible. The structure of a linguistic state therefore appears as a sort of *achronic* mechanism used to produce an indefinite number of messages—and to convert these into messages of a different type—thus filling a corresponding historical space with events.

Although this interpretation of the linguistic state introduces a certain parallelism between structure and history, it does not establish a relation between the two concepts. It is true enough that it enables us to see that a large number of "changes" often considered to be historical transformations, are not. Moreover, this interpretation also specifies the conditions for a structural description of history. It in no way establishes, however, the historical specificity of such and such a structure that subsumes a historical period. It does not indicate why such a model precisely accounts for the functioning of Old French (a unique historical structure) and not of another state of another language. As a matter of fact, it is not impossible to imagine that there exists an identical linguistic structure somewhere in Amazon or that a comparable one existed in linguistic prehistory. Instead of explaining the historical character of structure, such an interpretation restores the dignity of structure to the signifying totalities localized in history.

The Historicization of Structures

It seems that the relation between structure and history, along with a methodology common to the social sciences and the historical sciences, can be defined only if two orders of questions can be answered satisfactorily. Of what does the historical nature of social structures consist? How can we account for diachronic transformations situated between structures juxtaposed at the same level of temporal succession?

We know that the greatest success of nineteenth-century linguistics was the reconstitution of families of languages, founded on criteria of historical relations. This reconstitution went so far as to construct an original Indo-European language of which there was no written trace—in short, to reconstruct a historical structure that can do without evenemential history. Although this enterprise was a considerable task, patiently undertaken by several generations of linguists, its structural reinterpretation was attempted only in 1943 (and published twenty years later) by Hjelmslev. In itself this suffices to assess the distance that continues to separate both linguistic traditions. Because of the importance of the attempt, we feel obliged to summarize the main lines.

It is recognized that the historical (or genetic, according to Hjelmslev's terminology) relationship of languages is exclusively situated at the level of the signifier and consists in recording correlations between the elementary elements of this plane, phonemes defined both by their commutability and their behavior within more important units of the signifier, namely, syllables. The units constituting the signifier, but also the contextual frames within which they function, are the basis of comparison permitting the establishment of what used to be called affiliation. Moreover, the inventory of the syllables from which phonemes are extracted to establish this correlating comparison is restrictive. The only syllables taken into consideration are those that can, either alone or combined, function as segments of the signifier related to contents, that is, syllables used to constitute the signs of language.

Such a definition of historical relation has an undeniable explanatory value. First of all, it enables us to see that such a relation is quite different from a purely *typological* one, by the very fact that the corpus of syllables retained for the description is *restricted*. Among the large number of combinatory possibilities each language has to constitute its syllabic stock, only the syllables actually realized as supports of signification are taken into consideration. The historical anchoring of a structure, its nature as a structure that is actually manifested in a certain historical *hic et nunc*, is, in the structuralist formulation, therefore defined as a limitation of its possibilities for manifestation.

On the other hand, this limitation of the virtualities that entail the historicization of structures is situated at the level of signs, that is, at the level of "semantic effects," the form taken by every manifestation of the signifying universe. It is not difficult to transpose our remarks from the plane of expression to that of content, and to speak of historical relation with respect to units of the signified and to units of the signifier. The structures of signification will be historical only insofar as the inventory of semantic effects happens to be restricted. Relatively speaking, within the human universe, the sign takes on the same role as Descartes's piece of wax in the natural universe. Although the sign takes on the aspect of an indisputable and immediate reality, the union of the signified and signifier institutes an unusable level of reality that is nonpertinent for scientific description. For semioticians, signs—words, messages, texts—constitute the same screen of real appearances as do the objects of the world and their varied reconversions for physicists. Just as the atomic structure can easily be imagined as a combinatory of which the present manifest universe is only a partial realization, imagined according to a comparable model, the semantic structure remains open, and its closure is sanctioned only by history.

If this exploratory chain of thought has any value whatsoever, instead of being an opening up as has been endlessly repeated, on the contrary, history is a *closure*. It closes the door to new significations contained, as virtualities, in the structure on which it depends. Instead of being a driving force, history is a brake. As we noted at the beginning of this chapter, we therefore find, not to our surprise, that instead of the expected newness only permanencies are found in manifestation. Redundancy, which at every moment solidifies structures into functions and transforms them into idiom, is certainly one of the explanatory elements of historicity. And the popular wisdom that claims "the more things change, the more the more they stay the same" has a large measure of truth to it.

Structures and Usages

If we start from the Hjelmslevian dichotomy, new extrapolations, opposing structure (= schema) to usage (which have hardly been explored up until now), are possible. Operationally, by usage we can understand the use a linguistic community makes of the structure of signification at hand. The concept of usage is then identified with the historicization of structure. But, like Hjelmslev we can also use the term "usage" to designate the *structure closed by history*, and in this case the problem of the relations between structure and its partial historical manifestation is situated at a homogeneous level of reflection. The relations between these two concepts can be specified in terms of a twofold observation: if we chose a certain usage as object of description, from this usage we can only explain a single structure immanent to it. Conversely, because of the diversity of possible limitations, a single structure can appear in the form of several usages. In other words, it can give rise to several historical structures.

If this is the case, we can see that a single social structure, for example, feudalism, can appear as particular usages that can be designated as French, Japanese, or Indian feudalism. Hence, a certain *comparativism—both historical and achronic*—seems easier to imagine than historical and diachronic comparativism. Far greater theoretical difficulties would arise if one attempted to apply the same descriptive procedures to two structural states succeeding one another and situated along the same temporal chain. In this case one would have to establish comparisons, no longer between two usages, but between two different structures. Taken separately, each state has an immanent structure that is not exclusively limited to it. The transformations of structures, and not the extension of usages, are changes that allow us to speak about the succession of two states, since by definition an interruption in the course of history can occur only if the existing model no longer accounts for new events that appear and a new model needs to be postulated. The categories of signification on which these transformations operate are not necessarily those that are already realized in the *ab quo* state, or even in the two usages that succeed one another. We should proceed with caution. It is not at all impossible that a certain correlation exists between two successive and separate historical usages, but structuralist methodology currently does not seem able to specify its status.

The Transformations of Structures

A properly historical investigation that would attempt to introduce the concept of structure into the list of its operational instruments cannot ignore the following order of priorities: the *description of the static structures* inherent to usages is logically *prior to the procedures of comparison of the successive structural states*. But at first glance this second stage is no different from the achronological methodology used in typological comparativism. In both cases, it is a question of comparing historical contents reduced to their form as models. In both cases, especially, the establishment of correlations between two structures of content constitutes a metalinguistic operation with respect to the contents described. These differences in attitudes and terminologies should not lead us astray. In the first case, using a metatheory of signification that would subsume both the structured contents and the transformations carried out, it is a question of accounting for the transformations identified between the two models. In the second case, we are obliged more or less explicitly to acknowledge a translinguistic subject whose interventions justify the diachronic transformations separating the structural states, within a temporal continuum.

Comparativists concerned with their descriptive tools do their best to maintain them at homogeneous levels of generality and are obliged to recognize the metalinguistic nature of the models of transformation. Not wishing to take themselves for the subject of the transformations they are simply describing, they multiply verification procedures and progressively transfer all responsibility to the model they are trying to make objective. Historians, and especially Marxist historians, posit history as an immanence. For them the structures of content and the (dialectic) models of transformation are immanent to the manifestation of history. The need to clarify them remains in its entirety, however. Construction and explication of the models are merged in the praxis of discovery and description. What historians and comparatists are lacking most is a better understanding of the models of transformation they both need. For descriptive praxis has a knowing-how-to-do in the form of a list of models that can be used as one wishes. It is from this perspective that we can understand better the meaning of Claude Lévi-Strauss's investigations. Instead of negating history and especially historical comparativism, as some have implied, his research aims at integrating them into a general typology of structures of signification. By highlighting the existence of "concrete logics," he has given us a precise idea of how repertories of the constituent elements of these historical structures of content, which as we saw was a prior condition for any description of their transformations, could be imagined.

The comparison, currently taking place between mythical narratives belonging to distinct societies, is of interest to semanticists from two points of view: not only as an attempt to get beyond usages by extracting the structures that make a typology of the superstructures possible, but also as a progressive clarification of the models and types of transformations that can be identified. Far from constituting an ahistorical or even an antihistorical enterprise, structuralist methodology is probably preparing a revival of historical research. For a better understanding of the general rules of structural transformations is necessary before one can reach a clear verdict about the specific nature of diachronic transformations. This is the price to be paid for the movement from the philosophy of history to the science of history. Linguistics experienced this when, for want of descriptive models, for centuries it reveled in the contemplation of its general concepts.

Diachronic Transformations

It is possible that the originality of diachronic transformations can be found in the *irreversible* nature of their unfolding. For this, all one has to do is to define precisely a certain type of correlation enabling one to rule as follows: given two structures of content S_1 and S_2, and the correlation R that exists between them, the structure S_2 can be the transformation of the structure S_1 and not the inverse. Unfortunately, we are still far from being able to imagine such rules. We do know, it is true, that there exist compatibilities and incompatibilities between the elements and the categories of signification, and that knowledge of them would enable us to establish rules of selection and restriction at the level of manifestation. The debate about their asymmetry that has recently been instituted in linguistics can, perhaps, bring some element of clarification to the problem. We also are aware of the difficulties encountered by logicians when they come across oriented relations that prevent them from constructing a logic freed from discourse. This is perhaps another domain where history could seek its justification. One should note, however, that the dialectical enterprise that, at first glance, appears as the very model of diachronic transformation, does not present sufficient guarantees of irreversibility. After our first investigations, it would seem that the dialectical enterprise (which some considered as having devastated mythical correlations), insofar as it negates the conjunction of contrary terms and affirms the possibility of new articulations of discrete contents, has the inverse mythic process as corollary, that is, the creation of symbolic correlations that reconcile the irreconcilable.

Without being excessively optimistic for the time being, we believe we have

exhausted the main possibilities of methodological extrapolation that can be envisaged. This attempt at bringing them together highlighted the lacunae and de-
ficiencies of structuralism as well as those of the conceptualization of history.
The task of integrating history into the methodology of the social sciences will
take place only when the historical sciences adopt the concept of structure as one
of their fundamental concepts.

Chapter 6
The Semiotic Analysis of Legal Discourse: Commercial Laws That Govern Companies and Groups of Companies

In collaboration with Eric Landowski

Introduction

A Naive Gaze

We initially undertook as a wager the semantic analysis of the law regulating commercial companies (Law Number 66-537 of July 24, 1966) with the idea in mind of trying to determine the semiotic status of a "group of companies."[1] Neither our training nor our prior experience in descriptive practice nor again research carried out by others could serve as a model — nothing had prepared us for such an enterprise. However, the implicit postulate underlying the search for a method of semantic analysis that we have been pursuing over the years urgently required that such discourse analysis be founded only if its procedures could elucidate any discourse whatsoever, and only if the models we proposed could account for the modes of the production, the existence, and the functioning of any text.

This apparent contradiction between the competence of the models and the procedures available, postulated a priori along with our avowed incompetence regarding the contents invested in legal texts, can be overcome simply on one condition. It must be understood that the analysis in question can give only naive results, that is (by giving the term "naive" its scientific meaning), can lead only to either banal or unexpected conclusions. *The naïveté of the analyst's gaze* is consequently the first edict of this investigation.

Methodological Choices

The fact that the text to be analyzed is short presents another difficulty. Although the text of the law governing commercial companies is a sufficiently long example of legal discourse, the segments of this text referring to groups of companies are few and far between.[2]

Even if we brought greater logico-semantic rigor that is sometimes lacking to the methods of content analysis employed by certain sociologists, nevertheless such methods would still not be applicable to our corpus. In principle, content analysis proceeds *inductively* and seeks to generalize observations from data extracted from texts by establishing an inventory of its constants. What can these methods give us when dealing with a text that is only a few paragraphs long?

Consequently, it is necessary to carry out a methodological inversion and abandon the inductive method with its generalization procedures for a *deductive approach*. Among all possible and realized discourses, legal discourse is simply a particular case that can be defined in its specificity by some or other natural language. Starting from what we know about the general properties of discourse we can deduce certain general and specific characteristics of legal discourse. Beginning with our relative knowledge about the mode of existence of conceptual structures called "collective subjects," we can ask ourselves about the nature of these "legal beings" that commercial companies happen to be and try to determine the specific status of groups of companies that are also "collective beings" but that the law seems to have some difficulty creating.

Our own methodological preferences here converged with the requirements imposed by the nature of the text to be analyzed. Therefore, with the explanation of the text in mind, the analyst will successively use very general models and procedures that are sufficiently powerful to account for the organization and the functioning of the text in question.

Methods

The task of the analyst, entailing the more or less elegant presentation of results while at the same time disguising them, is long and arduous. For all intents and purposes it requires the establishment of a team. Yet it has to be recognized that "team work" remains a fashionable phenomenon and a mystifying word, at least in the social sciences where the distribution of tasks it presupposes is rather delicate because of the major role still played by intuition. It has to be one thing or the other: either the *descriptive procedures* are solidly established and formalized and the analyst ends up with tautological results bordering on the banal, or else the procedures are confused with *discovery procedures*, making it impossible to hierarchize and coordinate tasks so ill defined that they merge with the vagueness of the dimensions of the partial objects under study.

We were therefore very careful not to distribute tasks by carrying out an a priori division of the objects of analysis. To begin with, we simply asked that each member of the team establish a preliminary report on how, if he were given that responsibility, the analysis would be carried out and what hypothetical results could be expected. The four reports, written separately and without consultation, were then distributed, examined, and debated during joint meetings, with the idea of establishing a strategy of analysis that included an inventory of the models and procedures to be used, as well as a list of provisional hypotheses and conclusions to be examined and verified. Eric Landowski, one of the researchers, was given the task of writing up the final version of the text. He reworked the analysis once again from beginning to end and wrote a 181-page document of which the following is a sort of synopsis, completed and reworked by the person in charge of the investigation, who has to shoulder the responsibility for the conclusions whether they happen to be collective or stem from personal points of view that needed to be introduced.

The team of co-workers was not founded on the division of tasks, and discovery procedures took precedence over descriptive procedures. The team had to be constituted in such a way that a collective "naive gaze" emerged and that a reading, even though not unique, but at least relatively homogeneous was possible. *Pluridisciplinarity*, another myth in the social sciences, had to be overcome. Although the researchers making up the team that was constituted in an ad hoc fashion came from different backgrounds—sociology, literature, political science or linguistics—the team itself should not be considered as being plurdisciplinary since over the years all of the members in different disciplines, had practiced a semiotic approach founded on a set of common epistemological postulates. The only pluridisciplinary research that seemed possible to us was to accept a single methodology.

A Few Simple Questions

The analysis carried out attempts to answer several simple questions: What are the specific properties of legal language? What is a commercial company? What does the legislator of these groups of companies "think"? The analysis can be considered to be successful only if all the answers are included in the text that we have attempted to interrogate and clarify.

Legal Language

Legal Discourse

The analysis of a specific legal text, such as the law governing commercial companies, presupposes reflecting on the semiotic status of legal discourse as a whole. It is only if we have at our disposal a certain number of operational concepts clarifying its properties and the mode of its linguistic existence that we will be able to determine a specific discursive "object" or "place" where commercial law is situated.

The very expression "legal discourse" already contains a certain number of presuppositions that need to be clarified. First, it suggests that by legal discourse one has to understand a subset of texts that are part of a larger set, made up of all the texts that appear in any natural language (in our case, French). Second, it indicates that we are dealing with *discourse*, that is to say, on the one hand, the syntagmatic, linear manifestation of language and, on the other, the form of its organization, which includes, in addition to phrastic units (lexemes, syntagms, utterances), transphrastic ones (paragraphs, chapters, or, finally, actual discourses). Third, qualifying a subset of discourse as *legal* in turn implies either the specific organization of the units constituting it or the existence of a specific connotation underlying this type of discourse, or, finally, both at the same time.

Legislative Discourse and Referential Discourse

To say that legal discourse is a subset of a set, the infinite text unfolding in French or in any other natural language, amounts to admitting that, while incorporating certain properties that distinguish it from other discourses taking place in French, it nevertheless possesses everything making it possible to define it as discourse in a natural language. From this point of view, its status is not fundamentally different from literary, political, or economic discourses produced in French.

A natural language enables one to speak not only of the world and of humans, but at the same time, using its own materials, makes it possible to constitute specific discourses endowed with a certain autonomy. It thus appears as a relatively distanciated referential locus to which refer particular significations produced by second-degree discourses, such as legal discourse. It also appears as a locus where significations depending on different metadiscourses converge and intermingle in a polysemy that originates from every period in time. This phenomenon accounts for the fundamental ambiguity of a French person's everyday discourse, be he a professor of law or not, made up of an extremely complex mix of elements belonging to legal, economic, and political discourses, for example.

The question that has caused much ink to flow, regarding the relations that legal discourse can have with social or economical "reality," is not pertinent from our current point of view. If legal discourse seems at every moment sullied by a sort of duplicity, it is because it unfolds along a *dual isotopy*. The first is represented by *legislative discourse*, composed of performative and normative discourse, instituting beings and things along with licit and illicit rules of behavior, whereas the second appears in the form of a *referential discourse*, which, although being only an ideological construct—a discursive cover of the world—passes off as the social world itself, prior to the language that articulates it. These two isotopies are of a linguistic nature and are not separated by a difference in kind. Often confused in the same legal text, these two discursive levels are also the only "realities" semantic analysis has to deal with. The dependencies of one isotopy on another, and their mutual interferences, on the contrary, constitute a structural problematics the elucidation of which, in a certain measure, makes it possible to define the specificity of legal discourse as such.

The problem of the referent (i.e., the relation between words and things, between actual processes and the verbal predicates covering them) is part of general semiotic theory and does not come into play at the level of the definition of discourses and secondary semiotic systems supported by natural languages. On the other hand, taken within the totality of significations they manifest, they can and must be examined from the point of view of their adequation to "natural" semiotic systems, that is, nonlinguistic (social, economic structures, etc.), to which they are more or less isotopic in their subarticulations. That a particular "vision of the world," understood as a certain organized semantic investment appearing through a natural language, happens to be "twisted" and "deforming" in relation to the natural semiotics to which it corresponds—and this for historical reasons (a linguistic semiotics that survives the transformations of natural semiotic practices) or for social reasons (a linguistic semiotics corresponding to the natural practices of the dominating classes and milieu)—is an extremely important problem. It is, however, a problem that falls under general semiotics and can be clarified only by comparing linguistic and nonlinguistic systems. Such a comparison can be envisaged only after the isomorphic description of the two systems.

From the preceding, we shall retain the distinction of the two constituent isotopies of legal discourse: its legislative level and its referential level. While the relations between these two levels need to be examined more closely, nonetheless, at first glance, they appear as follows. Legislative discourse constantly refers back to the significations of referential discourse, as though it were not only isotopic, but also isomorphic to the "reality of the world," prior to legislative discourse, that would simply be language on things whose existence is evident. What we are dealing with here is a relation of logical presupposition that is of the order of *semiotic seeming*. In fact, it is legislative discourse that, in selecting the referential elements of a natural language, confers on them the status of referential level and, by bringing about their closure in relation to surrounding significations, integrates them into legal discourse. From the point of view of *semiotic being*, the legislative level consequently has the right of antecedence and is presupposed by the referential level.

A Connoted Discourse

As we have seen, natural language is a complex semiotic system because it allows for development of secondary metasemiotics, such as legal language, whose discursive manifestation remains to be analyzed. A new concept, connotation, can help us better understand certain mythicizing characteristics of legal discourse. A system of connotation is made up of a set of secondary signifieds that, in addition to its denoting and openly intentional meaning, every text generated by any semiotic system can have. Hence, when we are dealing with law, it is as though independently of what it wants to state, in unfolding, the legal text conveys a set of vague connotations accepted by the reader as a mixture of incomprehension, respect, implicit threats, and so on, that could be called the "judiciality" of the text. The latter allows it to be classed without any precise reference to its content, as a legal discourse, distinct from all other comparable discourses.

This is probably also the case for the sentiment of "reality" of the referential isotopy of discourse. It imposes itself on the reader as social verisimilitude, or even more so, as a logical a priori that simply describes an organized legislative language. Moreover, this illusion of reality covers the totality of legal discourse in another manner, by conferring the status of autonomous *semiotic objects* endowed with personality and quasi-organic functions to the legal denominations and definitions (company, board of directors, assembly, etc.), in short, by transforming these *discursive objects*, language artifacts, into *semiotic objects*, agencies, or institutions. It is possible that social connotations are only a set of semantic effects; nonetheless, it still constitutes an autonomous symbolic dimension that accounts for the weight of legal discourses and the credibility of legal institutions.

Law: A Semiotics

Leaving aside the problem of connotations, we can say that legal discourse can be recognized as such if it has a certain number of recurring structural properties that differentiate it both from any everyday discourses and secondary discourses having other specific properties. These recurring properties can be either grammatical or lexical.

The recurrence of grammatical properties allows us to extract them from discourses and formulate them as a set of grammatical rules. Conversely, we can say that a system of grammatical rules allows us to produce all sorts of discursive units and formally recurrent discourses, independently of the contents that can be invested in these units and these discourses. Consequently, if such recurrences can be noted in legal texts, we must infer that as far as its form is concerned, every legal discourse is produced by a *legal grammar* that is distinct from the grammar of the natural language in which this discourse appears.

In turn, lexical recurrence makes it possible to postulate the existence of an autonomous *legal dictionary*. This dictionary is then only the manifestation, in a lexical form (words, expressions, etc.), of a certain semantic universe that we shall call the *legal universe*. If this is the case, if legal discourse refers back to a legal grammar and lexicon (grammar and lexicon being the two components of language), we can say that it is the manifestation in the form of message-discourses, of a language, of a *legal semiotics*.

This constitutes our initial hypothesis. We postulate that the text to be described is part of a legal semiotics, that it is produced by a grammar and is the manifestation of a specific semantic universe.

Certain consequences immediately follow from the preceding. For example, contrary to what happens in the case of literary semiotics, which seems to be a pure grammar, indifferent to the contents it deals with, legal semiotics has a semantics in addition to its grammar. The grammatical rules of law do not apply to just any content; they operate only within a present legal universe, in a more or less explicit way, at the referential level and under the purview of legislative discourse. The legal universe can be articulated as a microuniverse in which are included the laws governing commercial companies that we will now investigate.

Legal Grammar

The comparison of legal semiotics with other semiotics brings out a new particularity. Insofar as most often the grammar of social semiotics is implicit, and subjacent to the discourses it produces (this is the case, for example, with the code of table manners), *legal grammar attempts to be explicit* and ostensibly exhibits the body of its rules. It not only claims to be known by all, it also appears as a well-made grammar, leaving no room for ambiguity at the level of intentions, it goes without saying.

As far as its presentation is concerned, legal grammar, however, somewhat resembles a schoolbook. It takes the form of a very badly organized inventory of definitions and prescriptions, and not of a hierarchy of concepts or a deductive series of rules. It appears as a syntagmatics, essentially concerned with the proper formation of utterances and more important discursive units (for example, of the type: *if . . . then*) and leaves the taxonomy of the fundamental categories implicit, which, as system, produces the grammatical discourse of law. The *legal code* (taking the term in its linguistic meaning) that generates the grammatical discourse (or the *code* in the legal sense) is absent, although it remains implicit in the discourse itself. One of the first tasks of the semiotic exploration of law is in fact the formal reconstruction of the legal system underlying these numerous discourses.

The explicit form of grammatical discourse is actually one of the specific criteria of legal semiotics. For example, we know that all the French can speak French, without necessarily knowing a single grammar rule of the language. But we are unable to question the existence of the grammar they obey. This is not the case regarding legal grammar, which is a *constructed grammar* and displays itself as such. The initial enunciation of the law of July 24, 1966—"The President of the Republic promulgates the law with the following content"—is not only the expression of a delegated collective will; as enunciation, it institutes, much in the manner of the divine fiat, the set of legal utterances that will exist only by virtue of this original performative act.

We can also see that this initial *wanting to say* is reflected on the entire corpus of legal discourse, by covering it with a *modal grid* that is one of the components of the grammatical taxonomy. We can distinguish two types of fundamental utterances: *qualifying utterances* (which constitute discursive objects into semiotic objects by attributing determinations to them) and *functional utterances* (which determine the sphere of activity that these objects can assume). Hence these two types of utterances are modalized (much like the modalities of the true and the false, which govern the utterances in binary logic) by the categories proper to legal language (or an equivalent distinction seems to appear at the lexematic level through the opposition of "formal dispositions" and "imperative dispositions").

In the *nature of the being* that characterizes the qualifying utterances, the utterance (considered as the *expressed* of the legislator's *expression*) is identified with the term "existent." Only what is explicitly said has the status of existent. Moreover, the same type of equivalence is established between the *nonsaid* and the *nonexistent*. Thus, for example, by creating (or believing to create) something that does not conform to the legislative model, the formulators of the statute do not "violate" the law, and do not even say something "false"; what is not the legal company does not exist at all. The notion of legal invalidity here conjoins with the term "nonexistent" of the modal category:

existent vs. *nonexistent*

which in legal grammar is identified with that of:

said vs. *nonsaid*

and founds legal grammar as an *arbitrary and explicit construction*, the explicit being the arbitrarily chosen criterion of its existence.

Although the "grammatical objects" of law exist only by virtue of the said, we can see that to *name* and to *define* the objects constitute one of the essential aspects of legal practice, understanding by *practice* the two dimensions of legal activity: the production of law and the verification of the conformity of the utterances on the world with the canonical utterances of legal language. We shall return to this later.

In the *nature of doing*, where by means of functional utterances it is necessary to fix the operational sphere of the semiotic object that is called into existence, the predictable set of behaviors is subjected to the evaluation of a modal grid. Theoretically the inventory of behaviors the legislator is attempting to regulate is part of the more or less explicit referential level and is supposed to cover the totality of the justiciable universe. Two procedures are therefore possible. The first consists in considering only *prescribed* behaviors as legally existent (as is the case, for example, regarding the execution of liturgical or magical rituals); the second, in considering all *forbidden* behaviors as legally nonexistent (this is the case for a structure of kinship that would not have any preferential rules). Taken separately, both solutions are theoretically possible. There is a chance, however, that they produce considerable gaps, since they can barely exhaust the combinatory of the events anticipated. It follows that most often legal systems mix both types of rules, while demonstrating variable preferences for particular modal categories of legal regulation. This could, moreover, serve as a criterion for a typology of these systems. As a hypothesis, one is quite free to suppose that all the modal categories of this type could be integrated in the following elementary model:

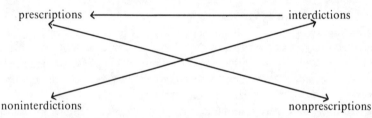

It would be interesting to test the French legal system from this point of view in order to see: (1) what type of regulations it prefers; (2) whether the use of a specific type of rule (prescriptive, interdictive) is free or linked to any class of legal objects or any specific legal microuniverse (commercial, penal law, etc.).

Legal Practice

Considered at its source, the legal system appears as an absolute performative language, instituting a conventional and explicit order of the world. Considered from the point of view of its organization, by the very fact of expressing beings and things, it seems to call them into existence by ascribing specific functions to them, delimited by prescriptive and interdictive rules. As such the legal system appears as a solid and immobile architecture with the immutability of law being one of its principal connotations. Nonetheless the system does evolve, accrue, and transform itself because of the constantly renewed legal discourses whose innovations are reflected at the level of their underlying system.

From this perspective, legal practice is a *production of law*, of new legal rules and significations. But legal practice is at the same time a *recurring procedure of verification* of the validity of the instituted legal language. From this point of view, compared with other semiotics, it has undeniably original characteristics. The validity of a grammar can be tested in two different ways: either by means of a metalanguage that is called on to rule on the internal coherence of its concepts and its rules, or by comparing all the utterances generated by the grammar in question with the established canonical forms. But, as in principle the grammar can produce an infinite number of actual utterances, we do not see how such a procedure can be put into practice. On the contrary, the strength of legal discourse resides in the fact that it considers and constantly puts into practice such procedures of verification. This can be done through the specific structure of the delegation of power, by substituting the original sender of legal messages that the legislator happens to be, for a surrogate sender who reiterates the law, and that is called "justice."

Although distinct as to their purposes and as to when they appear in the legal process, as soon as we attempt to clarify their mode of functioning the two practices in question nonetheless raise comparable problems and have structural affinities. Legal discourse, which as we saw is the result of the convergence of its two components, a grammar and a lexicon, produces legal utterances (in the broadest sense of the term) that are defined both by their canonical form (resulting from the application of the rules of grammatical construction — this is what constitutes their *grammaticality* [G] and by their legal content, considered as part of the semantic universe that legal language covers (this constitutes their *semanticity* [S]). Only utterances that satisfy *stricto sensu* the two criteria of grammaticality and semanticity will be recognized as being legal. Indeed, these two criteria seem sufficient to define the two legal practices of the production and the verification of law: legislative practice and jurisprudential practice.

From this perspective, *legal production* appears as the construction of *grammatical* discourse that, in well-constructed utterances, integrates contents considered as *asemantic* ($\bar{S}$), that is, as not yet fully belonging to the legal universe. These contents can only come from the virtual referential level of legal language that is immersed in the discourse of natural language where heterogeneous elements from different semantic universes are jumbled together. To transform an *asemantic* ($\bar{S}$) word, expression, or sentence into a *semantic* (S) term or utterance consists in transferring it from the referential level to the legislative level of legal language. Consequently, the procedures consist in correctly naming "things" and inscribing predictable "events" into the modal grid of prescriptions and interdictions, the legislator's word being sufficient to give a legal existence to what is expressed.

Although *legal verification* is part of the same conceptual framework, it proceeds differently. From the indefinite number of "facts" and "events," which as soon as we talk about them, as descriptive utterances, seem to be part of the referential level of legal language but are nonetheless *agrammatical* ($\overline{G}$), the practice of jurisprudence consists in verifying the conformity of the utterances that can *grammatically* (*G*) produce legal discourse. In other words, once the semanticity of the *related* event has been acquired, verification is carried out by the translation of a nonlegal utterance into an utterance conforming to the rules of construction of legal utterances, and this, in order to show that among all the utterances that the legal grammar can generate, there exists at least one utterance matching the one stemming from the translation of the nonlegal utterance.

That we then find a distribution of roles among the speakers, a more or less complex interplay and dramatization—opposing parties contradictorily representing two desires to verify and falsify the utterances and the arbitrator acting as the legislator's delegate—no longer falls under the jurisdiction of legal discourse but under that of narrative stylistics.

We can try to summarize these observations and present them by means of the accompanying schematization:

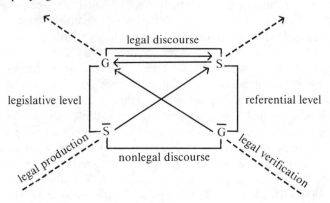

G = legal grammaticality

$\overline{G}$ = legal agrammaticality

S = legal semanticity

$\overline{S}$ = legal asemanticity

G + S = legal discourse (made up of a grammar and a semantics)

$\overline{G}$ + $\overline{S}$ = nonlegal discourse (legally agrammatical and asemantic)

G + $\overline{S}$ = legislative level (legal grammar, without content)

$\overline{G}$ = S = referential level (virtual legal universe, without legal gramar)

$\overline{S} \rightarrow S$ = legal production $\Big\{$ transformation of a virtual content into a legal content, implying the use of the grammatical form

$\overline{G} \rightarrow S$ = legal verification $\Big\{$ transformation of agrammatical into grammatical utterances, implying legal semanticity and their content

Narrative Grammar

The legal grammar whose main outline we have just sketched is not the only one governing legal discourse. It is a sentence grammar that accounts only for the construction of the utterances and, at best, for their concatenation into discursive sequences. At the same time, during our reading of the text to be analyzed, we think we have recognized numerous manifestations of a different form of organization of discursive significations that belong to what we called narrative semiotics.

This is actually a general form of the articulation of contents, prior to their linguistic or nonlinguistic (e.g., cinema, dreams, etc.) contents, that we can consider as a form of the organization of the human imaginary. Once realized in various discourses, these narrative structures appear as implicit or explicit narratives that, although they seem to be more or less spontaneous productions, in fact recur from one text to another, from one semiotics to another and from one culture to another. In spite of important structural and functional variations, these recurring narrations seem to be subjected to a system of regulated organization, and hence fall under a general narrative grammar.

In passing, we have already recognized a narrative sequence in the organization of jurisprudence that appears as a dramatization, the parties and the tribunal acting much as characterized *dramatis personae*. In a general way, we can ask ourselves if what we designated as *procedures* do not correspond to narrative units as they appear in legal discourse. The micronarratives encountered in legal discourse are descriptions of programs of behavior, organized in terms of logical and/or temporal relations, the unfolding of which is instituted as "appropriate." Obviously, we are dealing not with actual behaviors but with the *exemplary* unfolding of procedures, models of legal doing, which possess a legal existence by the fact that they are described. Subject to prescriptive or interdictive regulation, they constitute various molds ("forms" in the legal sense of the term) into which nonlegal behaviors of the referential level can be poured to test their conformity. Except for this particular narrative organization, the legal status of the narrative sequences and the syntactic units constituting them hardly differs from those of the utterances produced by legal grammar *stricto sensu*.

We must insist, however, on the dependence of the legal micronarratives with respect to general narrative grammar. Legal narrative sequences are simply particular manifestations that sometimes have the variations and the specifications of general narrative algorithms. To take examples only from the text under consideration, the constitution of a commercial company and the procedures describing its creation correspond to the narrative sequence of the establishment of the contract and the institution of a subject endowed with a performative *wanting*. The same holds true regarding the modalities of *being-able-to* and *knowing* that characterize some social agents and organs and even the procedures of the verification of accounts that, according to a terminology ill suited to legal discourse, but whose use is excusable at the level of metadiscourse on law, can be interpreted as the "glorification of the hero" or the "revelation of the traitor." It is as though the company, from birth to death, underwent a series of stages and tests, conforming to rules of behavior that are both anthropomorphic and legally exemplary.

Two things can be retained from these observations. First, a theoretical remark: while strictly obeying the rules of legal grammar, legal procedures also fall under narrative grammar. Consequently, their analysis demands that an appropriate methodology be used. Second, a working hypothesis: the recognition of the narrative properties certain sequences of legal discourse have authorizes one to use general narrative models to account for the organization of certain legal discourses, and more particularly, those regarding commercial groups and companies.

Subsequently, the methodological hypothesis adopted makes it possible to substitute a deductive approach using the insights gleaned from general narrative semiotics to examine particular realizations of narrativity in legal discourse — for investigation into vague analogies between several disparate domains, legal language and literary language, for example.

The Commercial Company

The Collective Actant

Legal discourse defines a commercial company both in its "being" and with regard to its "doing."[3] The company is indeed an object of discourse, that is to say, an "entity," but it is also a "moral person."[4] Yet, at the same time this "person" can receive successive predications, it is supposed to behave in a certain way and obey a certain number of explicit rules.

Such discursive objects are called "actants" in semantics. They have qualitative configurations that define their specificity, and they are also defined by the domain of their functions. In the broad sense of the term, an actant can be either the linguistic representation of a human person or the character of a story or again an animal or a machine.

Furthermore, an actant must be individualizable: a person can be represented in discourse as John Doe, born the . . . , domiciled . . . , etc., a machine can be constructed by . . . , in use since . . . , situated . . . , etc. We shall designate by the term "actors" those that represent the corresponding actants, by their typical behavior, and at the same time are distinguished by a specific *historical anchoring* (inscription in space and time, name, etc.).

On the whole, the commercial company corresponds to such a definition: it appears as a characterized actant in the legal text. It is a *collective actant*, and the actors it subsumes are also *collective actors*.

The problem we are dealing with here is that of the status of the "moral person," as opposed to the "physical person." Contrary to what is generally thought, these are not characteristics of individuation: its uniqueness and its historicity make it possible to determine the individual actant in relation to the collective actant. The latter can also be individuated and generate individual actors.

Elsewhere we have attempted to distinguish two types of collective actants: *syntagmatic actants* and *paradigmatic actants*.[5] If the actant is defined only by the set of its functions, that is to say, by the virtual program it is able to actualize, we note, for example, that the Régie Renault (or any other automobile manufacturer) can be considered as a syntagmatic actant insofar as, within a single program of construction, different actors (engineers, supervisors, skilled workers, etc.), subsequently replace one another and carry out a single program to produce the object-automobile.

This is not the case when one wants to account for the collective actants we proposed to call *paradigmatic* actants. A class in the last year of high school or a social group in society is not characterized by the possibility of integrating the individual actors making it up into a programmed process of the whole. It (1) belongs to a classificatory partition of a wider and hierarchically superior collectivity (high school, national community), and (2) functions on the basis of determination criteria that the actors have in common (their functional field or their specific qualifications).

This amounts to saying that the possibility of constructing collective actants depends on our very general faculty of imagining different modes of existence of "quantitative beings," in the continuum of the world, of conceiving different segmentations as discontinuous units and totalities, unit and *totality* being universal categories that make such a segmentation possible.[6] Contrary to what happens during the institution of the syntagmatic actant where the unit-actors are totalized much like ordinal numbers, the paradigmatic actant is not a simple addition of cardinal numbers but rather an intermediate totality situated between a collection of units and the totality transcending it.

The Logical Construction of the Collective Actant

The recognition of the formal structure of the collective actant is of utmost importance to us. It not only allows us to determine the status of the commercial company at the deep level, but it can also serve as the basis for considerations on the nature of a group of companies.

Let us suppose that there exists a collection of discrete individuals characterized as *units* (*U*) by the fact that they are discontinuous, and as *integrals* (*i*) because they possess features of individuation. For these individual actors to be considered as part of the collective actant representing a new totality (*T*), which we shall call partitive (*p*) (that is, a whole of which they are the parts), they must both maintain their identity as units (*U*) and abandon their integrity (*i*). They can then be considered as partitives (*p*), that is, as individuals who share common determinations with all others belonging to the same set.

These transformations constitute a series of operations that can be represented within a more general logical model:

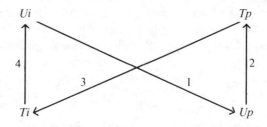

We can see that to get from the collection of individuals (situated at point *Ui*) to a new collectivity (*Tp*), the syntactic trajectory makes provisions for two types of operations:

> *Operation 1.* The transformation of *Ui* into *Up*, that is, the negation of the integrity of the individual and the assertion of its partitive nature.
> *Operation 2.* The implication of *Up* in *Tp*, that is, the conjunction of individuals defined as parts with the totality their properties logically presuppose.

The Semantic Investment of the Collective Actant

The purely formal transformations we have just described are supposed to account for the construction of any paradigmatic collective actant. Only the semantic content invested will allow us to distinguish these actants from others.

As is the case in our text, insofar as legal discourse deals with commercial companies, it organizes and manipulates a certain microuniverse of signification as content, which it improperly designates as "commercial." Subsequently, the collective actant instituted by this discourse will have semantic determinations that found it in its specificity as a "commercial company." These determinations will appear and be recognized in our model in the form of a particular semantic investment of the term p, of the qualification common to all the elements of the collection that is substituted for the integrity of the individual and retains only what allows him to participate in the new totality.

Narrative semiotics distinguishes two types of qualifications that actants can have: (a) *permanent* qualifications recognizable by the verb "to be" (and its synonyms) that express the relation of attribution (for example, "This man is good"); and (b) *temporary* qualifications, attributed to the actant by the verb "to have" (and its synonyms) (for example, "This man has a house"). Commercial law seems to be characterized by the quasi-exclusive use of *temporary possessive attributions*.

On the other hand, even a superficial reading of the texts concerning commercial companies reveals that they come about from the conjunction of two sets: a human and a monetary one (contributions in kind can sometimes be substituted for parts of the latter).[7] Every individual part of the human set who wishes to be transformed into a company manifests his partitive determinations (p) and, at the moment his integrity is abandoned, is characterized by the possession of a part of the monetary set. We can say that every possible *participant* in a company ceases to be an individuated person and is defined uniquely as the holder of a portion of the capital.

The expression "holder of a portion of the capital" that we have just used is part of natural language and for this reason is not exempt from ambiguities. It is therefore necessary for us to subject it to semantic analysis.

The canonical form of the semantic utterance in which all sorts of qualifying predications can be expressed is:

$$Q \ [A; \ O]$$

where:

Q = the relation of attribution of a qualification
A = the syntactic actant to which the qualification is attributed
O = the object value attributed to the actant.

If we invest a content such as "holding" in such a canonical utterance, we note that the semantic investment can take place in three different manners:

1. The relation Q, which is a formal one, can be endowed with a content "to

hold," "have." In this case, only the relation Q will have a determined semantic content, the other terms of the utterance will subsist as "empty boxes":

$$Q \text{ ("holds") } [A \text{ (someone); } O \text{ (something)}]$$

2. The actant A can be invested semantically and named "holder." This investment is sufficient in itself and logically implies both the relation of the holder and the existence of the object held:

$$Q \text{ ("from") } [A \text{ (holder); } O \text{ (something)}]$$

3. The object of value can be invested with the content "asset." As does the preceding one, this investment implies the existence of other terms of the utterance. Although it is sometimes difficult to manifest in French the absence of content of the presupposed terms, their formal nature can be recognized because of semantic redundancy:

$$Q \text{ ("holds") } [A \text{ (someone); } O \text{ (assets "held")}]$$

This somewhat tedious examination makes it possible to define the status of the *participant* in a commercial company. The participant is neither an individual that is part of the human ensemble making up the company nor the portion of the capital (of the monetary ensemble) he contributes, but rather a structural relation implying both terms at once, that is, an original *semiotic object*. As soon as it receives a semantic investment this form appears as a *structure in an unstable state*. Initially, as a relation of "possession," it seems to be the metasemiotic apprehension of a possible link between beings and things, a certain principle, among others, of the signifying organization of the world. But the relation itself can be polarized and the semanticism invested clarified by one or the other of the two terms. If the content is transferred to the actant, the world appears as a universe of owners where every object is defined by its virtuality of being possessed; and if, on the contrary, the semantic weight bears on the object, the owners begin to search out possessors. We shall say that in the first case term A is *dominant* and term O *dominated*, whereas in the second one it is term O that is dominant, and term A that is dominated.

The unbalanced nature of the structure of the *participant* and the variations of dominance of the terms "holder" and "held" should allow us to account for different forms of companies and establish their *typology*. Indeed, between these two extreme poles corresponding to two types of dominance, *human resource companies* and *capital companies*, it is possible to institute discontinuities characterizing subclasses of companies, either by specifying the number or the holders' special functions or by establishing distinctions between different categories of "property titles." We have to admire the ingenuity of legislators when dealing with this in legal discourse. Nonetheless, the ideological support for such an enterprise seems to be the category of *privatization* vs. *collectivization*

which connotes the contradictory concerns of legislators both to preserve the traditional fiction of individual owners (which they were before becoming *participants*) and to recognize the new forms of ownership where capital assumes the role of integrating the persons.

Be that as it may, it is the structure of ownership over the object that allows us to interpret the second operation of the construction of the collective actant, which the conjunction of the terms is

$$Up \rightarrow Tp$$

This operation, which at the level of the surface narrative grammar corresponds to the *transfer of the object of value*, is conceivable only if the participant is envisaged as being under the dominance of the object held. The object in question, separating itself so to speak from its former holder, is attributed to a new actant, the company, which thereby becomes the holder of all the portions of the capital transferred. With the institution of this new actant as holder, the company can define itself according to the same canonical formula, as

$$Q \text{ (holding) } [A \text{ (company)}; O \text{ (totality of the portions of the capital)}]$$

A final observation: it was noted in passing that as a relation between persons and things, possession is a *temporary attribution*. It is of the order of having, of accidental qualities, and not of the order of being, of permanent characteristics. During the constitution of the company, the relation established between the human ensemble and the monetary one is not therefore a fixed relation—property titles can change hands, one of the two ensembles can increase and the other diminish, or conversely. While remaining relative, the stability of the relation of possession can consequently be polarized on the categorical axis (more or less)

permanent vs. *temporary*

and employed as a complementary criteria of the *typology of companies*. At one of the poles we shall find companies whose participants are characterized by indissoluble links between holder and held; at the opposite pole are limited companies tending to consider this link as simply accidental and part of the basic fiduciary circulation of symbolic titles. We can now understand that when both criteria are present the dominance of the object at the expense of its holder and the accidental nature of the relation of possession could easily destroy the unstable structure on which commercial companies rest, and transform it into an agglomerate of anonymous capital.

The Collective Legal Actant

It would perhaps be appropriate to insist once more that the syntactic rules accounting for the construction of the collective actant are formal and, consequently, apply to the construction of any actant of this type. If, afterwards, we examined the semantic investment of the model constructed, it must be understood that, from the point of view of legal language, the investment in question describes only the *referential level* of legal discourse, that is, what in this discourse is presupposed as taking place in "economic reality."

As we have said, there are two distinct levels in legal discourse: the referential level and the legislative one. The former is the discursive projection of a "reality" made up, so to speak, of *natural* things and events, which the latter attempts to make accede to *culture*, by giving objects and behaviors appropriate forms and rules of functioning.

In legal discourse, the passage from nature to culture takes place at the legislative level. At the referential level, the recognition of a newly constituted actant gives rise to the legitimization of its birth and to its integration in the world of legally identified and recognized "persons." By employing a slightly metaphorical vocabulary to characterize the legislator's cultural activity, we simply want to underline the analogy that exists between his behavior and that of parents who extract newborns from the "state of nature" by conferring on them a civil status in conformity with the law. The regulations that make provision for the naming of the company, its registered office, and so on, follow exactly the same procedures. In order for the "natural" collective actant to be transformed into a "cultural" actant, a new syntactic trajectory must be envisaged that, while following the first one, exhausts the totality of the model proposed (see earlier in this chapter, "The Logical Construction of the Collective Actant").

Operation 3. This operation consists in transforming the collective actant considered as *Tp* (a totality composed of parts) by conferring on it the status of individuated actor. At the level of surface grammar, this operation finds its equivalent in the procedures of denomination of the company that can be interpreted as the attribution of characteristics in conformity with the law. We shall note, however, that the operation of integration of the "savage" collective actant into legal culture results in its retrogression at the level of *legal actor*. The same holds true for the domain of "nature" where every participant is an actor in relation to the collective actor. In the hierarchy of collective beings, the notions of actor and actant are relative and only the change in level should be retained: in the state of "nature" participant-actors are in relation to the company-actant; in the state of legal culture, individuated society-actors are referred to the legal actant— society.

Operation 4. This operation is a conjunction that integrates a specific company with the commercial company as a class. The company apprehended as a whole is a true moral person, a complete legal actant.

Once again, within legal discourse problems of relations arise between the referential and legal levels and their logical anteriority. The procedure we followed falls under legal "seeming," according to which there exists first of all a "referential reality" that the law simply organizes. As we have said, legal "being" is somewhat different. It is by naming things that the legislator calls them into existence, and gives them a virtual and for the most part implicit referent as their horizon, which is basically his vision of things and not their "reality."

Consequently, legal language develops its discourse on commercial companies deductively, and the operations we have just described are inverted. Legislators first of all construct the company as a moral person considered as a class and then provide for the rules of its constitution as specific companies, in accordance with the established model. Finally, they set up a typology of the companies and at the referential level describe the set of predictable relations between the participant and the company.

The Collective Subject

At first, the commercial company was envisaged only as a collective actant, that is, as a semiotic object comparable to other objects of the same type. Then it was specified, by means of a particular semantic investment, appearing as the form of different articulations of the category of *possession*. Taxonomical contours of this collective actant were finally traced without any consideration whatsoever for the syntactic role it can be called on to play within the framework of the narrative grammar that, as we saw, governs legal discourse in a certain way.

Now, it is as though the company were not any actant, but rather an actant invested with determined syntactic functions that make it a *subject-actant*. By subject we understand an actant endowed with a *wanting* (who is subject of a desire) and who wishes to obtain an *object* (object of desire). It seems that the commercial company is such a subject, that it develops intentional activity and, as the text expressly states, pursues a "purpose" or "object."[8]

Adopting the same discursive strategy as before, we need to answer two questions: what are the conditions for constructing a collective subject, or, what comes to the same thing, how can we account for the constitution of a *collective wanting*? And moreover, what is the content of this wanting, or, formulated in a different way, what is the specific object of desire of the commercial company? Since the procedures are the same, we shall use an existing logical model and we shall also keep essential observations to a minimum.

It seems obvious that to establish a company it is not sufficient just to pool capital resources, but rather that the will of the individuals wanting to join forces also plays a comparable role.[9] We shall therefore say that individuals (Ui), by transforming themselves into possible participants (Up), each bring not only their share of *objective values* (portion of the capital) but also *subjective values* (their wanting). Wanting can be partitive in nature (p) insofar as it is considered as a specific partial desire that is consonant with the specific object intended, and not with the totality of desires with which an individual is normally invested. It is the pooling of these *partial wantings* that makes it possible to envisage the attribution of a *corporate wanting* to a collective actant that is constituted at the same time by the totalizing acquisition of the objective values (capital). Narrative semiotics here provides for the appearance at its surface level of the more or less explicit narrative sequence called the "contract." The contract, a concept employed in its semiotic sense that is more general than in the legal sense, is defined as the transmission (followed by the acceptance) of a sender to a receiver, of a *wanting-to-do* and the programmed content of this doing. In the case of the commercial company, the collective actant is assigned a collective wanting and a particular mission. The latter are both transmitted by the participants, and this is what invests it as a *collective subject*. The transformation of the (savage) collective subject, who will carry out the orders transmitted by the participants in a disorganized and excessive manner, into a "civilized" subject by the legislator, follows the same trajectory. Law endows the actant-subject with organ-actors of the company that in its name are supposed to carry out *appropriate* performances in pursuit of the object of collective wanting. A second implicit contract is signed between the actant-subject and the legislator who, in prescribing the canonical forms of behavior and by anticipating sanctions in case of transgressions, in part transforms this *wanting-to-do* into a *having-to-do*.[10] The a priori nature of legal discourse appears here more clearly than elsewhere. In dictating the law the legislator institutes the company and offers it a contract as a having-to-do (a contractual form among others). The "savage" wanting-to-do is transformed into a "culturized" having-to-do by the will of the legislator (who represents the wanting of the national community).

The Semantic Investment of Corporate Wanting

The second question we asked concerns the semantic investment of corporate wanting. Corporate wanting must be understood in the semiotic sense, as the logical modality of doing, that is, as a modal utterance that overdetermines another utterance whose predicate function has a minimal investment called "doing." We shall therefore say that an utterance of the type

$$F \text{ (wanting) } [S \text{ (someone); } O \text{ (something)}]$$

modalizes another utterance, if it is equivalent to the object-actant of the modal utterance, in other words, if

$$O = F_1 \text{ (doing) } [S_1 \text{ (someone); } O_1 \text{ (something)}]$$

on condition that the subjects S and S_1 of the two utterances be identical. By calling this subject "other" we can exemplify what we have just said by "Peter wants Peter to do something."

As we have said, in its taxonomical being the commercial company is defined by the category of holding:

$$Q \text{ (holding) } [C \text{ (company)}]$$

Subsequently, the passage from *being* to *doing*, from statics to dynamics, can be considered as the transformation of the content invested in the relation between subject and object:

$$Q \text{ (holding) } \rightarrow F \text{ (acquisition)}$$

and the company's doing can be formulated as:

$$F \text{ (acquisition) } [C \text{ (company)}; O \text{ (goods)}]$$

If wanting, as a modality, bears on an utterance of the type doing, and if corporate doing is invested with the content "acquire," corporate wanting is then semantically specified as the desire to acquire goods. The canonical formula of corporate wanting can be transcribed as follows:

$$\textit{corporate wanting } = F \text{ (wanting) } \{C \text{ (company)};$$
$$O \, F \text{ (acquisition } [C \text{ company), } O \text{ (goods)}]\}$$

To simplify things, we can designate this formal structure of corporate wanting by the term "interest" and attempt to establish a *taxonomy of interests*, according to the types of wanting subjects that appear in the corporate space.

1. Thus, prior to their desire to participate in a collective enterprise, "physical persons" have the status of "third parties" in a national collectivity where their "legitimate interests" are protected by the fact that the *general interest* is confused with the legitimate interests of the third party.

2. From the moment they express a desire to acquire new assets through participation in collective activity, they bring to bear their desire of appropriation, which we can call *personal interest* insofar as it is not regulated.

3. The pooling of personal interests confers the attribution of subject to the collective actant, making it the expression of *corporate interest* that remains in a "savage" state and that is capable of all excesses.

4. The legislator recognizes this corporate interest but transforms it into a *legitimate corporate interest* by regulating it using a system of prescriptions and interdictions.

5. Legitimate corporate interests are then assimilated with the legitimate interests of third parties and become part of one and the same *general interest*.

The schema distributing these various interests can be transcribed as follows:

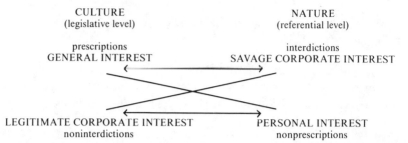

CULTURE
(legislative level)

NATURE
(referential level)

prescriptions
GENERAL INTEREST

interdictions
SAVAGE CORPORATE INTEREST

LEGITIMATE CORPORATE INTEREST
noninterdictions

PERSONAL INTEREST
nonprescriptions

Such a distribution of interests should allow us to understand both the legislator's normative system and the type of conflicts that jurisprudence has to resolve.

At first glance it is curious to note that the rules the legislator institutes in the form of various prescriptions and interdictions are distributed in conformity with a taxonomical model of interests. This is due to the fact that as prefigurations of behaviors, interests can be categorized as licit and illicit, just as the behaviors they actualize can be. What is more curious is that corporate savage interests are regulated in the form of interdictions (culture being defined as the negation of nature). This allows us to consider legitimate corporate interests as belonging to a vast undefined domain of nonprohibited behaviors and giving them at the same time liberty that is limited only by specific interdictions. The same holds true for prescriptions. Because only what is expressed has a legal existence, prescriptive rules simply institute model behaviors, corresponding to legitimate interests, whereas the joint holders' personal interests (abuse of power, misappropriation of funds, etc.), because they are not prescribed as conforming to the general interest, fall under the interest of the law.

Interests can be considered from a different point of view, no longer as pre-configurations of appropriate behaviors, but as contents of *subjects* endowed with economic wanting (see this chapter, ''The Semantic Investment of the Collective Actant''). In this case, the taxonomic distribution of interests corresponds to all the various manifestations of subjects having different and individuated interests. Hence the narrativization of ''economic life'' that legal discourse institutes appears as a closed domain of *predictable confrontations between willing subjects*, each representing its own interests. If we consider as *subject-heroes* those subjects that pursue legitimate interests and as *traitor-antisubjects* those pursuing illegitimate interests, a typology of legal performances (tests) can be established. The predictable confrontations can be of two sorts: (a) the subject representing legitimate corporate interests can enter the lists against the antisubject, the incarnation of personal interest (joint holder, accused of abuse of power, etc.); or (b) the subject representing the general interest (the legitimate interest of the third party, whether physical of moral persons) can confront the antisubject acting on behalf of savage corporate interest, at the expense of the rights of the third party. What characterizes this very elementary syntax of legal confrontation is the interchangeability of roles of subject and antisubject common to all syntax. As long as the company defends its legitimate interests, it assumes the role of hero, but when it exceeds its powers and misuses its power, it changes into a traitor. The same can be said with respect to roles assumed by "third parties."

The Actantial Structure: The Structure of the Legislator

Thinking about a commercial company in terms of a narrative subject naturally leads one to ask the question regarding the status of another actant of the narrative, the *sender* evolving along the syntactic axis

sender vs. receiver

An actant becomes a subject only by virtue of assuming first of all the status of *receiver*, receiving and accepting from the *sender* the contractual message that gives him a certain wanting-to-do. It seems to us that the institution of the collective subject that the company happens to be results from the convergence of two contracts. Consequently, it presupposes the existence of two senders, the first of which represents the totalization of the partial wantings of everyone participating in the common enterprise, whereas the second one, in which we recognized the legislator, assigns the corporate actant with a having-to-do that is both imperative and restrictive. These two senders, however, are far from exhausting the inventory of formally recognizable senders who grow in number as the hierarchized organs of the commercial company are set in place.

To begin with, the concept itself of legislator is not exempt from semantic ambiguities or syntactic polysemies. From the point of view of narrative grammar, it appears as a *collective subject* because a wanting of a "national will" is expressed as the syntactic exponent of the corporate actant to which the national community corresponds. This collective subject does not exhaust the totality of collective wanting, however: its doing is of the order of the word. Its wanting to say that is not direct, but mediated by all the instances of the structure of this collective actant, shall not be examined here but shall be seen reflected in the organization of the functioning of the commercial company. This mediation is brought about by a series of descending operations that go from sender to receiver, and end up in the last receiver, instituted as *the subject of enunciation* of legal discourse.

Although the legislator as subject of the *enunciation* produces legal discourse, this discourse is his global *utterance*, which is an emanation from the subject, his imaginary projection that can manifest itself only by means of certain forms of the canonical narrative structure, forms that can be read between the lines of the legal text as subtext, or metatext.

The legislator is therefore present in legal discourse as the *receiver-subject* of a legal wanting-to-do (we shall say that he is the incarnation of the "acting law''). By his discursive performances, he pursues a legal 'object,'' which is, as we alluded to on several occasions, the institution and the maintenance of a certain *legal culture*, that is, of ''good legal manners'' (in the same way as there exist table and conversation ''manners,'' etc.). The order instituted by law is, in a certain way, the reign of the acceptable.

There exists a parallelism between this legal conventionalism on the one hand, and initiation rituals such as the qualifying tests of folktales on the other. There is no doubt that the rites of passage from nature to culture (to which youth ''in the state of nature'' is subjected), or the imaginary performances that the subject of the tale must undertake to prove that he knows how to behave appropriately, are entrance exams into culture envisaged as such, and are, in fact, very general cultural forms.

If the subject conforms to this general form of the qualification, it transforms him into a hero who can realize the performances expected of him. This not only accounts for the last phase of the institution of a commercial company but also confirms the general semiotic status of the agencies of control of the verification procedures anticipated by the legislator. Along with the *instituting actant* of legal forms, we are obliged to acknowledge the *control actant* that is one of the substitute forms by which the legislator is present in legal discourse (an actant that covers numerous actors such as ''justice'' security council and auditor). In the very different area described by Vladimir Propp in his *Morphology of the Folktale* it corresponds to the *donor*-actant who is responsible for verifying the competence of the subject and his acceptance of properties.

The *legislator* therefore assumes multiple roles in the legal discourse he produces as subject of enunciation. They can be summarized in the following actantial schema:

This schema is meant to describe the distribution of semiotic objects — actants endowed with precise functions — situated at the highest hierarchical level of legal narration. The legislator, who is not a simple actant but a complex actantial construct, communicates with hierarchically inferior semiotic objects as a dual sender: commercial companies apprehended as receivers. The legislator does this in two different ways: As *sender 1*, the legislator institutes the company as a collective subject endowed with a having-to-do; as *sender 2*, he transmits a certain *knowledge* to the company regarding the conformity or nonconformity of corporate practice. We shall return to this later.

The Actantial Structure: The Structure of Corporate Power

Just as the wanting defining it, the company instituted as collective subject is basically a virtual project and a desire to actualize its doing. According to the narrative model, its effective functioning presupposes the *mediation of an actant* that is distinct and personalized in a certain manner, and the investment of this actant with a new modality of *being-able*. Wanting-to-do must be enhanced with a being-able-to-do in order to produce a doing.

As is the case for the effective manifestation of "national will," discrete and individuated organs, new subjects of power are necessary to assume the mediation between corporate will and its realization by means of procedures of doing. No matter if these organs that have been anticipated for exercising power in the name of the commercial company reflect the organization of the powers of parliamentary democracy, this means only that other forms of organization can be applied to the functioning of companies.

The originality of corporate power, which as we can see it shares with political power, resides in the fact that two actants are provided for by the legislator to exercise this power: the *decisional actant* (the general assembly) and the *managerial actant* (the set of management organs). As the names we have proposed are arbitrary, we shall highlight the most salient features of their syntactic and semantic structure defining and differentiating them.

As a decisional actant the *general assembly* is the sovereign holder of corporate power in conformity with the law. Its configuration also corresponds to that of the "body of shareholders," that is, the participants defined by the relation of possession.[11] It should be noted, however, that the participant who assists at the meeting of the general assembly is characterized by the dominance of the term "object held." It is not a shareholder but a share representing a vote that will participate in decision making. The power of the company therefore appears as a *modality determined by its relation to capital* and secondarily only to its holders. This already suggests to us that the problematics of groups of companies is situated at the level of corporate power and not of will. We should add, however, that legal discourse seeks to valorize, at least symbolically, the term "holder" by demanding the physical presence of the stock "holders," and by also establishing the historical anchoring of decision making (making provision for meetings, their regularity, etc.).

As could have been expected from the very general narrative models at our disposal, it would be wrong to think that the power of the general meeting is a being-able-to-do, and that its vocation is to transform a virtual project into an actualized one. The functions peculiar to the actant-assembly constitute an intercalated syntagm between being-able-to-do and doing itself. Its power is a *decisional power* whose exercise ends up in decisions and not in performances.

Subsequently, we can see that the relation of logical implication that normally exists between doing and being-able-to-do, when the subject of power is an individual, in the case of exercising corporate power is mediated by *decisional performance* that takes on the form of a performance. Corporate power is broken down into discrete elements of votes, whereas voting draws out groups of antagonists, and confrontation determines the victory of one of the protagonists. The consequence of the test basically results in making corporate power that was implicitly present at the beginning, explicit. There is no need for us to insist on the character—both formal, because it did not end up in a doing, and conventional, because it is only a rule of the game—of this procedure. If we now consider the object on which decisional power is exercised—the decision being the taxonomical application of another dichotomized set of the content-object—we note that the list of objects subjected to the decision of the assembly is *prescriptive* in nature. As the law expressly states, contrary to the being-able-to-do with any object whatsoever (whose regulation is of a *noninterdictive* nature), *being-able-to-decide* covers a functional field that is delimited and granted by the legislator. The assembly's decisions bear on: (a) the existence of the collective subject itself (modification of the statutes; dissolution and amalgamation of companies); (b) the quantitative dimension of the collective actant (increase and reduction in capital); and (c) the object of wanting of the collective subject (distribution of dividends). For the most part decisional power is exercised (with the exception of the distribution of dividends to which we shall return later) on the *being* of the commercial company and not on its *doing*. The most important decision of the assembly appears to be the *transmission of the power* it has to a new receiver-actant, the true *subject of doing* to the managerial actant.

The *managerial actant* holds the power that can be considered, first, as an integral type of power because it is delegated as a whole and is not subject to the vague impulses of partition; and, second, as a limited but not prescribed power. It is limited only negatively, by the domain reserved to the decisional actant, on the one hand, and by the formal interdictions regulating the manifestations of savage corporate interest, on the other.[12]

The fact that the manager can neither modify the dimensions of the company nor decide whether it should disappear makes it possible to establish an equivalence between his doing and the company apprehended in its functioning. In other words, the collective subject that a company happens to be can conceive of the expression of its power and the actualization of its doing only by the institution of a subject of doing that is both distinct from and coextensive to itself. Thus performances of the company that make up the essential aspect of its "life," but that take place at the referential level of law, are recurrent performances of the managerial actant. Law, and it is its right, is not interested in economics. Therefore, the performative doing of the subject (which is the essential characteristic of the narrative structure) is present in legal discourse only through its consequences: the acquisition of object-values and their transfer to the sender (distribution of dividends).

Contrary to the decisional actant whose participant actors appear under the dominance of the object possessed (stocks), the participants in the managerial actant are defined as permanent possessors. Their structure is dominated by the term "holder," and the stocks they hold are "unalienable, nominative, guaranteed by management" (Article 95). The organization of power within the company therefore appears in the form of an archi-actant, as a relational structure with two terms, where the anonymous power of the stocks is counterbalanced by the personalized power of the director-stockholders. Although commercial law does not concern itself with corporate doing per se, this is not the case with respect to its formal framing. By making two modalities of narrative grammar explicit—*being-able-to* (which is at the origin of doing) and *knowing* (which bears on the modes of its actualization)—legal discourse exhausts the requirements of the narrative model.

The communication of *knowledge about doing* that the manager owes his sender (assembly) and that is one of the highlights of legal narration—the legislator even delegates his own representative-controller—seems to have a dual significance. From the point of view of the managerial actant, this is the final test the outcome of which, in other nonlegal narratives, when positive, is designated as the "glorification of the hero," and when negative, as the "revelation of the traitor." As we can see, this is the test for conformity between the project of doing and its actualization, made possible by the mediation of *knowledge*.

From the point of view of the decisional actant we can note the parallelism between the two transfers that characterize its relation with the managerial actant. A transfer in return for the *knowledge* that is supposed to compensate *power* corresponds to the transfer of the latter, prior to economical performances. This syntactic equivalence of transfers constructed along the axis of the reciprocity of exchanges, without the transferred contents being identical, has certain mythicizing connotations.

The last actant we need to examine is the *object-actant* of corporate wanting. According to the canonical formula of the narrative, initial desire is founded on the acknowledgment of a lack (in our case: loss of profit). The reason for the subject's activity is to liquidate this lack by the mediation of the hero-performer on his own and followed by a *gift*, that is, the transfer of the object of value acquired from the company where this lack appeared.

The interpretation of this structure of compensation, as it appears in the law that regulates commercial companies, is not without problems. Thus the law reserves the power to distribute benefits for the general assembly. Although it is the managerial actant who is responsible for the performance the consequence of which is the acquisition of the object of value, the function of the *gift*, the attribution of benefits belongs to the decisional actant, and the attribution itself belongs not to the company instituted as a collective actant but to individual shareholders as participants. The company therefore seems to dissolve symbolically every time benefits are distributed.

This is what happens when the results of the performance are positive and the object of value (benefits) is acquired. If, on the contrary, performance ends up in a failure (deficit or absence of benefits), it is not the decisional actant but the management actant that can be held responsible and, possibly, disqualified. This is the moral of the tiny prince who alone is praised, whereas his small friend the beggar is punished.

A third possible case is that of the nondistribution of benefits that are devoted to self-financing the company. The function of the gift is fulfilled, but for the benefit of the company itself as collective actant, and no longer for that of the participants considered individually.

Considered as the reaffirmation of the contract between the subject of power and the company from which he emanates, the function of the gift is a relation between a sender-subject and the receiver-company that allows for the transmission of the object of value from one to another. A very simple schema can account for all the cases envisaged, by letting the two actants in question appear as variables:

decisional actant   *company 1*
in case of success   as a collection of participants

SENDER ⎯⎯⎯⎯⎯→ OBJECT OF VALUE ⎯⎯⎯⎯⎯→ RECEIVER
                              (benefits)

managerial actant   *company 2*
in case of failure   as a collective actant

We can clearly see the appearance of vagueness in commercial law: (a) the sender is the general assembly in the case of success and the manager in case of failure; and (b) the sender-company is conceived of in two different ways, either as a temporary semiotic object whose role symbolically ends with the periodical obtention of the desired object, or as a permanent collective actant whose corporate being one attempts to enrich and increase.

Groups of Companies

The Notion of Group

The group of companies appears on the referential horizon of legal discourse as a social object that is still implicit, but about to emerge at the surface, that is, be named, defined, and called into legal existence. We have already seen that legal discourse is steeped daily in natural language where it is in permanent contact with the segments of economical and political discourses—to mention only these—that it can integrate into its referential level. What we call "groups of companies" are necessarily part of this virtual horizon, if only because these are companies, legally recognized semiotic objects. The expression "group" simply suggests one of the possible forms of their organization.

In its wider meaning, the term "group" seems to designate the set of discrete elements apprehended as a whole, due to the fact that each element, taken separately, possesses characteristics common to all. Hence we can speak of a "group of trees" or of a "group of students" because each element of the set has determinations that allow it to be called "tree" or "student." But it is asemantic to speak of a "group of trees and students," since the elements constituting the group are not homogeneous and cannot be apprehended as a whole.

However, the qualifications common to all the elements of the group can be not only *objective*, as is the case when we speak of groups of students or groups of trees, but also *subjective*. The common denominator making it possible to apprehend a "group of onlookers" or a "group of demonstrators" as a whole can be constituted either as a "desire to see" or as the "fact demonstrating." Consequently, the group can be constituted either by the existence of a *wanting* or a *doing* common to all the elements of the whole.

Insofar as such human or personalized wholes appear only as collections of *wantings* they are not *organized* and correspond more or less to the idea we have of the "crowd." The actualization of wanting-to-do into a manifest doing, on the contrary, seems to give rise to what social psychology calls "group dynamics." Although they stem from an identical *wanting* and consequently have the same *object*, individual *doings* have to be different from one another, since the virtual program of doing is not transmitted by any sender. Subsequently, differentiated behaviors oppose each other, and comparable behaviors are coordinated or subordinated, creating recognizable subsets within the group. This means that the elements constituting it, which initially have only the relation linking each element to the set of which it is part, as a formal element, are progressively enriched with new structural properties. This is so because they are covered with a network of internal relations, which, although temporary, are nonetheless relations of dependency, complicity, and domination.

This seems to be the image that legal discourse projects onto the horizon of its referential level when dealing with groups of companies that are recognized only negatively as manifestations of "savage corporate interests" (negative recognition in the form of interdictions and restrictions regarding conventions between companies, notably by third parties).

Archicompanies?

Insofar as the group of companies can be assimilated with an unstable structure of economic doing that manifests a collective wanting recognized as a particular form of savage corporate interest (see this chapter, "The Semantic Investment of Corporate Wanting"), it finds itself, as we can see, in a situation comparable with that of the commercial company under the responsibility of legal culture. Subsequently, the question arises naturally as to whether legal discourse can once again, but at a hierarchically superior level, take on the responsibility for this new collective actant and make it into a legal subject, notably according to appropriate forms, by naming and integrating it among other legal objects (physical and moral problems), covered and protected by the general interest.

Nothing prevents us from agreeing on such a procedure of integration. An archiactant whose contents would be constituted by bringing together the participants (= company-actants, defined by the possession of capital) would be transformed into an archisubject endowed with corporate wanting. The denomination and the setting up of organs of power (power of decision and being-able-to-do) would allow for the institution of an *archicompany* that would be the explicit legal form of a new "moral person" situated at a hierarchically superior level of the companies making it up.

At first glance, legal discourse seems to have left a gap that permits us to introduce this type of conceptual framework. Hence, the interdiction of dual participation, according to which one company cannot hold more than 10 percent of the capital of another,[13] can be interpreted as the expression of the legislator's will to guarantee the autonomy and especially the integrity of semiotic objects that commercial companies happen to be, a primary but not sufficient condition for their transformation into participants, founders of an archicompany. Such an ideal company would, however, be logically coherent only if its constituent elements were homogeneous. Just as only students, and not trees and students, can constitute a "group of students," the participants in the archicompany could be only companies and not companies and stockholders at the same time.

Even if the legal establishment of this type of *company of companies* were desirable and by imagining that a new collective subject could be constituted in a homogeneous manner with the help of mechanisms establishing distinctions between possessor-companies and possessor-stockholders, their functioning could not help but highlight the fact, well noted by commercial law, that at this level the real game can be played neither in terms of possession nor in terms of the collective wanting, but rather *in terms of power*.

The Dual Nature of Companies

In analyzing the structure of a commercial company, we isolated two fundamental configurations and identified two types of actants that, although linked by a relation of subordination (*sender* vs. *receiver*) and complementarity (the actant of power working on behalf of the actant of wanting), could end up in a situation of conflict because of their autonomy.

We were able to define the content of a company as a totalization of the *participants*, understanding by participants the relation of possession between the subject and the object value, a relation constituting an unstable structure. This instability of the structure of possession, which was dominated by the term "object" (= "action") during the installation of the collective actant, made it possible to attribute it to a new subject-company by instituting it as the holder of the capital.

Note: If we can imagine the object value serves as mediator between the original holder and the holder-company, by establishing a relation of *dual possession*, we can see that the installation of a third holder-archicompany can only result in the neutralization of the first term, by completely depersonalizing the structure of possession.

The holder-actant so constituted is endowed with a corporate wanting-to-do, but can actualize it only by means of delegation (sender-receiver), by drawing out the actant of power. Although this actant of power enjoys an autonomy in relation to its sender, it nevertheless realizes the "corporate object" for which it is responsible. Nothing, in principle, would have prevented the legislator from instituting this actant of power by closely following the narrative model, as a single individualized actant, as a sort of enlightened monarch acting for the good of the company. We have seen that commercial law opted for the "parliamentary regime" by instituting the decisional actant (the general assembly), which, although in large part it served as the driving force of the managerial actant's being-able-to-do, nevertheless constitutes an autonomous instance of the organization of power. Indeed, although being-able-to-do is entirely transmitted by the company as collective subject and to the assembly as decisional actant, it is arbitrarily broken down and segmented, according to the principles of formal democracy (a share of stock = a vote; the "law" of majority).[14] As we have said, power distributed in this way can be defined by its relation to possession characterized by the dominance of the object, and no longer of the holder. At this level, however, it ceases to be a corporate power and appears only as a collection of discrete fragments of fragmented power, which nonetheless will be reconstituted later during its transmission to the managerial actant. This recapitulation seemed necessary to give prominence to the *dividing in two of the company* considered as a collective subject and to show that during its installation, we witness a sort of twofold birth. At first, the participants are transformed from a collection into a totality, creating the subject of corporate wanting. Then the participants come together to make decisions and transmit corporate power to a subject of doing (the manager).

We can now understand better the legislator who, no longer able to apprehend the "group of companies" as a holder-subject, attempts to define it at the level of the actant of power. It is the holding of more or less important "portions of power" that determines the relations between companies, and the term "group" now makes sense in this context. If the group is a set of elements having common characteristics, the first common characteristic that appears is the holding of a portion of power that allows taking part in decisions relative to the being and the doing of the company. A second characteristic should be added, however: these holders of power must be both collective actants and companies. As an initial approximation we shall therefore say that *a group of companies is a whole whose discrete elements are made up of companies holding a portion of the power within a given company.*

The distinction we previously established between the two forms of actantial articulations of companies—companies characterized by the holding of capital and companies characterized by the exercise of corporate organized power—appears to be immediately exploitable. It allows us to disambiguate the definition of the group of companies, where the term "company," used twice, must be understood in two different ways. In fact, companies that hold fragments of power distributed within a given company, and that thereby constitute a group conforming to the definition we proposed, are not external to this company. The group of companies contains an additional element, namely, the founding company within which power is shared and which also holds a portion of the power it displays during the general assembly. If we call the particular company within which fragmented power is exercised the *holding company*, we can see that this same company (with all its participant-shareholders), in the same way as the external companies, is holder of a portion of the power, and must be considered as an element among others that constitute the said *group of companies*. In its new functions it can be designated as a *power-holding company*.

Definition and Typology of Groups of Companies

The distinction we have just established between *holding companies* and *power-holding companies*, notwithstanding the purely arbitrary nature of the terminology proposed, rests on the essential differences recognizable in their actantial structure and in their workings.

That the same company can be both a holding company and a power-holding company changes nothing. It only indicates that, in what can be called the "normal" situation, it is articulated in two actantial organizations, linked by the relation *sender* vs. *receiver*. When foreign company participants intervene, however, the dimensions between the two manifestations of the same company—holding capital and holding power—are no longer isomorphic. Hence in the theoretical case of affiliation of companies provided for by commercial law, and insofar as this affiliation can be carried on infinitely, the relation is inverted between the importance of the power held by the central company (and whose capital can be limited, just sufficient to ensure the holding of more than 50 percent of the capital of its subsidiary) and the importance of the capital held and manipulated by the last of the subsidiaries (whose decisional power will be void): *the company holding power hardly possesses any capital; the company holding capital cannot exercise any power.*

We can now understand that the legislation regulating groups of companies (power-holding companies) must by very different from that which institutes and organizes commercial companies (holding companies). In fact, the law on commercial companies has simply established a very brief typology of groups of companies.

By hypostatizing the rule of the democratic game it instituted itself (but which, it goes without saying, does not have any universal value), the legislator provides for two types of groups of companies according to the decision-making procedure: (1) groups of companies that exercise power over companies with capital by means of a permanent majority (or *domination groups*), and (2) groups of companies where power is exercised by means of temporary and relative majorities (or *participation groups*).[15]

By schematizing to the extreme, it is obvious that two elements suffice to constitute a whole. Hence, the legislator binarizes groups of companies, providing only for the elementary relations of domination or participation, between *two* power-holding companies, that exercise it within a single holding company.

As we know, this elementary typology is of the order of the *word*; consequently, it corresponds to the legal recognition of groups of companies. It also defines them by situating them at a determined structural level (the instance of decision making) and by legitimatizing the power relations through the reaffirmation of the majority rule. Its apparent clarity, underscored by the dichotomous principle of classification, adumbrates an explanatory flaw that seems important to us with respect to the future development of legal discourse on groups of companies.

It is rather curious to note that when the legislator speaks of commercial companies, he uses a surface grammar, which presents his words as explicit legal utterances. When he is dealing with groups of companies, however, he stays on the other side of discourse and describes the groups in terms of the taxonomic model that is part of deep grammar. The distinction established between two types of groups of companies (domination groups and participation groups) is pertinent at the level of the deep structure but ceases to be so at the level of the surface manifestation. It is obvious that these two types of groups are not always and necessarily found in a pure state and that their "normal" state is that of mixed groups. In the case of domination, for example, if the central company is a dominant company, considered in terms of holding power, the subsidiary company is still a participating company since it holds less than half the capital, which is the definition itself of participation. We can even ask if it is not better to go further and question the dichotomy *domination* vs. *participation* established by the law. We can claim that the general structure of the group of companies is a *structure of participation* and the constitution of groups is simply an individual case of this structure. The existence of a dominating company, we saw, logically implies the existence within a same group of a participating company. The existence of an absolute majority within Parliament does not dissolve the various groups of the opposition.

The same holds true for the binary relations constituting the groups dealt with under commercial law. This oversimplification is valid only at the level of the deep structure when it is necessary to determine taxonomic criteria taking into consideration only the minimal units where these relations take place. It is obvious that the entities made up of groups of companies, at the level of the manifest structures, can and do contain, more than two element companies. Starting from a simple taxonomy, legal discourse can produce a combinatory of groups and provide for more or less complex cases of participation, if only by imitating once again the parliamentary game as it appears in the case of coalitions and unstable majorities. Evidently, everything depends on the conception the legislator has of *general interest*: defending minorities and thirds, proper business operations, national interest, and so forth. In groups of companies made up of power-holding companies, it is the exercise of this decisional and managerial power that will be enunciated by the legislator who specifies its appropriate forms when giving an opinion on groups of companies.

What seems fundamentally lacking in legal discourse on groups of companies, and what is implicitly written between the lines of the text, is the distinction between the two types of companies that we arbitrarily designated as holding companies and power-holding companies. Polarizing these two types, we can say that as collective subjects the former are endowed with a *wanting-to-do* (where the modality of *being-able* has only the function of mediation between desire and its realization), whereas the latter, collective subjects of a different nature, are characterized by a *wanting-to-be-able* (where doing is simply a secondary consequence of acquired power that, as we saw, essentially appears as a *being-able-to-decide*). At the same time—and still taking these extreme cases—a differentiation is produced at the level of the *objects* intended by company activity. If the final object of any commercial company is economic, it is modalized differently in both cases. It is understood that the interests of the holding company are satisfied by the mediation of doing (on the mythical plane, the president's "being-able-to-do-on-things"); in the case of power-holding companies, mediation takes place thanks to the exercise of power (cf. at the same level, "power takes fundamental decisions" from the president of a financing company).

> *Note*: The mythical reactions we note (cf. our *Structural Semantics*) are interesting insofar as they refer back to the value systems invested in the corresponding managerial actants.

These supplementary distinctions have been highlighted to illustrate the fact that, by indirectly defining groups of companies by their participation in power, perhaps without wanting to explicitly, the legislator has introduced a qualitative transformation in his discourse on companies: participation groups are structurally different from commercial companies. This is a sort of topological distinction. There do exist groups of participation, but there also exist companies that are *semantic loci* where these participations meet, cross, and are realized. Without any reference whatsoever to "economic reality" we can therefore anticipate two different types of relations:

First, by distributing its participations, a company extends its network of relations of power (which are not necessarily relations of domination) that cover an ensemble of commercial power-holding companies of variable dimensions.

Second, a holding company is the meeting place for participants from an ensemble of power-holding companies of variable dimensions.

In the first case, holding companies *are grouped* together by a power-holding company; in the second case, the power-holding companies *are grouped* together by a holding company. It should be noted that these are only elementary logical applications carried out on two sets, one of which is constituted by a single element. While being certain not to stray from "economic reality" it is relatively easy to complicate things by postulating a first set composed of n elements and the second of two elements, and so on, in order to have an idea of the theoretical possibilities of the combinatory. We would like to believe—and have the reader believe—that these last remarks, which appear as suggestions with the possible prolongation of legal discourse on groups of companies in mind, are not pure hypotheses, but that in the law on commercial companies they logically stem, almost always implicitly, from what little the legislator says about them.

Chapter 7
Toward a Topological Semiotics

Introduction

If it is true that all knowledge of the world begins with projecting the discontinuous on the continuous, we can perhaps provisionally once more take up the age-old opposition:

expanse vs. *space*

and say that *expanse*, taken in its continuity and plenitude, filled with natural and artificial objects, made present for us by all our sensorial channels, can be considered as the *substance* that, once informed and transformed by humans, becomes *space* (i.e., *form*) and can serve as signification because of its articulations. Space as form is therefore a *construction* that chooses only certain properties of "real" objects and only one or other possible levels of its own pertinence, to signify. It is obvious that all construction is an impoverishment and that the emergence of space makes most of the richness of expanse disappear. What it loses in concrete and lived fullness is compensated for, however, by multiple increases in signification: by becoming *signifying space*, it simply becomes another "object."

In investigating not the origins of space, which is meaningless, but its simplest articulations, we note first of all that any *place* can be apprehended only if it is situated in relation to another place, that it can be defined only by what it is not. This first disjunction can be either indefinite and appear as:

here vs. *elsewhere*

or take on specific contours such as:

enclosed vs. *enclosing*

It really does not matter what form it takes; the appropriation of a *topics* is possible only if a *heterotopics* is postulated. It is only after this that discourse on space can take place. For space that is instituted in this way is only a *signifier*; it is there only to be taken up and to signify something other than space, that is, humans, who are the *signifieds* of all languages. Consequently, it does not matter what types of contents, which vary according to cultural contexts, can be differentially instituted because of this gap of the signifier. Whether nature is excluded and opposed to culture, the sacred to the profane, the human to the superhuman or, in our desacralized societies, the urban to the rural, changes nothing as to the status of signification, and as to the mode of articulation of the signifier and the signified, which is both *arbitrary and motivated*. Semiosis takes place as a relation between a category of the signifier and a category of the signified, a relation that is necessary between categories that are both indifferent to a given context and determined by it. It also goes without saying that the binary articulation of these categories is suggested here simply to exemplify the minimum conditions of signification. Intermediate spaces (the suburbs, for example) can be instituted or a transcendental space, such as the pictorial representation of Saint Georges founding the city, can be imagined in contrast with immanent space. It is important to understand that conditions are ripe to consider space as a form that can become a spatial language making it possible to "speak" about something other than space, in the same way that the function of natural languages, which are sonorous languages, is not to speak about sounds.

If once again we take up the naive distinction according to which every object can be considered and studied either for what it is or for what it signifies, we can say that space will appear differently according to whether it is constructed as a *scientific form* or as a *semiotic form*, the former only registering articulations of a discriminatory nature, the latter attempting to found signification on discontinuity. Two topologies, mathematical and semiotic, are therefore possible. To avoid terminological difficulties and ambiguities, we could just as well designate the description, production, and interpretation of spatial languages by the expression "topological semiotics."

While maintaining the principle that at least one binary articulation of space is necessary before a minimum of meaning is "spoken" through it, we must nonetheless recognize the existence of a phenomenon of focalization. For example, when we distinguish a space *here* and a space *elsewhere* the first articulations are established from the point of view *here* (the *here* of the city dweller not being the *here* of the nomad examining the city). Consequently, every topological study must first of all choose its point of observation by distinguishing the *place of enunciation* from the *enunciated place* and by specifying the modalities of their syncretism. Topical space is both the place we are speaking about and the place from which we speak.

Space therefore initially appears as a language by which a society conveys its own significations. In doing this, it proceeds by exclusion, by spatially contrasting itself with what it is not. This fundamental disjunction, which only defines it negatively, makes it possible to introduce internal articulations that enrich its signification. As Claude Lévi-Strauss has shown, the social organization of a village is also spatially signified in this way.

Spatial language is far from being the only means of expressing this *social morphology*, however. It is not by chance that when sociologists attempt to establish a classification of "social languages" (kinds of sublanguages employed by a single society whose differences can extend from simple stylistic variations to the use of distinct natural languages), on the whole they find the same categories:

> *sacred* vs. *profane*
> *private* vs. *public*
> *external* vs. *internal*
> *superior* vs. *inferior*
> *masculine* vs. *feminine*

which seem operational to establish a typology of structures within a preindustrial city or to account for the distribution of spaces within a spatial complex. We are dealing here with a static social morphology that seeks to manifest itself by all these languages or, rather, that takes on signification because of these languages.

It was only after the appearance of merchant and industrial societies that stable social morphologies were progressively replaced by the dynamics of mobile social groups. It was also at this time that sociosemiotic *syntaxes* developing into specific discourses, spoken and listened to within the framework of systems of *communication*, replaced spatial or linguistic *taxonomies* apprehended as systems of *signification*. The city, which *constructed* itself, *is constructed* by an individuated instance, distinct in itself.

Two sorts of *utopias* arise from the fact that the city can be thought of as an *unhealthy city* and the space that envelops and signifies it is considered to be a *negative space*. Above and beyond the diachronic transformations specific to each semiotic system, a contentious metadiscourse is established that puts into question established human space, a discourse that negates space as the signified of a social signifier. Whether we are dealing with More or Le Corbusier, the goal of the metasemiotic project is the same.

Methodological Approaches

As can be seen, the foregoing brief remarks are intended only to present, in intuitive and simplified terms, the problematics of a possible topological semiotics, rather than to answer the question every researcher has asked: how and where to start exploring such a vast, complex, and promising domain?

It is as though the object of topological semiotics were twofold, as though its project could be defined both as the inscription of society in space and as the reading of the society in question through space. Two dimensions, which we provisionally called the spatial signifier and the cultural signified, seem to constitute this semiotics. Although these dimensions can be dealt with autonomously, it is only their correlation that makes the construction of these topological objects possible.

Considered in itself, the spatial signifier is coextensive with the natural world, which is also called the world of common sense. It is through this world that we read an infinite number of significations that appear as figures of the world, as objects beyond their apprehension. Within this vast spatial network, it is possible to delimit a zone of signification specific to topological semiotics only if a specific signified is posited for it at the same time.

In addition, this spatial signifier is used not only to categorize the world, to construct the world of objects as it appears in natural languages (in the form of an inventory of lexemes such as "forest," "prairie," "road," "house," "roof," and "window,"). It can also be established as a true spatial language ("a spatial logic") that is both natural and formal and that makes it possible to speak "spatially" about things that have no apparent relation with spatiality. We are aware, for example, of the particularly rich semantic investments that spatial categories such as *high* vs. *low* or *right* vs. *left* or the multiple semantic articulations of the cardinal points in what Lévi-Strauss calls concrete logic can take on. The contents manipulated by the spatial categories go far beyond the limits of signification that we would like to assign to topological semiotics.

Because the spatial signifier appears as a true language, we can readily understand that it can be used to signify and especially to signify the presence of humans in the world and their activity that informs and transforms the substance of the world. Hence, if for example we start from the rather commonly held idea that an architect's ideal is to use space to "create beauty," then we will undoubtedly misunderstand the semiotic project. All human activity, whether it is simply "digging a hole," for example, is significant in two different ways: first of all for the subject of the activity and second, for the one who observes the activity in question. All social practices that are organized as programs of doing take on signification both as project and as result. Conversely, all transformations of space can be read as signifying.

If these partial practices are organized into systems of competence the question of the global goal of doing, or what is done, automatically arises and sets off either conscious or unconscious, individual or collective reflections on the value of this activity. Just as in the case of the spatial signifier that developed into a natural autonomous logic, the immediate signified, present in the process of the transformation of space, frees itself from its signifier, takes on new articulations, and becomes a series of autonomous discourses to speak about space. For example, when a builder "constructs" his new city, this discourse can use spatial language as its signifier, but it can also extend beyond this signifier and make use of other languages of manifestation—pictorial, cinematographic, and especially natural languages—to "think" through the signification of human space. The place of ideologies and mythologies is instituted in this way: myths about the origin and purpose of the city, its various diagnostics and therapeutics to heal the city by applying spatial treatment.

Thus, starting with a language that informs space and confers meaning on it, two increasingly distinct and autonomous discourses emerge, but whose correlation with one another is nevertheless necessary for constituting a topological semiotics.

Even after the general framework for a topological semiotics has been established, it is still necessary that in their apprehension and construction specific semiotic objects obey formal and cultural constraints.

Formally, the first definition of the topological object is negative. To take into consideration a given space, it is necessary to oppose it to an antispace, the city and the surrounding countryside. Moreover, spatial focalization (i.e., the identification of the subject of enunciation with enunciated space) is necessary to ensure the latter's positive determination: an urban semiotics is just as possible as a rural semiotics.

Culturally, the appropriation and exploitation of space by humans are dependent on sociological relativism. A general model to account for the totality of possible topological objects, which would, at the same time, need to include restrictive rules justifying their cultural topology, seems both necessary and impossible to foresee for the time being. To constitute itself, topological semiotics needs a theory that deals with the status and structure of topological objects in general. Yet the only chance such a theory has of emerging is for it to break up into a large number of specific semiotics that, while studying certain classes of topological objects, would subordinate their exploration to a unifying semiotic project. This is the only way to ensure that a subsequent comparative enterprise can come into being.

That specific semiotics such as urban semiotics not concentrate on specific objects (the cities of Tours or Carcassonne), but only on classes of topological objects, seems self-evident: a grammar cannot exist for each utterance and even for each discourse. One therefore has to begin by noting *invariants*, recognizable both at the *syntagmatic* level as recurring phenomena, and at the *paradigmatic* level by identifying comparable phenomena in two parallel objects. The preceding is an example of methodological extrapolation, of "borrowing" from linguistics that some are suspicious about, and which nevertheless is part of the general epistemology of the sciences.

Concrete topological objects are often complex and ambiguous, if only because of the durable solidity of their signifiers, and because their "message," like Egyptian writing engraved in stone, is the product of mediating communication compared with immediate speech. This results in a *historical stratification* of the object with several substrata and superstrata coexisting within the present dimension. A "real" topological object can therefore be justified not by one but by several models. As we say today, it is the product of several grammars. This is another reason not to confuse urban semiotics with the study of particular cities, canonical cities with real cities, the organization of real objects with the construction of topological objects.

An Ideological Model of the City

It is not by adopting a scientific strategy, which supposedly would make it possible to work out at one and the same time a specific semiotics and a common methodological conceptualization, that we can hope one day to imagine a general semiotics. Nor can we hope to specify the limits of its project that appears either too vast, if extended to the totality of human behaviors that transform space, or too restricted, if it only includes artificial and secondary signal codes (arrows, signs, display windows, etc.) covering spaces that already signify with their overdeterminations.

Let us take as example, topological objects called "cities" as part of a specific semiotics that we can call urban semiotics. It is obvious that we have before us a complex and polysemic object that can be apprehended only as a global semantic effect. It is also obvious that its reading can be thought of only as the disarticulation of a whole into its constituent parts. And yet, the attempt to decompose the city into an infinite number of objects filling its space would not get us anywhere in our analysis. For two reasons these objects in part would also appear as complex and polysemic. First of all, an object alone cannot be apprehended semiotically and scientifically because a topological whole is made up not of objects but of their common properties. Second, a Dogon lock, for example, is a global object; that is, it is multifaceted and undifferentiated until the cultural context in which it is inscribed questions it by situating it at various possible isotopies of reading. It is only when it is situated before our eyes, surrounded by other objects that are part of our familiar space, that it can be questioned as to whether it is beautiful, good, or useful. Most often, however, our answers to these questions are false because they are founded on our implicit Europocentrism.

Since the epistemological revolution to which we referred (and an aspect of which we defined as the substitution of a discursive syntax for sociosemiotic morphology), perceived as global objects our cities are subjected to a pluri-isotopic reading. This phenomenon is moreover especially noticeable at the level of the mythic conception of the city. Formerly thought of as a euphoric molar object whose origin and destiny were its only problematic aspects, today the city is conceived of in terms of a profane mythology that articulates it along the general axis:

euphoria vs. *dysphoria*

as a triple discourse on beauty, goodness and truth.

This sociological triad serves as the starting point for the establishment of the major isotopies for reading a city. It also haunts the dreams and thoughts of producers (or so-called producers) of cities, at any moment likely to transform *descriptive* semiotics, which seeks only to explain the significations inherent in its object, into a *normative* semiotics. Articulated into positive and negative values according to the category *euphoria* vs. *dysphoria*, the three systems

aesthetic (beauty and ugliness)
political (social and moral "health")
rational (the efficiency of the working order, the economy of behaviors, etc.)

on the syntagmatic plane produce three distinct isotopies that make it possible to group partial objects constituting urban space and thereby disambiguate polysemic objects, which in turn can be analyzed along several isotopies.

An additional category complicates this pluriplanar reading of the modern city arising from the quite recent opposition of two concepts that, we are told, are endowed with a characteristic of universality:

society vs. *individual*

It is acknowledged that the archaic village is the spatial expression of its social organization. Whether we envisage it from a static or from a dynamic social perspective (like the Pilou-Pilou ceremonies) does not change the fact that the concept of "community" is coextensive with exploited space. This is no longer the case with our modern cities where the opposition *society* vs. *individual* is not isomorphic with the ancient morphosemiotic category of *public* vs. *private*. Nor is it the case even if we consider this category as being enriched with new significant subarticulations and appearing sometimes as the opposition of public and private places determined by criteria of their occupation (*walls, stairwells* vs. *buildings, apartments*), and sometimes as a typology of spaces corresponding to behaviors (place of work, leisure, habitation). On the other hand, in their opposition to the urban community individuals are not to be taken as numerical entities the sum of which constitutes society, nor as a "lived" and unique entity that cannot be substituted in space and time (although political mythologies readily "degrade" or "exalt" individuals by placing them in either of these categories). Considered as an epistemological concept the individual can be compared to the ideal Weberian type in sociology and to the ideolectal universe in semiotics. Individual and society, individual universe and cultural universe appear as coextensive concepts, as virtual uttered loci that can be semantically invested in the same way. Just as with the definition of topical space beginning with the opposition *here* vs. *elsewhere*, only the "point of view" (i.e., the co-occurrence of the place of utterance and the place of enunciation) will decide what type of discourse can be held on the city as it can be considered either as "urban culture" or as the city dweller's "life-style."

Because of its abstract and purely differential nature the opposition *society* vs. *individual*, by reason of its varied semantic investments, can give rise to multiple ideological interplay (society for the individual or the individual for society?) and produce a rich urban mythology. It can also be used as an epistemological category that dichotomizes discourses that can be held on the city—euphoric and dysphoric discourses distributed along aesthetic, political, or rational isotopies that can have either society (the urban community) or the individual (the city dweller) as subject. Just as the city can be beautiful, happy, or functionally organized, individuals in the city can also feel beauty, be happy or unhappy, and see their needs met according to the law of the least effort.

With two semantic categories (*society* vs. *individual* and *euphoria* vs. *dysphoria*) and three axiological isotopies (*aesthetic*, *political*, and *rational*) we can compose a reading grid and draw up an inventory of the elements of the combinatory producing a city. This grid and inventory are in no way exhaustive or necessary, but they can give us an idea of how, for a historically and geographically determined zone, one could construct an *ideological model* of the city. Such a model would not only generate multiple modern mythologies but, under conditions of manipulation of the signifier that remain to be specified, would also produce topological objects that are part of urban semiotics.

A certain number of remarks would be useful in order to specify the status of this model.

First, it must not be considered uniquely as a model for reading the city, but also as an abstract and deep structure from which an infinite number of urban canonical forms can be generated. Since it is not a normative model (i.e., it is independent of the science of beauty, goodness, and truth), it must be able to allow for the generation of beautiful as well as ugly cities, happy as well as unhappy ones, functional and dysfunctional ones, whether they happen to be realized or only possible.

Second, the categories that constitute the model situated at the level of deep structures are to be considered as formal categories; that is, they can be invested both with the semantic variables of different cultural contexts and with the sub-articulations of the invested contents giving rise to the appearance of true axiological microuniverses. Without raising the issue of aesthetic or political categories in general, whose relativity is self-evident, cultural differences appear at all levels and through all channels. For example, the thermic euphoria of an inhabited space will be different for an Englishman or an American, and the sonorous or olfactive euphoria of an oriental town will be considered to be dysphoric by a Westerner. The relativity of semantic investments and their articulations makes it possible for us to consider this type of model as a grammatical model.

Third, in addition to its taxonomic organization, we can see that the model has a limited number of rules that can orient the actualization of its combinatory. Thus, along with the *compatibility* of two social or individual euphorias or dysphorias, of communal culture or individual life-style, the rule of the *dominance* of one over the other can be formulated and applied. The same holds for rules of *priority* to be given to the different isotopies for constructing cities, rules that, when applied, can produce cities with a functional, political, or aesthetic dominance.

A Grammar: The City as Utterance

The model we have just proposed must be considered to be hypothetical for the following two reasons. Although grounded in the dominant episteme, it is nevertheless intuitively constructed from the redundant concerns of urban planners. As a model organizing the form of content at an abstract level, it remains incomplete, without any foreseeable links with the plane of spatial expression whose parallel articulations only can validate it. In fact, it is through this spatial language that the categories constituting this model must appear and/or be read. In turn, this is possible first of all only if an equivalence, the nature of which remains to be clarified, between the articulations of the deep content and those of the language of manifestation can be postulated and also if the distance separating them can be filled with procedures of generation and instances of construction that progressively conjoin the postulated model with the spatial manifestation. Possible solutions to this very problem need to be worked out in the near future.

Among the various approaches that make possible the analysis of a topological object as complex as a city, the setting up of a structure of communication appears to be one of the most viable. Within the framework of this elementary structure, made up of a sender-producer and a receiver-reader, the town can be inscribed as an object-message to be deciphered. This can be done either by imagining procedures that are prior to the message and end up producing the object-city, or by paraphrasing the reading operation that attempts to decode the message with all its inferences and presuppositions. In either case, the city can be considered as a text whose partial grammar will have to be constructed, at least in part.

However, instead of taking on the appearances of the surfaces and volumes that can be represented by maps and models, this text must first of all be imagined naively as a cluster of *beings and things* from which semioticians will attempt to identify relations that make the construction of a metatext possible. The metatext will take the form either of inventories or of a series of *utterances* whose *subjects* are humans (the users of the city), and the things (with which subjects are in contact and manipulate) the grammatical *objects*. The identification of iso-topical levels of organization at which the objects can be analyzed, and especially the recurrence of observable relations linking subjects and objects, will then make it possible to establish lists of canonical utterances and their semantic investments.

In the main, this is the general outline of the simplified operations leading to the construction of a textual grammar of the city initially taken as a global utterance. The text-city to be analyzed appears as spatial language, which, as we have seen, is a language that enables us to read the world of sensorial qualities. The objects that enter into relation with the recognized subjects of the text will not be of interest as such, but only their sensorial properties will be, whether visual, sonorous, thermic, olfactive, and so on. At this stage, space itself is conceived of as a concept totalizing all of these qualities, and in turn the user can be defined as the interpreter of urban space.

We can see that at the level of sensorial reception, such an approach makes it possible to meet up with the category *euphoria* vs. *dysphoria*. First applied to the city as totality, the category can then be applied to individuals insofar as they are in a euphoric or dysphoric relation to urban space. We can also see that the vague and undefinable terms that are frequently used, such as "live," "feel," and "perceive" can be reduced to this *relation of the subject to space*, to this "use of space" about which we cannot say whether it is conscious or unconscious, thought or lived, but which is, in a word, *significant*.

All we have said nonetheless can be applied to any space that acts on humans. Consequently, urban space cannot be defined in its specificity but only by the "qualities" it produces and communicates to humans and by the *constructed* (but not necessarily "built") nature of the objects that act as supports for these qualities. The analysis of spatial language into pertinent features, into minimal phemic units (the "qualities of the world"), therefore constitutes a level that is both pertinent and insufficient to describe the signifier of urban space. It is pertinent because the world is significant for humans at this level; but it is insufficient because the process of production of a city cannot be described without first of all establishing the constructed objects and systems of objects that support and condition the establishment of sensorial isotopies.

Hence *utterances of state* that make possible the formalization of the relation of the subject to the world presuppose the existence of *utterances of doing*, which can account for the production and/or the transformation of these states. For example, to create a state of thermic euphoria, the subject is supposed to get some wood, light a fire, and so on—that is, to carry out an entire program of behaviors, with the goal of producing a thermic state. These finalized somatic behaviors are therefore *signifying programs*. They can be characterized by the fact that they are stereotypical programs that are both recurrent and can be carried out by any subjects, considered as syntactic roles (and not as flesh-and-blood individuals), and also by the fact that these are programs for which human subjects can be replaced, in whole or in part, by automatons.

There is no need here to enter into sociological considerations describing the process of industrialization, showing how, starting from the tool that extends the hand, humanity has constructed substitution automatons that in turn presuppose other somatic or mechanized programs of doing, thus instituting new forms of social organization that function by successive mediations and substitutions. To do so would be to encroach on other disciplines, more precisely on a certain branch of sociology, only the research results of which could be used in topological semiotics. However, the identification of the substitution of segments of somatic doing by automatized programs is already of interest to semiotics insofar as this "thingification" of social practices facilitates the segmentation of the urban text into autonomous and isotopical instances of doing.

We can also see that the semiotic manifestation of urban space, which roughly can be illustrated as the setting into relation of

(thermic signifier) + (euphoric signified)

presupposes a certain *doing of the subject* (which can simply be an operation of pressing a button) carried out on a *support object* (central heating furnace), a localized substitute of a somatic program. This *individual instance* of doing in turn, however, presupposes a new *collective instance*, with a new *support object* (the urban distribution of gas or electricity), manipulated by a *collective subject* (gas or electric company). We are therefore faced with two types of support objects that make it possible to distinguish two forms of participation of subjects in an urban space that, for the purpose of analysis, constitute two autonomous syntactic individual and collective instances.

Seen from this perspective, individual instances appear to be made up of all the relations of an individual with the surrounding objects that make him the center of this relational network. On the contrary, the collective instance appears as the set of networks (electricity, gas, water, sewers, telephone, mail, subway, streets, etc.) whose terminals constitute a series of individual instances.

Two types of individual and collective practices are linked to these instances that ensure the maintenance and functioning either of individual or collective networks. Two types of subjects considered no longer as individuals but as *syntactic roles* corresponding to programs can be equated to these two types of support objects and programs. Just as objects are of interest to semiotics only because some of their properties make it possible to group them into topological sets, subjects also can be broken down into roles, according to the programs they have to carry out. It is only at the price of this dual "destruction" of objects and subjects that a semiotic syntax is possible.

The grammatical approach we have just sketched has a number of advantages, probably the most important one being the integration of human subjects into the text of the city. While providing a semiotic interpretation of the "users of the city," in a way by allowing us to imagine *the city as a set of interrelations and interactions between subjects and objects*, it enables us to make our representation dynamic. In addition, distinguishing two canonical forms of the transcription between subjects and objects — utterances of states and utterances of doing — it specifies two distinct manifestations of meaning. If individuals experience space within utterances of state by conjoining with the qualities of the world, then the existence of utterances of doing, whose function it is to produce the states, brings to the fore a new instance of signification. The practices of individuals, in fact, are significant for themselves and for others.

In our modern cities, however, this signifying practice, which consists in producing, setting into place, and manipulating objects with the view to constituting signifying states, is replaced for the most part by programs carried out by automatons. This gives rise to an invasive *desemanticization* of cities, which, when dysphorically experienced, appears as alienation. Yet one should not assimilate too quickly these two concepts of desemanticization and alienation, since the former is simply an acknowledgment of existence, whereas the latter includes, in addition, an axiological judgment. Desemanticization is a general semiotic phenomenon. We can say that part of our life is spent in replacing our signifying behaviors by desemanticized programs that are basically automaticisms. The economical and rational exploitation of our bodily activities can give rise to the abolition of meaning, but it can either be euphorically or dysphorically experienced.

To return to the problematics of urban semiotics, we can say that those semiotics programs that survive or are replaced by automatons are not always and necessarily endowed with more meaning than the programs of substitution that can also produce euphoric meaning. However the functionalization of the city, situated on the isotopy of the rationality of individual or collective life, is neither good nor bad in itself. That being the case, the phenomenon of desemanticization, like that of resemanticization (for example, the reintroduction of fireplaces along with central heating), appears as a semiotic fact that can be analyzed independently of all ideological considerations.

It seems to us that the major inconvenience of this grammatical approach resides in the fact that it cannot give a clear picture and a satisfactory metatextual representation of the collective component of the city. It is true, however, that the collective instance is clearly distinguished as being presupposed by the individual instance and characterized by a particular class of support objects appearing as multiple urban networks that are governed by forms of autonomous organizations. Although this partial image of the city, constructed from localizations in the form of networks, of support objects considered as substitutes for real human activities, can give an idea of the maintenance and operational structures of a town, we fail to see how the "meaning of the city" can be apprehended from this. It is as though such a grammar, centered on the term 'individual'' (of the epistemological category *society* vs. *individual*), were unable to change points of view and to account for the social dimension of the city. It is also as though another grammar and another ideology were necessary to define the relations of humans to urban space, no longer in terms of "life-style" but in terms of "urban culture."

It is true that in examining the practice of subject-citizens, along with individual roles, we were able to identify social roles by which individuals participate in collective tasks. Consequently, we can say that these social roles are "lived" in one way or another and that these social activities are significant for the individual. But such an analysis cannot be pushed too far, if only because social activities are participatory, each role and each program being inscribed within the framework of collective practice that goes beyond them. Social roles can obviously be referred back to the individual, who can interpret them in terms of fatigue, boredom, and so forth. But the problem remains of knowing if and how individuals as social role "live" their participation in the common practice, what meaning they give to themselves and to their practice as part of a whole.

From the problematics of the individual actant we now go on to that of *collective actants*. Because we are familiar with concepts of "society" and of "class" and with anthropomorphic attributes such as "class conscience" with which we endow them, we can ask ourselves whether a grammaticalization of these collective entities and the representation of social groups and social organizations as collective subjects could not give urban semiotics a tool that makes it possible to account for the modes of existence of "social beings," that is, humans engaged in social practice and participating in the social being. A number of investigations in narrative semiotics tend to show that it is not impossible to describe economic and social organizations, political and cultural institutions as collective actants endowed with the modalities of wanting, being able, and knowing, and invested with axiological contents that are experienced as such by the participants in this "moral person." Urban social organization can therefore be broken down into different actants and collective actors whose descriptions, initially partial and then comparative and totalizing, would provide numerous insights into communal signification. The syntactic models so obtained would serve as a framework for the semantic analysis of the "collective representations" of the city.

The advantage of such an approach[1] is that it clearly posits the object of urban semiotics. By refusing the traditional views according to which the city is a thing, a complex of objects lived and perceived by humans, it substitutes a city-text made up of individuals and things, of their relations and interactions. Human subjects whose presence in the text can only account for its signifying character are therefore differentiated from the subject of enunciation, the producer of the city; and the grammar of the enunciated-town can be completed by a grammar of enunciation. This is all the more possible as the hierarchized instances of generation that presuppose one another are already theoretically anticipated. In short, all one has to do is to take the procedures, which starting from the conjunction of the individual with the qualities of urban space, posited the existence of support objects constructed on several levels, and inverse them by using opposite procedures that illustrate collective mechanisms, before going on to the objects constituting the individual's immediate environment.

Another Grammar Project: The Enunciation of the City

In spite of the specificity of the object considered ("the architectural ensemble" is only incidently inscribed in the problematics of urban semiotics) it is Jean Castex and Pierre Panerai's project[2] that can best illustrate this generative process. It is obvious that the analysis of such a limited object is valid only insofar as all the restrictions that made it possible to clarify the thrust of the project are clarified beforehand, that is: (a) that for the intents and purposes of analysis the architectural ensemble is considered separately, as an enclosed object with the enclosing being provisionally bracketed off; (b) that the delimited object is considered only on a single isotopy, the visual one, and moreover: exclusively of the subisotopy of forms, excluding those of color and light; (c) that the description deal solely with the plane of the signifier of this object; and (d) that the global undertaking be inductive and generalizing, from the description of actual objects, with a view to establishing an inventory of forms and a list of rules of derivation that at a subsequent stage would serve as materials to construct a grammar of the production of canonical "architectural ensembles."

These restrictions admitted, in the general economy of urban semiotics, Castex and Panerai's project occupies the place reserved for one of its subcomponents, which the individual instance filled with objects and systems of support objects happens to be. These objects and systems are constructed with users of the space in mind and exclude all signification resulting from their participation in communal life.

From this perspective, the organization of spatial forms appears as the final instance of the generative trajectory situated just before their manifestation as "built space." For the entire procedure can be envisaged only as starting from an ideological instance situated at a deep level whose architectural ensembles are simply surface realizations. The ideological model, semantic in nature, can manifest itself spatially only if it coheres with the signified of the language of spatial manifestation that is expressed by means of the "phonological" component, that is, the architecture of the spatial forms that it will ultimately receive.

Linked by these cursory remarks to the textual grammar that was previously sketched out, Castex's undertaking is a good example of the generative process. This is so, if only because it posits that the architectural text is the result of the expansion and combinatory of one or several simple structures of signification, connected to the elementary spatial articulations. It is only afterward, by successive subarticulations and overdeterminations, that the topological object becomes more complex and takes on the form of some or other architectural ensemble.

Such a construction entails a first order of difficulty found in the choice of the units and the levels of analysis, for the initial choice determines the *strategy of the description* in its entirety. In Castex's example of the George Barton House, we can see that the analyst has three possibilities. Three spatial structures can be considered as *ab quo* structures from which the procedures of the generation of the whole can be initiated. In order not to complicate things, if we admit that the description can be undertaken "from plans" and not "from models" and, after a reductive transposition, that architectural space can be treated as a surface and not a volume, the three structures are: (a) first the *cross* ("six spatial units grouped together as a cross"); (b) next, at a lower level, the *square* (a unit of which the cross is basically an expansion); and finally (c) at least the *straight line* and the *right angle*, which are the constituent features of the square. Beginning with these three types of elementary spatial units and these three distinct levels of analysis, one has to choose the type of elementary unit and the optimal level of depth at which to begin the descriptive procedure. At first sight, we do not see which criteria of pertinence would oblige the analyst to consider any particular units or any particular levels as initial units and levels.

In theory, it is the level of distinctive features, that of *phemic categories* such as (only for the sake of suggestion),

straight vs. *curve*
right (angle) vs. *nonright* (angle)

drawn from typology, that ['both approximate and rigorous science" (Guilbaud)] that makes it possible to produce *squares*, *triangles*, and *circles* by combining their terms. This level must be considered elementary. Indeed, it is at this level that baroque architecture is defined in part by means of the category *convex* vs. *concave*. It is also here with the oppositions—straight lines and curves, vertical and horizontal lines—that the first articulations of signification, isomorphic to spatial oppositions, appear. It is as though to engender *spatial figures* such as the square and the triangle by means of the rules of its combinatory, the grammar of the production of spatial forms had to begin with these elementary categories.

As in the case in point, it is only if the architectural corpus to be analyzed happens to be relatively restricted that the spatial figures possibly can be chosen as the point of departure from which to construct a limited number of topological objects. In fact, we can see that the choice of the square as an elementary figure best satisfies the rule of simplicity of description, because it is from the square that the greatest number of rules of derivation can be formulated in the simplest way. Nevertheless this rule is only pragmatic and therefore subordinated to the principles of coherence and exhaustivity.

Moreover, if *spatial categories* can generate *figures*, they in turn can produce composite figures or *configurations*, such as the cross of the George Barton House, which is coextensive with the actual architectural ensemble described. Following the *decomposition* and *overcomposition* of the figure chosen as base structure, a hierarchy of spatial units is instituted that in large measure justifies the analyst's strategic option.

However, although it seems to be an expected extension of the process generating the architectural ensemble, the recognition of this third level of overcomposition does create difficulties when interpreting constructed objects. An "architectural ensemble," which is defined only intuitively, can be produced either by a configuration (= the cross) or by interrupting the generation at the level of simple figures (= square building) or, finally, by the coordination of two figures (= two square buildings juxtaposed). For want of a definition of the "ensemble," instead of speaking about contradictory models or the "exasperation of an architectural code," we could see the simple effect of the passage of a figurative level to a configurative level, of sentence grammar to discursive grammar. Since derivation is a procedure of decomposition of the utterance (figures could be assimilated with semantic utterances), overcomposition of base units produces configurations that correspond to expansions of the utterances of discourse, it being understood that the discursive level once recognized, the utterance-figure is already a discursive unit that can be substituted for the entire expanded discourse. Consequently, the rules of a discursive grammar that would deal with the compositions of architectural ensembles, but also with much more complex objects, must be worked out independently of those of the elementary grammar.

On the other hand, and without excluding the theoretical possibility of contradictory codes that would imply the production of a topological object starting from at least two autonomous elementary structures, we can envisage the existence of objects characterized by the complementarity of spatial figures, of which some would be, for example, constructed from straight lines and others, from curved lines (the Pantheon in Paris). In this case, the strategic choice of the level of figures, as a starting point for the generation of architectural forms, could be maintained only by adding new rules of transformation to the rules of derivation, and by positing, for example, that at such and such a level of derivation, square figures are transformed into circular figures, a principle that would presuppose a strict hierarchization of different types of figures and would inevitably limit the domain of application of the descriptive procedure considered. Only the procedure of the production of forms from spatial categories can guarantee the coherence of the description, even if it apparently seems less economical that the one we have just examined.

The interest in the formalization we have proposed, however, exceeds the framework of the architectural ensemble and the cases analyzed. We can see that the same approach and the same procedures can be applied to the more important objects studied by urban semiotics, as long as a clear separation is established between the articulations of the figurative and phrastic level and those of the configurative and discursive level. Identification of several semiotic levels of organization of forms allows for a surer approach when tackling problems of the topological signifier. It clearly demonstrates that, because a spatial language can appear at all the levels of the identified articulations, it produces multiple and graduated significations (the right angle, the square, and the cross each signify separately) whose organization produces a global semantic effect.

The Sender and the Receiver of the Urban Message

Of the two possible methodological approaches (the interpretive approach and the generative approach) corresponding to the two poles of the structure of communication—the city considered as a global utterance readable by the receiver and the city enunciated by the sender—it is the latter, for reasons that are not all of a scientific nature, that interests most architects who wish to investigate urban problematics from a semiotic perspective. In adopting this perspective, it is as though town planners naturally found themselves once again in a familiar ideological landscape. By identifying with the sender-enunciator of the city, in their own eyes they are transformed into *producers* of the city, thus misrepresenting their fundamentally individualistic and reactionary ideology. We know to what degree the myth of the individual creator, which dates only from the eighteenth century, is deep-rooted and self-serving. The subject of enunciation, the semiotic locus that can legitimately be privileged by adopting a specific semiotic methodological procedure, is transformed into an obsessive focalization for all ideological, aesthetic, and sociological ills. Such a focalization ensures delaying the actual establishment of urban semiotics.

For we forget all too often that the communication schema that will facilitate a semiotic apprehension of the city is first and foremost a formal model that institutes the instances of production and of reading only as empty spaces. Moreover, the task of urban semiotics is to describe neither real cities nor their producers in flesh and blood, but canonical objects and syntactic actants. Sociological investigations that undertake the contextual analysis of the actant-producer are nevertheless necessary, even if they happen to be subject to socio-cultural relativism. If we can say in brief that in a Bororo village, the same populations simultaneously or successively play the syntactic roles of producers and readers of their topological space, it is much more difficult to answer the question of who constructed the city of Paris. The construction of new cities by such and such an architect should not delude us: on the aesthetic isotopy, to inscribe his city of Grigny, Mr. Aillaud certainly did not choose the triangular form, generally read as dysphoric, or the model of the dormitory town, on the political isotopy. He is simply one of the *actors* (whose role has to be determined) of the complex *collective actant*, the analysis of which would bring to light economic and political components that are much more powerful than the architect-town planner.

This could be one of the objects of urban semiotics. For example, insofar as the producer can be considered as the subject of enunciation, a subject endowed with competence that ultimately can be broken down into a *being-able-to-do*, a *wanting-to-do*, and a *knowing-how-to-do* of the producer. Having no real power, town planners would be in part exonerated or at least would not confuse the two syntactic roles they can be called on to play.

The structure of the collective actant is made up not only of the dispositions of the modalities of being-able, wanting, and knowing; it also consists in an investment of an ideological nature. The study of the process by which various particular wills constituting this actant succeed in amalgamating sometimes contradictory values and give rise to an ideological model of the city to be constructed, makes it possible to describe the decisional mechanisms that end up constructing cities along the three previously examined isotopies. This ideological model is implicit and corresponds only remotely to what architects think and especially what they do. For if we know, or even believe we are more or less acquainted with, problems related to the political finalities of town planning, such research would also make it possible to situate aesthetic problems in their proper light, notably by describing the various systems of constraints imposed on architects: so-called natural constraints, pressures of actors making up the collective actant, as well as the self-censorship exercised by this imaginary model of reading that the implicitly recognized and accepted "user's taste" has to be.

Finally, a third type of analysis is possible, consisting in the syntagmatic decomposition of the global program of the production of the city into collective or individual actors or into automatized substitutes. In adopting the generative form, such a description appears as the inverse path of the process we have already described, when we proposed the model of textual grammar. In its generic form the description would aim at giving a representation of the processes and programs actually realized by various actors and ending up in the construction of a city in case.

Methodological difficulties increase when one abandons the point of view of the sender for that of the receiver. The same terms generally used to designate this instance — "reader," "user," "consumer" — belong to ideologically different disciplines and attitudes that lead to their constant metaphorical or analogical use.

It should also be added that even the semiotic conception of the city as object-message is not without ambiguity. We are too used to interpreting communication in linguistic terms not to have difficulty in imagining that meaning can be communicated without the intermediary of natural languages. We have already emphasized that to receive spatial messages is not, or is not only, to perceive them; rather it is what could be called by the vague term "to experience" the city, by reacting in a significant way to all spatial stimulations. Even though such an interpretation of the signification of nonlinguistic messages may appear clear at the moment of its formulation, nonetheless it must be used with caution in practice. It is necessary that the primary "meaning" of the city not be confused with conscious thought or with discourses on the city. It implies that the boundary between what is conscious and what is unconscious about the way one experiences the city be abolished or at least suspended. It is only at this price that the concepts of *reading* and *usage* of the city can be considered as synonymous and that the *consumption* of the meaning of the city, while maintaining its metaphoric form, ceases being an exclusive reference for a society based on commerce.

We have seen that for the individual to live in the city signifies the place where all spatial messages converge. Yet it is also to react to these messages by becoming dynamically engaged in the multiple programs and mechanisms that solicit and constrain individuals. In principle, it is therefore in developing a *life model*, a semantic representation of what one could understand by a citizen's life-style, that one can hope, at least partially, to understand the structure of the content of the receiver actant. Nonetheless, we are aware that such a model can be only *topological*, that along with a certain number of constants, it will have a certain number of variables corresponding both to social stratification and to the historical relativism of urban communities. We can even go further, by introducing new variables and by multiplying the number of possible readings of the city. We can, for example, by means of the category *external* vs. *internal*, oppose the reading of the user of the city to that of the passerby and distinguish a particular reading proper to a social category of tourists and even create a typology of them. We can also examine the aesthetic attitudes of the "elite": architects or interpreters of their esthetic aims, and so on. Just as the analysis of the instance of the sender, that of the receiver is situated beyond the concerns of topological semiotics proper, and is part of considerations on the social structure in correlation with axiological systems that have a collective status.

As we have said, the concept of life-style does not exhaust all the possible significations of the city, if only because the totality of the "immediate experience" that it attempts to subsume is at each and every moment superseded by constructions of the imaginary that humans project outside themselves. Filmed space "beyond the frame" (which is progressively constituted during the projection on the screen of partial visual spaces that finally end up as metonyms of an imaginary global referent) can give an idea of the mediated apprehension of urban space. Whether we represent the citizen as a stroller stocking partial views of the city, as a user disapproving of the conveniences or their lack of comfort, or as social beings engaged in different activities constituting their lives, a global image of the absent city is formed, an image accepted as the locus of its spatial inscription. It does not matter what physiological or psychological status we attribute to such mediated representations of topological objects, it does not seem possible to question the existence of the city as *global imaginary referent*.

This global referent is obviously consolidated by metasemiotic transpositions of all sorts—maps, postcards, panels indicating panoramic views (Alençon, city of facades), and so on—without mentioning the innumerable discourses on the city. It is also nurtured on other ideologies that are formed in other circumstances (alienation, pollution, promiscuity) and serves as a pretext for multiple *secondary elaborations* that appear as diverse urban mythologies (Paris, City of Light). An entire architecture of significations is built up on urban space, and in large measure they determine its acceptance or refusal, the happiness and the beauty or the unbearable misery of urban life.

Consequently, it would be wrong to represent the receiver of the city as a naive reader, as a sort of tabula rasa on which the sender inscribes the first of his spatial hieroglyphics. On the contrary, the receiver appears as a structure of reception possessing a complete code by which to decipher messages, but that is not necessarily identical to the sender's code that served to produce the messages. Just as in linguistic communication, two actants encountering one another are supposed to ensure the emission and reception of messages filled with possible misunderstandings.

Topological Discourses

As space does not have to be spoken in order to signify, terms such as "message," "discourse" or "text" that we have used in connection with it are simply names of semiotic concepts that must be defined, as structures and not as terms, at the level of an epistemological language establishing the principles of the analysis of all semiotic systems. In relation to this primary "spatial text," all discourses on space are always secondary. Whether they happen to be more or less faithful transpositions of a spatial language into another language or autonomous manifestations of original modes of spatial construction—or, more often, both at the same time—verbal, graphic, pictorial, or cinematographic discourses on space are always situated adjacent to spatial discourse proper.

Verbal discourse, the dominance of which need not be underscored, since through it all other languages can be compared and since they can be translated into it, constitutes the principal concern of semioticians. It is their responsibility to work out a twofold and paradoxical task. At the same time, semioticians need to recognize the distance that separates spatial discourse from the discourses paraphrasing it, but also, since their own discourse takes place in a natural language, they need to attempt to suppress this distance or to nullify its effects.

In the first instance, to recognize this distance is to distinguish the properties of signifying space from the properties that characterize verbal discourses dealing with space. For no matter what is said about them, discourses are defined not by the contents they manipulate (to speak of political, social, or religious discourses is to establish a typology of value systems) but by the forms of their organization. The typology of discourses, which is of a grammatical nature, is therefore a problem of general semiotics on which discourses on space depend. They do not, however, constitute a separate class of discourses. Hence the dissenting or prospective, descriptive or normative utopian discourses that can be held on space could easily find their equivalents in semantic loci other than space.

To nullify the effects created by the distance separating "discourse on things" from discourse on this discourse is first of all to clarify the conditions of the scientificity of the latter, so that the semiotic discourse one is attempting to construct can be subjected to the rules that make it possible to satisfy these conditions. Hence, contrary to what happens in the production of nonscientific discourse, where, for example the temporalization and the spatialization of the models are procedures of normal enunciation, semiotic models are considered to be *achronological*, realizable at all times and in all places, but independent of their realization. Contrary to what happens in prescientific times where sometimes extremely judicious theoretical models have been worked out that can be subsequently modified, semiotic models must satisfy the principle of *adequacy*. In a way, scientific discourse must be equivalent to the primary discourse it transposes, and thereby can be validated by means of procedures or indispensable complementary discourses. However, the principles for the validity of discourse and the procedures for its validation also fall under the purview of the general epistemology of sciences.

Chapter 8
The Challenge

Rodrigue, as-tu du coeur?
Corneille, *Le Cid*

If we agree that to the empirical distinction between man's action on things and man's action on other men there corresponds, at the semiotic level, a distinction based on bringing into play sometimes the category of *transitivity* (causing-to-be) and sometimes the category of *factitivity* (causing-to-do), then for any discourse under analysis we can identify segments that, in many different ways, manifest the elements of factitivity. We can also seek to construct, by clearly identifying and explaining them, a model or models of the phenomenon of manipulation that can be put to generalized use.

Conceptual Framework

Factitive doing is one of the defining elements of manipulation as long as what is at play is a *cognitive* and not a pragmatic doing. "Physical constraint," while being the action of one person upon another, at first sight does not have to do with manipulation. There is nonetheless a resemblance: the challenge, which we have chosen to study closely by considering it to be one of the characteristic figures of manipulation, is indeed defined spontaneously and intuitively as a "moral constraint."

This intuitive definition is, however, not confirmed by our dictionaries. For them, a challenge is a "provocative declaration by which you signify to someone else that you consider him incapable of doing something" (*Petit Robert*). As we can see, the dictionary takes the challenge to be a simple utterance and does not consider the modal nature of the two subjects facing each other. Neither does it consider the specific link established between them as a result of such a declaration. In other words, the dictionary does not take into account the "doing" aspect of this "saying." Only if we make clear the "provocational" nature of the declaration can we understand that a challenge is, first, an act of "inciting someone to do something," where the verb "incite"—with its figurative *parasynonyms*, "push," "lead," "drive'"—appears at the surface of discourse as the lexicalization of factitivity.

Given this, this incitement can be brought within the general framework of the contract, and there, more precisely, it can correspond to the first part of a contract, the *contract proposal*, which we can formulate as follows:

$$S_1 \rightarrow S_2 \cap O_1 \, [O_2 \, (O_3)]$$

or

O_1: a cognitive object (the transmitted knowledge);
O_2: $S_1 \cap d$ (the manipulating subject's *desire*, which is communicated to the manipulated subject);
O_3: *realization* (the NP of S_2) (the object of desire being the realization by S_2, of a program developed and transmitted by S_1)

Such a message is obviously of a purely *informative* nature. Knowing what S_1 wants in no way obliges S_2 to do anything. The contract proposal thus constitutes a neutral cognitive first stage that then authorizes our conceiving of the receiving subject as being modally sovereign, free to accept or reject this proposal.

It is within this contractual framework that we can place manipulation and see it at play.

Persuasive Doing

Between these two contractual instances—proposal and acceptance—is a problematic locus where we find intersubjective tensions and implicit affronts. Here is where the interpretive and persuasive doing of the two subjects takes place, eventually giving rise to a contract that is either sought after or imposed.

In the case of provocation by challenge, which now holds our interest, the persuasive message of the manipulating subject that accompanies the contract proposal consists in informing the subject that his lack of competence is about to be manipulated. The subject S_2 is thus invited to carry out a certain program (NP), and at the same time he is warned as to his modal insufficiency (his "not-being-able-to-do") for the carrying out of that program.

The persuasive utterance that, as object of knowledge, is transmitted by S_1 to S_2 at the same time as the contractual utterance can be formulated as follows:

$$S_1 \rightarrow S_2 \cap O_1 [O_2 (O_3)]$$

or

O_1: epistemic judgment (S_1's certainty);
O_2: object of knowledge (S_1's knowledge);
O_3: $S_2 \cap \overline{\text{batd}}$ (S_2 is deprived of being-able-to-do).

Note: If the epistemic modalization of the persuasive utterance is obvious, we must still not forget that epistemic modalities can be ranked gradationally. The manipulator can claim to be "certain," but he can also "claim" or "allow to be understood." The epigraph quoted from Corneille ("Rodrigue, do you have heart?") shows that a simple question that shows doubt is enough to set off the manipulating mechanisms. The force of the epistemic judgment is thus not a decisive factor for the effectiveness of persuasion.

Elsewhere we have already had the opportunity to sketch out an initial articulation of persuasion:[1]

deixis of persuasion	*deixis of dissuasion*
persuade to accept	persuade to refuse
dissuade from refusing	dissuade from accepting

We can see that the *challenge* is a particular instance of *antiphrastic persuasion*. The persuasive utterance appears as *persuasion to refuse* with the hidden intention of having it understood, following on the interpretive doing of the manipulated subject, as being *dissuasion from refusing*. It is a kind of "arguing in favor of what is false in order to obtain what is true." The denial of his competence is supposed to provoke a "salutary reflex" on the part of the subject, who then becomes the manipulated subject.

We have often noted that the narrative schema offers a useful reference by which to situate and eventually interpret any narrative sequence we wish to analyze. In our case, we see that the behavior of the manipulating subject as seen in the two utterances of proposal and persuasion, corresponds to two main interventions by the sender, the giving of a *mandate* and the *cognitive sanction*. This latter is the essence of what occurs when the sender recognizes or chooses his subject. The challenge is thus a kind of short form of the narrative schema, one in which *recognition is anticipated and inverted*. As sanction, recognition thus has to do with the competence and not the performance of the subject, and it is unjustly imperious and negative.

This anticipation of sanction allows us to consider the manipulating subject as a syncretic actor who subsumes the two actants: the mandating sender and the judging sender. The inverted nature of his judgment in turn raises the delicate question as to the veridictory status of this sender for whom lying is one of the essential elements of his strategy.

Interpretive Doing

A Constraining Communication

The reaction of the subject on receiving a persuasive message consists of bringing into play his interpretive procedures. This interpretive doing is inscribed within a particular form of communication that we might call constraining communication. Indeed, in certain circumstances, the receiver to whom a certain kind of message is addressed finds himself constrained to answer, to act on, the message he has received.

There are many examples of this situation. In the first instance we have the general problem, one much discussed, of apoliticism and noninvolvement or noncommitment. It is generally agreed that any refusal to become involved constitutes a negative involvement. A good example is Jesus' silence before his judges, the silence of Maupassant's "two friends" when facing the Prussian officer's accusations. In these cases the constraint has to do with the impossibility of maneuvering oneself into a position of neutrality by in some way withdrawing from that situation of communication.

The *challenge* we are studying belongs to this type of communication, as does, perhaps, all provocation. When faced with an affirmation of his incompetence, the challenged subject cannot avoid answering because silence would inevitably be interpreted as an admission of that incompetence. In other words, he faces a *forced choice*: he can choose, but he cannot fail to choose.[2]

If we consider choice to be a *decision*, and if we believe it to be a cognitive act, we can see that this obligation to choose can be interpreted as being part of the modal competence of the challenged subject, and that it consists in his modalization according to his /being-able-to-do/. This latter is situated at the cognitive dimension, where it occupies the position of /not-being-able-not-to-decide/, a position that can be homologated with /having-to-decide/.[3]

Let us sum up. Faced with the twofold message sent by the manipulating subject—notification of what he wants in terms of a specific narrative program and a statement as to the manipulated subject's incompetence to carry out that program—the receiver can neither accept nor refuse the proposed contract without first pronouncing on the "challenge" itself. We are suggesting that he finds it impossible not to pronounce, and we want to study the mechanisms that produce this constraint.

The Objects of the Choice

The challenged subject thus faces a dilemma that the dictionaries define as "an alternative between two contradictory propositions between which the subject is *placed in the position* of having to choose." The choices in our case are found, on the one hand, in the utterance produced by the manipulating subject S_1, which we can formulate as follows:

$$S_2 \cap \overline{\text{batd}}$$

and, on the other hand, its contradictory, which the manipulated subject himself constructs:

$$S_2 \cap \text{batd}$$

A dilemma can thus be formulated in this way:

$$S_2 \cap \overline{\text{ba}} \; \overline{\text{decision}} \; (S_2 \cap \overline{\text{batd}} \text{ vs. } S_2 \cap \text{batd})$$

Such a formulation is, however, incorrect because, if we look at it more closely, we see that the entities included by the symbolic label S_2 are not identical. The S_2's that are endowed with /being-able-to-do/ or with /not-being-able-to-do/ are in a way objects of value between which the challenged subject's choice has to take place, whereas the S_2 that faces the dilemma is in fact the subject of a doing and is endowed with a particular cognitive competence, that of /not-being-able-not-to-decide/. Therefore we have to distinguish, on the one hand, the *subjects of communication* S_1 and S_2 who are facing each other in negotiations over an eventual contract and, on the other hand, *subjects of representation* (whom we might designate as S') who are within the cognitive space of S_2 and of which the first one ($S'_2 \cap \overline{\text{batd}}$) has just been received in the form of an utterance produced by S_1, while the second one ($S'_2 \cap \text{batd}$) is produced by S_2 and is the contradictory of the first.

We can see that the cognitive space in question is peopled with actants that are just more or less convincing representations of the subjects of communication. Can this space be seen as a kind of interior discourse or as its reconstructed hypothetico-logical simulacrum? Does it constitute, in part, what other disciplines sometimes call the "autonomous imaginary dimension"? Because this simulacrum makes us think of the "brand-name image," an expression created and used outside semiotics. If the comparison is suggestive, it teaches us more about differences than it does about resemblances. Thus, the brand-name image is situated along the axis of seduction rather than on that of provocation. It is created to be used transitively, whereas the simulacrum we are dealing with is instead for the *ad usum internum* of the subject who seeks to recognize himself in it.

Nonetheless, in arguing for the resemblance, we can say that to describe the simulated subject using the form of his modal competence cannot always be done using only that subject's abstract anthropomorphic representation. With the help of "imagination," the image of this subject often receives new semantic determinations, acquires a figurative overlay, and even becomes endowed with narrative trajectories in which final positive or negative sanctions can be foreseen.

Encompassing Axiology

It would be too much to say that the choice of the "right image" (that of the subject endowed with positive competence) depends exclusively on the challenged subject, on his desire to recognize himself in it. This choice is also affected by the "view of others" and must conform to the supposed projection of the manipulator's values. It does not matter if this is a simple intersubjective structure, that we have present an observing actant or a judging sender that is, at least implicitly, accepted by both parties. If the challenge is to work properly there must be an *objective complicity* between manipulator and manipulated. In other words, if S_2, the challenged subject who is accused of incompetence, seeks to establish a conformity between his manner of being (his modal competence) and the projected representation, he can do so only within an axiological framework that has already been posited by S_1 and ratified by S_2. It is unthinkable for a knight to challenge a peasant, and the converse is unthinkable also. Likewise, if a given author raises the issue of the *American Challenge* for the French, he is implicitly accepting, and requires that his readers do so too, the American system of values. Without that, the challenge would make no sense.

The example of Jesus provides us with a countercase. If his being slapped, as we are told in the Gospels, represents a challenge and a provocation, there apparently are only two possible responses: he could have acted by returning the challenge (thus affirming his being-able-to-do), or he could have done nothing (thereby accepting the judgment of his helplessness). Now, Jesus opts for something else: he turns the other cheek. This is not only a "refusal to play the game." He is also proposing a new code of honor.

For we see that, in all these cases, we must speak of a shared *axiological code* and, because we are involved in the problematic of power, of a *code of honor*. What used to require that a gentleman accept a duel, what today obliges a gangster who is winning big to agree to prolong the poker game until he loses everything, is a sense of honor, a word the dictionaries have not been able to completely define.

Thus we can provisionally propose a likely articulation of this code of honor, one that can be obtained by putting the modality of /being-able-to-do/ on the semiotic square, with the understanding that the terms thus distributed over the four points will be considered as modal values:

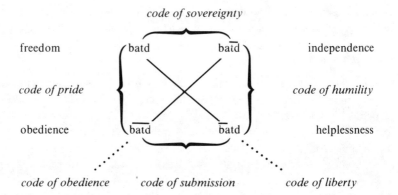

This model allows us to recognize, along each axis, schema, or deixis, an honor subcode that can develop into an *autonomous axiological system*. We should also note the particular status of humility subcodes (Jesus) and pride subcodes (Vigny: ''Honor is duty's poetry''). These are developed out of the structure of the deixes and are distinguished by their deviant nature.

Valorization

This proposed axiological model is an organized ensemble of reference codes within which subjects of communication choose and take values that can be the basis of their complicity, a complicity that is not necessarily freely chosen by both. However, these values are only virtual ones, they are known to be values, but are not yet effective. In order to be actualized, they must be ''converted into something else'' by moving from one generative level to another and satisfying two essential conditions: (a) they must be narrativized, inscribed within the syntactic relation constitutive of the subject and object. This will alter the subject and object's paradigmatic and syntagmatic status; and (b) within the narrative utterances they must at the same time affect both subject and object, transforming the first into a desiring subject (or a subject with a duty), and the second into a desired object (or one that is owed as a duty, that is indispensable within the order of ''things needed'').

Thus only values are actualized, and the simulacra

$$(S'_2 \cap \overline{\text{batd}}) \text{ vs. } (S'_2 \cap \text{batd})$$

become, for the challenged subject S_2, objects of value. From being objects of knowledge, they move to becoming objects of desire or of duty.

Identification

Now we have modalized S_2 that is inscribed within a value universe in which he can carry out the cognitive operation of choosing between two values, an operation for which, it will be remembered, he is endowed with a negative competence, that of /not-being-able-not-to-choose/. He will therefore choose the positive value contained in the image he has of himself as one who /can-do/, and will exclude the negative value that makes up the image of his helplessness.

We have thus arrived at a stage in the construction of the simulacrum at which the subject finds himself in a position of "he who knows what he wants." Now, "what he wants" in reality is not to be "powerful" but rather to *see himself and be seen* as such. In other words, the problem now posed is situated at the level of cognitive sanction and presupposes the existence of a sender that is common to both subjects S_1 and S_2, a sender whose sanction corresponds to recognition by S_1 of S_2 as being ($S'_2 \cap$ batd). It will also correspond to the identification, by S_2, through a sort of self-recognition, with his image as ($S'_2 \cap$ batd). Of course this sender is no more than the incarnation, at the level of anthropomorphic grammar, of the value universe — and more precisely of the code of honor — whose existence we have already noted.

Now we can see that in order to bring about recognition of the sender, the subject can do nothing else but *prove* his /being-able-to-do/ competence by *testing* it. This will require /doing/ itself. The realization of the NP proposed by S_1 will then become, for S_2, the means by which to attain quite another goal. In other words, the same narrative segment, having the same articulations, belongs at the same time to two NPs: the NP of the manipulation of S_1 and the NP of S_2's honor.

This NP is in fact a *use NP* for S_2. Considered in itself, this NP is a matter of indifference for S_2 in the best of cases, but it can be repulsive or deadly (for example, the knight's descent into the lion's cage in order to retrieve the glove dropped into it on purpose by the lady). Thus we cannot say that in this case the subject's modal competence is determined by /wanting-to-do/. As for any use NP, the subject will carry it out only when moved by /having-to-want-to-do/. We can see that in our case, the deontic obligation to do has added to it the need to "save one's honor." The subjectivizing /having-to-do/ is accompanied by a /not-being-able-not-to-do/.

Thus, through a kind of inversion, performance, by preceding competence, ends up proving and in a way even constituting that competence.

Toward Discourse

This paradox sees the program that S_2 has to realize in order to save his honor as being the same program initially proposed to him by S_1. The realization of that program will then, at least at the surface, allow it to be inferred that the contract itself, as proposed by S_1, was accepted, because the obligations flowing from it were all lived up to. Now, this is not at all the case and, in fact, we have only a *contractual illusion* such as we often find in everyday life when we see various cases of manipulation.

For, in this kind of situation, while appearing to be a constraining contract that was freely accepted—an accepted constraint being, as we have seen, the price of liberty—what we really have is a provisional solution to a polemical state. A challenge is a confrontation that is perceived as an affront.

A new problematics now faces the semiotician. It arises out of the need to describe ''in context'' the structures of manipulation, once they have been modalized at the semionarrative level. He must describe those structures as they are inscribed within the framework of their ''historical'' workings. Contrary to what is usually thought, and despite the fading power of the vocabulary that has to do with honor, this concept is more real in modern societies than ever before. Without mentioning the great powers who are afraid of ''losing face,'' and leaving aside the ''high mass'' of weekly sporting events at which national honor seems at stake, this unnamed, implicit, and/or carefully camouflaged concept nowadays shows a diversification and refinement such as to make the heroes of Corneille appear crude. This is even more so for Charlemagne's ''pairs.''

It is analysis of discourse that should eventually allow us to account for this richness. It is discourse, in effect, which by introducing the categories of intensity and aspectuality allows us to order antiphrastic persuasion in graduation— because the least little doubting of his competence will affect the challenged subject's response, a response whose meaning effects, in part because of the danger involved, in part because of the difficulty of the task or the humiliation suffered, are many and varied. The challenge, bringing into play modal organizations that are quite sophisticated, has as corollaries pathemic consequences that are no less important and that, in turn, will require that we engage in new investigations within the semiotics of passions.

Chapter 9
On Nostalgia: A Study in Lexical Semantics

Footfalls echo in the memory
Down the passage which we did not take
Towards the door we never opened
Into the rose-garden . . .
T. S. Eliot, *Burnt Norton*

Preliminaries

If we take that concept of Hjelmslevian theory according to which definitions are simply the expansion of denominations and, therefore, can be substituted for each other, we can imagine the right way to use dictionaries and, more generally, the right way to describe the lexical level of natural languages and can carry out semantic research that will help us to understand better the discursive organization of those languages. As definitions in dictionaries of common usage are not always rigorously constructed, it is obvious that the necessary precautionary measures must be taken. Hence one often needs to complete the methodological approach used by introducing elements of semantic analysis, by reformulating the definitional segments of dictionaries in terms of actantial and narrative structures — in other words, by inscribing the lexical study in a more general epistemological and methodological framework.

Definitions of "Nostalgia"

The first definition the *Petit Robert* gives of "nostalgia" can easily be broken down into three utterance segments:

//"state of wasting away and languor//
   //caused by obsessive longing//
      //(longing) for one's native land,

//for the place where one has long lived"//.

Although the second definition lexicalizes its components in another way, it is possible to recognize the same ternary distribution:

//" . . . melancholy . . . //
  //longing for . . . //
    //(longing) for something past or
    //for what one has not experienced"//.

It is easy to see that we are dealing with (1) a *pathemic state* (wasting away, languor, melancholy) that presupposes (2) another *pathemic state* (longing, obsessive or not) caused, in turn, by (3) a *disjunction with an object of value* (native land, something past, etc.).

We therefore have a three-level syntactic construction that, in spite of the "causality" (which we would like to interpret as logical presupposition) displayed between each level, appears concomitantly as a hierarchical superimposition. We shall examine each of them in turn.

State of Wasting Away

Following the procedure that substitutes definitions for denominations, and referring to the dictionary, we note first of all that we are dealing with the "state of wasting away of a person," which appropriately reminds us that we have before us an utterance of state endowed with a *pathemic subject*.

Although the definition of "wasting away" as the "state of what wastes away" simply refers to the verb, "to waste away" is explained as "to become weakened by gradual wasting." Moreover, the definition of "wasting away" is consolidated by a series of parasynonyms—"weakening, loss of weight, anemia, exhaustion, *languor*"—that are almost the same ones we find when we attempt to define "languor," and even "melancholy." It is interesting to note that these last two lexemes have a dated primary meaning (a pathological state of a somatic nature), which according to Descartes denotes a *bodily passion*: it is only later on, by a "metaphorical" transposition, that these will designate a *passion of the soul*, a *stricto sensu* patheme.

The enumerated parasynonyms themselves all have a common feature, that of /diminishing/, /to diminish/ signifying "to become smaller," whereas the antonyms of "languor"—"activity, animation, ardor, heat, force, life, vivacity"—inform us of the semantic value this diminishing undergoes: we are dealing here with one of the terms of a pair of semantic universals /life/ vs. /death/. In fact, the "state" we are attempting to describe is the *gradual passage* from one state to another—in other words, *becoming*, so dear to Bernard Pottier, which can be apprehended only at the categorical level. It is only when moving to the more surface discursive level, that is, after its inscription in discourse, that the categorical articulation formulated in "states" is *aspectualized* and appears as a *process*. This can be stated as follows:

$$\text{/life/} \rightarrow \text{/durativity/} \rightarrow \text{/detensivity/} \rightarrow \text{/death/}$$

where "life" or "death" represents the terms of a semantic category, and "durativity" and "detensivity," the aspectual notations.

Obsessive Longing

This gradual diminishing of vital forces by which, first of all, nostalgia is defined, is caused by "obsessive longing." We shall now turn to the semanticism of this lexeme, even if it means returning a little later on to the "obsessive" character that overdetermines it.

In the definition of "longing" — "distressing state of awareness caused by the loss of a possession" — we can distinguish two instances, if not two states:

(a) state of awareness
(b) state of distress

The State of Awareness

This "state of *awareness*," which is the "immediate recognition of one's own physical activity," falls under the cognitive dimension — or rather of its meta-cognitive level, since we are dealing with knowledge bearing on its own cognition — of the apprehension of signification. We have here before us a *cognitive metasubject* dominating from on high a cognitive "state of things." This is nothing more than the apprehension of the "loss of a possession," that is, of the disjunction of the subject and the object of value with which he was previously conjoined. The structure of the comparison of the two states of the subject — conjoined and disjoined — carried out by the metasubject, which appears situated on the axis of temporality

$$\underline{S \cap Ov} \qquad \underline{S \cup Ov}$$
$$\text{/past/} \qquad \text{/present/}$$

must therefore be detemporalized and the past made present in the form of a cognitive simulacrum in order to be confronted with the present marked by an absence. The cognitive subject of *lack* (a state well known since Vladimir Propp's work), lexicalized here by "loss" (with its parasynonyms: "misfortune, deprivation, damage, harm," etc.), on the thymic dimension is connoted by *dysphoria*, the "state of distress" of the dictionary.

The State of Distress

(Moral) distress, defined as a "painful feeling or emotion resulting from un-satisfied tendencies, needs" that parallels cognitively recognized lack, can be translated by aspectualized /dysphoria/, in addition to /intensity/, the degree of which will be proportional to the value of the object lost.

In the case of nostalgia, caused by "distressful, obsessive longing," intensity attains an acute degree: *obsessive* longing is what "torments incessantly" and "imposes itself without respite."

The appearance of these active verbs—"to torment" (which denotes origi-nally pragmatic doing), "to torture" (which provokes "bodily passions"), and "to impose oneself" (which designates an ineluctable power "that cannot be rejected")—signals a disruption introduced in the pathemic ensemble described. We can see that by its intensity the dysphoric *subject of state*, which we discov-ered under the lexical cover of *longing*, was transformed into a competent *subject of doing*. The latter was endowed with the modality of being-able, but not pro-grammed to recover the object of value, and to carry out durative and iterative thymic performances of torturing the subject of state whose wasting away he pro-vokes and pursues. The mechanism that we have just analyzed illustrates well a phenomenon that has not been studied enough in narrative semiotics—the trans-formation of the subject of state into a subject of doing—and, following here Jacques Fontanille's suggestions,[1] enables us to investigate the possibility of en-visaging the autonomous existence of the thymic dimension of narrative.

The Convened Simulacrum

We still need to examine a little more closely the status and the form of the "pos-session" whose the loss sets off these pathemic disruptions. We shall remind the reader that the first definition presents *nostalgia* as the "obsessive longing for one's native land, for the place where one has long lived," that is, for objects that, separated in space and time, are both complex and vague. Their figurative representation can evoke familiar landscapes, loved ones, happy moments expe-rienced. The second definition, which is much more general, speaks of the long-ing "for something past" and insists on the accomplished nature, separated from the present of the "something," or of longing "for what one has not experi-enced." If we have understood properly, this corresponds to an imaginary expe-rience that one has not had but that one would *like* to have had. In passing from the first to the second definition, we can see that the shift in meaning, which retains only the temporal distance that needs to be made present, occurs by the suspension of the seme of spatiality.

A more attentive examination of the content of *longing* makes it possible to understand better the status of the object-simulacrum at the origin of nostalgia.

Thus, regret defined as the "sorrow"/"morally distressing state"/ for having done or for not having done (something) in the past" tells us that the regretted object of value appears, or can be interpreted, as a *narrative program* that, once made present and compared with the actual state of the subject, entails unfortunate consequences. We have already noted that the "longing for one's native land" conjured up a series of narrative simulacra of a figurative nature, marked by the conjunction with the subject. In the cases where the NP is considered to be realized (= regret for having done), the dysphoric state resulting from a lack can be situated on the *ethical* plane and be lexicalized either as *remorse* (= regret "accompanied by shame") or as *repentance* ("desire for expiation and reparation"). But it can be without this type of connotation and simply come up against a "state of things" where the subject of *wanting* and *having-to* is powerless to reactivate the former program.

The case of nonrealized NPs (= regret for not having done) is more complex. Although we can obviously also be dealing with a regret of an ethical nature, cases of other figures are possible where the unfinished NP, having "subjective and affective" motivations (cf. reverie), seems to belong to an *aesthetic* isotopy. This type of NP, present in the last definition of "nostalgia" as a succinct form of "unsatisfied desire," has a euphoric connotation: the subject of wanting, with a life project and a program of action sketched out, is in a state of felicitous expectation. The euphoric program, while coming up against *not-being-able* or *not-knowing-how* of conjunction with the desired object of value, nevertheless maintains traces of the happiness glimpsed and, in formulating a "melancholic longing," indicates the complex term /euphoria + dysphoria/ where revivified desire, impossibility of realization, and the sorrow of unfulfillment come together.

Two complementary conditions are necessary for the narrative simulacrum that commands the institution of nostalgia to attain a sufficient degree of generality: the suspension of the temporal link that ties it to the past and the emptying of the object of value, which, while remaining a syntactic object aimed at by the subject, can receive various axiological investments. As Antoine de Saint-Exupéry would say, "Nostalgia is the desire of the ineffable." Without going as far, we can say that the subject of wanting, in his quest for the "happiness of being sad" — this is how Victor Hugo defined melancholy — has a certain liberty in the choice of the values used to feed his imagination.

Summary

The mechanism set in place to produce the complex passional "state of soul" that nostalgia is, can also be represented as a string of states and operations linked together (if we consider the resultant state as the synchronic superimposition and syncretism of the set of pathemic disruptions) by a series of presuppositions, constituting a prior generative moment. The base of this structure that the "state of wasting away" happens to be—which is made up not of state but of a durative process—is the locus of an iterative harassment, carried out by a subject of dysphoric doing. The latter suddenly appears because of intense dysphoria that connotes the cognitive operation of comparison, brought about by the metasubject causing the narrative position of the subject apprehended *hic et nunc* to interface with the narrative simulacrum convened and conveying a primary euphoria. The inadequacy of the two narrative programs sets off the cumulative process that ends up with the discursive subject's distress at a given moment of his trajectory.

Such a description, which is founded on only incomplete and elliptical dictionary definitions, cannot claim to be an exhaustive and reliable model of nostalgia. Nonetheless, it retraces, in the main, the entire configuration of a discursive-subject actor that can be considered as an encompassment within which thymic events put into play differently modalized syntactic subjects and cause determinable pathemic states to appear. Semiotics can hence try and postulate the existence of an autonomous thymic dimension of narrativity that can be syntactically articulated, and thus make it possible to undertake the description of the specific activities constituting an individual's "inner life."

A semantic study based on lexical data nevertheless remains incomplete, if only because analysis can neither be extended to the dimensions of discursive context nor question the *ab quo* situation of the specific disengagement that projects the subject toward an elsewhere the latter conjures up and reengages, thereby duplicating his passional trajectory with an imaginary isotopy. Although some well-known examples of such a convocation—Proust's madeleine, Buñuel's bells in *Belle de jour*—come to mind almost spontaneously, as can be imagined, its mechanism (which has recourse to different sensorial orders) remains very obscure.

A Lexicological Conclusion

This brief study is also a quest for a method. The exploitation of lexical data, simply because the lexematic level of language appears as a condensation underlying expanding discursive sections at all moments, seems immediately viable. The inadequacy of definitions found in dictionaries of common usage introduces hesitations that for the moment only the narrative models of semiotics can rectify. Although the description undertaken opens the way to an understanding of "French-style nostalgia," it does not, perhaps, yet allow us to make the desirable generalizations.

Chapter 10
Ten Years Afterward

Faithfulness and change: it is perhaps somewhat paradoxical for a researcher to want to remain true to himself, while a scientific project is the only domain where the notion of progress makes any sense these days. It is also the domain where renewal is what actually defines every theoretical effort. What meaning can be given to the desire for permanence when the semiotics of our dreams could not be satisfied simply with the pure contemplation of its own concepts, but urgently and at all costs had to get involved and confirm its efficiency by getting a handle on "reality." In this case, the object to be constructed determined to a great extent the objectives of the subject. More than that, however, the constant exercise of judgment we imposed on ourselves inevitably relativized the results obtained and shook our newly acquired certainties. The narrow path chosen became a sinuous route because the episteme of the times, the changing philosophical and ideological points of view, greatly shifted the grounds of its investigations and transformed the status of even the most secure formulations.

It is not without hesitation that we inscribed the number II on the title page of *Du sens*, as it suggests discrete numbers, the radical break between two "states of things." It is therefore advisable to read the distinctness of the title not orally but visually and ordinally, as it is supposed to display not the distance that separates fifteen years of semiotic inquiry but rather the continuity of the enterprise. Hence, the texts grouped in this volume bear witness to the meanderings of a true story, but at the same time and with some luck these landmarks make it possible to reconstitute a real history. The overview in the next few pages is inspired not by a genetic approach that retraces all the researcher's trials and errors but by a generative one. Starting from the end point and working back to the beginning, we have tried to find the main trace and subject of semiotic practice above and beyond specific attempts. This is perhaps the price to be paid if one hopes to reconstitute, or at least to give meaning to, one's own fidelity to self.

An Autonomous Syntax

If we begin with Vladimir Propp's description of the Russian folktale considered as an analogical model that can be interpreted in many ways, we can now reconstitute the major steps in the progress made over the years, giving them a quasi-linear form finalized after the event. We started by giving a *canonical succession of events* a more rigorous formulation than the one conferred on it by the status of the *narrative schema*. When we defined Propp's "functions" as simple utterances, and following Reichenbach interpreted "function" as a relation between actants, the schema appeared as a series of narrative utterances. As the schema unfolded, recurrences and regularities stood out. At the same time it became possible to construct a "grammar," defined as a model that organized and justified the aforementioned regularities. Moreover, the regularities quickly appeared as the projection of paradigmatic categories laid out on the syntagmatic development of discourse. To use a Lévi-Straussian expression, while giving it a certain dynamic orientation, such a framework both controlled and imposed closure on discourse.

An additional step was taken when the *event* was redefined to distinguish it from *action*. Whereas action is dependent only on the subject concerned with the organization of his activity, event can be understood only as the description of this activity by an actant external to action. This external actant is identified first of all with the narrator but, because of the complexity of his function, is then set up as an independent observer-actant accompanying discourse as it unfolds. Such an observer-actant accounts for the establishment and changes of points of view, the inversion of the actors' knowledge about past and future actions and, by aspectualizing them, transforms various activities into processes endowed with historicity.

The recognition of how discourse unfolded freed the subject from the ascendancy of the observer. A new interpretation of *doing* as *act*, and action as program of doing, became possible. Because of the new status the subject acquires in becoming a *nondescript syntactic subject*, the activities of any actors of a narrative, be they subject or helper, sender, representative, or judicator, can now be analyzed. Independent of all links with any specific sequence of the narrative schema inspired by Propp, a new syntax that can calculate simple or complex *narrative programs* (NPs) appears with its base narrative programs regulating the use NPs subordinate to them.

In the same way, the Proppian schema soon underwent another reevaluation. It was considered during the sixties and even now by a great number of narratologists as the model par excellence of narrative. It soon became evident that it was basically a clever interlacing of two narratives that opposed two subjects who, in different ways, each evolved along distinct and opposite paths. The distinction between hero and villain was in fact dependent on the moralizing nature of the narrator. From this time on, semionarrative syntax could take the principle of the confrontation between two subjects from Propp's description and interpret it as an elementary binary structure founded on either the contractual or the polemical — let us say, *polemico-contractual*—relation of two subjects whose paths are destined to cross.

Modal Syntax

In the Proppian schema, the circularity of the displacements of the object of value (of the princess, for example) that, leaving the space of origin, returns after having changed hands and spaces several times, almost inevitably led us to try and give narrative a *topological definition*. It was necessary, however, to reexamine the relations between objects and subjects before such a circulation of objects could give rise to a general and deductive interpretation of narrative, from a syntactic point of view.

A definition of subjects that was neither ontological nor psychological necessarily raised the problem of "semiotic existence." According to the theoretical postulate of the preeminence of relation over terms, we could say that relation alone was sufficient to define the two end terms of subject and object with respect to one another. We could also say that subjects existed only because they were in relation to objects and that, consequently, the first semantic investment subjects were endowed with was simply the value situated in the objects conjoined with them. This being the case, the *circulation of objects* then appeared as a series of conjunctions and disjunctions of the object and successive subjects or, what amounts to the same thing, as *communication between subjects*. The subjects were conjoined with the objects being defined existentially as *subjects of state*.

Yet such a definition of the subject was inadequate, since it remained static and axiological. A syntactic operator was necessary to account for such circulation, or communication. The *subject of doing*, complementary to the *subject of state* that appeared either as two distinct actors or was united in a single actor, emerged in the fullness of its functions. Moreover, axiology could be effective only if it were incarnated in the anthropological subjects of the surface-narrative syntax. Nonetheless, it was obvious they were present. All one had to do was to ask naive questions: What makes subjects pursue objects? They do so because the values invested in the objects are "desirable." How is it that some subjects are more desirous, more capable than others, of obtaining objects of value? It is because they are more competent than others. These trivial formulations, which reveal the existence of a layer of modalizations overdetermining subjects as well as objects, also indicate a remarkable semiotic phenomenon: the modal charge that is supposed to project itself on the predicate by modulating it (producing, for example, the alethic modalities) can be distributed in various ways in the utterance it modifies. When it modifies the subject of doing it constitutes *modal competence*, and when it modifies the object, because the object defines the subject of state, it accounts for the subject's *modal existence*.

If we distribute the modal mass into four modalities of wanting and having to, being able and knowing, we can envisage three series of modalizations: modalizations of utterance (by the mediation of the predicate constituting the utterance); modalizations of the subject of doing; and, finally, modalizations of the object (affecting the subject of a state). We can imagine the consequences of the integration of such modal systems in semiotic syntax freed from Proppian constraints. Whereas formerly we spoke of the circulation of objects, we can now start calculating the unequal modal competence of two subjects faced with an unequally appreciated object of value having its own modal attributions. Instead of being quantitative, change becomes qualitative. When reading Propp we were dealing with highly iconized beings and objects situated on the pragmatic dimension of narrative, but we are now dealing with cognitive competitions and interactions where modally competent subjects covet modalized objects, while the evenemential level of their activities is at most a pretext for much more important confrontations.

New Semiotic Systems

Yet when all is said and done the capacity of the analogical model that the Proppian model happens to be is not exhausted. Communication theory originating in topology can be readily applied to different dimensions defining society, the exchange of goods, but also of services, for example. We do not, however, see what would prevent it from dealing with intersubjective communication concerned with the circulation of the objects of knowledge that messages are. This is possible as long the neutral and unevenly modalized instances of sending and receiving, which partially explain the misunderstandings and the failures of communication between people, are replaced by competent but also motivated subjects directly engaged in the process of communication who exercise, on the one hand, persuasive doing and, on the other, interpretive doing.

The polemico-contractual confrontation that we consider as one of the fundamental organizing structures of the narrative schema is now transposed and established in the very heart of intersubjectivity where it seems to be able to account for the fiduciary, uneasy, groping, and, at the same time, cunning and dominating nature of communication. That the sender of the Proppian narrative appears at both ends of its unfolding and is separated into a mandator and an adjudicator situated at the two poles of the structure of communication—and assigns the subject first of all with a mission, controls his competence during the qualifying test, and then reappears to evaluate and acknowledge the events and deeds—does not change a thing. Communication is a game of role substitution, where, at any given moment, the enunciator assumes the role of enunciatee, and the instance of enunciation syncretizes both competencies.

We then see that the subject's doing proper is confined by two series of modalizable operations, each one activating two syntactic subjects, the first of which accounts for the behavior of the sender and the second, of the receiver-subject. The syntactic interplay itself consists, in the first case, in rendering the subject "competent," and in the second, in "sanctioning" his activity through epistemic judgments. By giving primary importance to a *semiotics of action* that can be either cognitive in nature and consist of a series of language acts, or pragmatic in nature and described as a series of somatico-gestural acts, two autonomous semiotic systems emerge: a *semiotics of manipulation* and a *semiotics of sanction* that are freed from the constraints of the narrative schema, as well as from the restrictions of verbal communication proper.

These new semiotic objects that have not been completely worked out are in fact modal organizations. They are indifferent to invested and manipulated contents, and they can be used as models of predictability in the analysis of verbal and nonverbal texts. They can also be used in the analysis of "behaviors" and "situations" as long as some order or regularity is detected so that they can be considered as signifying sequences.

It seems to us that the rather unexpected success of Proppian schemata can in part be explained by the fact that the Russian folktale, under the guise of various figurative dressings, in fact, dealt with a single obsessive problem, namely, the meaning of the life of an individual solidly entrenched in society. This actually corresponded to the concerns of various literary currents of the time that were ready to adapt a nascent semiology. The schema that initially corresponded to the three *periods* of life—qualification, realization, and recognition—was further refined, for example, by endowing subjects with a combinatory of modalities that constituted and typologized them (J.-C. Coquet).[1] However, the subject's status as an ideological framework for a *life project* was maintained. Subjects could be considered either in terms of the initial constraints defining them (and in this case their modal organization would evoke a genetic mechanism), or in terms of their divergent but predictable journey through life. New analyses of literary texts can only enrich the problematics of the *construction of the subject*.

A *semiotics of the object* must correspond to a *semiotics of the subject* concerned both with formulating his possible trajectories and topologically schematizing them. At first glance, problems related to appropriating and constructing objects seem to be situated at two distinct levels: the perception and the transformation of the world. Although it is no longer necessary to insist on the primordial role of subjects who, at the moment of perceiving see beyond objects and construct the natural world as they please, the problematics can nevertheless be turned around by asserting the "prior presence" of the figures of the world, which, because of their "salient" and "pregnant" nature (to use René Thom's terminology),[2] would not only incite, but would also actively participate in, the construction of subjects (Lévi-Strauss). No matter how alarming it can seem, this return of the pendulum will perhaps once again permit semiotics to exceed its set limits, if only, for example, by investigating the possibilities of an objectal, if not objective, aesthetics.

This transformation of the world and the question as to how objects come into being are naturally part of the domain of semiotics. Food, clothing, lodging—the primary concerns of individuals—have populated the natural world with manipulated matter and constructed objects. Their construction seems to follow the relatively simple model of the subject projecting a modalized value on them and subsequently supplying them with object covers by means of more or less complex programs of doing. Yet research attempting to explain and codify the "primitive" operations by which the subject exercises his ascendancy over nature has hardly begun. The way in which the subject manipulates the basic cosmological elements—water, fire, air, and earth—by making them act on one another or on the objects to be constructed (cooking by fire, rotting by water, etc., to mention only Lévi-Strauss's fundamental contribution), the elementary procedures of liquification and solidification, of kneading and mixing, make it possible for us to imagine a true "alchemy of nature" that can serve as the deep level of a figurative semiotics whose need is felt when reading poetic as well as scientific discourses.

The analysis of the discourse of experimental sciences currently being undertaken by Françoise Bastide[3] has both progressively brought to light these elementary operations and at the time increased the possibilities of working out an "objectal" syntax, by making other natural or already constructed objects come to the fore that in more complex programs perform the roles of operative or mediatory actants. Experiments appear as narrated events that reveal their true status of cognitive operations and end up constructing new objects of knowledge of a conceptual nature.

We can therefore see that the difficultly acquired autonomy of syntax transformed semiotic practice from top to bottom. At first it was cautiously concerned with elaborating and rigorously formulating a small number of canonical sequences. In the strategy of research adopted, it has progressively and slowly constructed new procedures and new ideal objects that are replacing semiotic explorations defined both by the channels of transmission of their signifiers and by the cultural domains they articulate.

Modal Semiotics

These semiotic systems have the distinctive characteristic of taking on the aspect of syntactic chains whose goal is to define and interdefine the principal semiotic actants: subject, object, sender, and receiver. This justifies in a formal manner, after the fact, the *molar actantial structure* that served as the starting point for the construction of narrative semiotics. As can be expected, considerable use is made of the modalities and their organization, but their paradigmatic definitions and their syntagmatic strings are more the concern of specific modal semiotics.

Deontic semiotics, which from the very beginning attempted to define its specificity, is the first of these semiotics, only because it appears to be the least questionable thanks to the existence of a logic having the same name. Deontic semiotics considers the values of modal logic simply as denominations underlying their syntactic definitions (interdiction, for example, being defined as a /having-not-to-do/), and situates its operations at a deeper level than logic. It is not satisfied with simple operations of substitution, but seeks to work out syntactic series with "increases in meaning" insofar as discourse retains the prior modal gains in its "memory."

When we attempt to apply such a semiotics to actual discourses, however, its homogeneity is often illusory. Hence, in the example chosen by chance for our analysis, legal discourse that is deontic to the *n*th degree had the following title: "the voluntary termination of pregnancy." After a series of persuasive manipulations, this title not only substituted a /not-having-to-do/ for a /having-to-do/, but in ways that need to be specified, manifested an individual /wanting-to-do/. If jurisdiction that begins to control the "voluntary acts" of its citizens appears somewhat suspect, it still indicates the absence of a *volitive semiotics* that is lacking in the analysis in question.

For the longest time semiotics refrained from dealing with anything that was even remotely connected with the domain of psychology. This bias, which was totally justified in the beginning when it was necessary to define the actants as simple "active agents" freed from the secular straitjacket of psychological determinations of "characters" and "temperaments," is no longer imperative. On the contrary, the absence of analytic tools when one tackles paper sentiments and passions, encountered in discourse, now appears as an arbitrary methodological limitation. Hence, the internal demands of the development of semiotics, to which should be added the ongoing refusal by psychoanalysis to work out a metapsychology that Freud himself longed for, forced us to undertake a systematic examination of the *theories of passions* that are present as integrating phenomena in all the major systems of classical philosophy. We noted that until Nietzsche and Freud all these theories had a common feature. Independently of the choice and of the hierarchy of the "passional" values they articulated, they were all *taxonomic* in nature and appeared as more or less successful lexematic classifications.

The temptation was great to give appropriate syntactic definitions to these lexeme passions and to their discursive expansions. We first noticed that, contrary to the implicit postulations of these classical theories, one rarely encountered "solitary" passions. They were almost never linked to a single subject, and their syntactic description always called for the establishment of an actantial structure. We then noted that the semiotic interpretation of these passions was almost exclusively undertaken in terms of modalities. The affectivity emanating from reading verbal or somatic texts could then be considered as a *semantic effect*, produced by pathemic structures of a modal nature. This was all the more the case as the boundary between what was considered pathemic and what was not was never clearly established, and the attitudes of various societies toward the question changed in space and time (if, for example, *avarice* had lived on as a passion until now, its contrary, *generosity*, the passion par excellence in the sixteenth and seventeenth centuries, has lost its affective force). Undeniable cultural relativism confirms what we have just said regarding semantic effects. Against the general backdrop of more or less complicated modal mechanisms—"attitudes" or "states"—each society traces the contents of its particular pathemic configuration, interpreted as a connotative social reading grid, whose task, among others, is to facilitate intersubjective and social communication.

The interpretation of the passions with the help of modal syntax constitutes a methodological tool making a more refined analysis of discourses possible. It also offers general semiotics new possibilities: for example, the hypothesis according to which the form of content of musical discourses would be pathemic in nature and could therefore be described as a syntagmatics of the modal systems of a semisymbolic language seems to be extremely promising. But the important aspect of this epistemological advance resides in possibly exploiting the analyses of passional discourses with the aim of constructing what, for want of a better term, we continue to call volitive semiotics.

Pursuing this insight, we naturally are able to account for a modal mass that can be articulated as a *semiotics of power* (being-able-to-do and being-able-to-be). Fortunately, this vast domain has already been explored by Michel Foucault, whose rich and pertinent analyses are often carried to an extreme by the ideological motivations of the philosopher and his disciples.

Perplexity is perhaps the word best suited to describe the attitude of someone faced with the problematics of *knowledge*, because the few certitudes one has appear so shaky today. Were it not for the fear of using pedantic terms we could speak of a radical change in the episteme that was taking place without our being totally aware of it and that consists in the substitution of the concept of efficacy for the fundamental one of truth. Far from having a uniquely technological origin, efficacy, considered not so much as a conquest but rather as a process enabling one to obtain results by taking into account all the explicit preconditions, in our age certainly benefits from the dominance of doing over being. In the domain of semiotics, it is already implicitly present in Hjelmslev's principle of empiricism and, in a more explicit manner, in the predictive requirement of generative grammar, where it sanctions the global enterprise of scientific practice.

Applied to our current preoccupations, efficacy takes on the name of *assumed communication*, which we borrowed from Lacan. In fact, communication is not a simple transfer of knowledge but a persuasive and interpretive enterprise situated within a polemico-contractual structure. It is founded on the fiduciary relation governed by the more explicit instances of believing and making believe, where confidence in individuals and in their words is certainly more important than "well-turned" phrases or truth conceived of as an external reference.

For communicational semiotics understood in this way, truth and its values are situated within discourse, where they represent knowledge, one of the domains of modal articulation. But then logical discourse as well as the "monstrative" discourse of science (the former governed more by knowing-how-to-be and the latter by knowing-how-to-do) occupy a space assigned to them by the primary condition of the efficacy of communication within the framework of global discursivity. A logico-monstrative *modal semiotics of knowledge* would then fulfill the function of providing the proper modal material or discourses of conviction—for example, much in the same way that volitive semiotics does for discourses of seduction, or the semiotics of power, for discourses of domination and provocation.

It is somewhat banal to say that the different modal semiotics, whose place and vague outlines have just been sketched in the general theory but have not all been worked out to the same degree, are not realized in a pure state in actual discourses and that the various modalities and/or their canonical sequences cross over and intermingle with one another. In fact, these semiotics are constructions that have only a virtual existence and belong to the universe of discourse as they are situated upstream, so to speak, from the instance of enunciation. Discourse draws on them as from a reservoir to constitute complex grammatical models and then attend to the various matters we attempted partially to identify when we spoke about specific semiotic systems.

Although theoretical reflection may be fruitful, it has the inconvenience of almost always outstripping the concepts it creates and the terms used to designate them. The concept of *narrativity* is perhaps the best example of this found in the semiotic domain. Its sole ambition at the beginning was to concentrate on a single class of narrative discourses, and to do so it naturally attempted to construct a narrative syntax. It was then noted that it could equally be used to account for all sorts of discourses: hence all discourse became "narrative" discourse. From that moment on narrativity was emptied of its conceptual content.

The same thing more or less happened *mutatis mutandis* with the instrumental concept of the *cognitive dimension* of discourses, which, at least in the beginning, enabled one to distinguish between descriptions of individuals participating in events and therefore falling under the purview of the pragmatic dimension and descriptions of their knowledge and its manipulations. However, things became complicated rather quickly. For example, we noticed that between subject-heroes and their doing, there existed a semiotic space that had to be filled by what we called modal competence. Even though it often brought out the modality of knowing-how-to-do, it could also include other modalizations. We could see that these modalities were not in the least "pragmatic" and that the definition of the subject—and we could say as much about the other semiotic actants—became a "cognitive" matter. It quickly became apparent that on the whole, surface-narrative syntax could be interpreted in terms of modal syntax, which in turn covered the entire cognitive dimension. The remainder that was part of the pragmatic dimension could probably be attributed to the semantic component of the grammar. Following the interpretation of the passions using modal structures, all affectivity was integrated into the cognitive dimension. Then, knowledge was replaced by the fiduciary as the support of all communication; by reducing the cognitive proper to the status of discursivity, all that remained of the "cognitive" in the cognitive dimension proper was the name, a metaterm defining a conceptual organization articulated in a totally different manner. It is as though after ten or so years of collective effort the heuristic value of certain instrumental concepts were exhausted and a new project, the construction of a semiotic modal syntax, one that can create its own problematics and define new semiotic objects, took over.

Whether we are dealing with a crisis that can be attributed to growth or a decisive turnabout, a new profile of semiotics is slowly being developed.

Notes

Notes

Foreword

1. A. J. Greimas and J. Courtés, *Semiotics and Language, An Analytical Dictionary*, trans L. Crist, D. Patte, et al. (Bloomington: Indiana University Press, 1982), p. 70. For definitions and interdefinitions of terms used both by Greimas and in this foreword, readers should consult this work.

2. In Greimas, *On Meaning: Selected Writings in Semiotic Theory*, trans. Paul Perron and Frank Collins (Minneapolis: University of Minnesota Press, 1987), pp. 3–16.

3. *Semiotics and Language*, p. 41.

4. Ibid., p. 42.

5. For an overview of the development of the general theory see the first ten chapters of *On Meaning*.

6. Unpublished paper, "Universaux et narrativité," given at a colloquium on the universals of narrativity held at the University of Toronto, June 1984.

7. In *On Meaning*, pp. 165–79.

8. Greimas and Courtés, *Semiotics and Language*, p. 302.

9. In *On Meaning*, pp. 204–13.

10. See "The Pathways of Knowledge" and the chapters in A. J. Greimas and E. Landowski, *Introduction à l'analyse du discours en sciences sociales* (Paris: Hachette, 1979), that examine, among others, texts by Claude Lévi-Strauss, Marcel Mauss, Lucien Febvre, Gaston Bachelard, Maurice Merleau-Ponty, Pierre Francastel, and Roland Barthes.

11. In *On Meaning*, pp. 192–203.

Chapter 1. The Meaning of Meaning

1. By isotopy, we generally understand a network of semantically redundant categories that are subject to the discourse considered. Two discourses can be isotopic but not isomorphic.

2. See *Structural Semantics: An Attempt at a Method*, trans. Daniel McDowell, Ronald Schlaifer, and Alan Velie (Lincoln: University of Nebraska Press, 1983).

Chapter 2. On Scientific Discourse in the Social Sciences

1. See Gilberte Gagmon, "Contribution à l'analyse lexico-sémantique d'un corpus des sciences de la terre: domaine français" (thesis) 1973, doctorat de troisième cycle, Paris).

2. Because the problem of truth is situated within discourse, we should speak in its connection about *truth saying*, in other words *veridiction*. The knowledge possessed by the subject of enunciation, as it is projected throughout its discourse, is in turn modalized into *true* or *false*, into *secret* or *lie*, and it is overdetermined by the modality of *believing* (persuading/assuming).

3. By "anaphora" we generally mean the recurrence, in a given phrase of discourse, of certain specific elements. This recurrence allows for the implicit reprise of contents that have already been uttered, or it can anticipate contents that are to be uttered at a later stage. The setting into place, by the subject of discourse, of this mechanism (which we consider to be one of the forms of discursive organization), will be called "anaphorization."

Chapter 3. The Pathways of Knowledge

1. See A. J. Greimas and E. Landowski, *Introduction à l'analyse du discours en sciences sociales* (Paris: Hachette, 1979), with texts by Greimas, Eric Landowski, Sorin Alexandrescu, Jean-François Bordron, Jean-Claude Coquet, Joseph Courtés, Ivan Darrault, Jean-Marie Floch, Jacques Geninasca, Pierre Geoltrain, Jean-Claude Giroud, and Louis Panier.

2. [The authors refer here to *Introduction à l'analyse du discours*. —Trans.]

3. As was shown in an analysis presented orally by Paolo Fabbri during one of the sessions of the Seminar at the Ecole des Hautes Etudes en Sciences Sociales (1976). Unfortunately this presentation was not written up.

4. [See note 2, this chapter. —Trans.]

Chapter 4. On Chance Occurrences in What We Call the Social Sciences

1. In adopting the term "narratee," proposed by Gerard Genette, we are suggesting that the terminology for enunciation be rounded out by introducing a pair of presupposed and implicit actants: *narrator* and *narratee*, set into and manifested within discourse through *actantial disengagement*.

2. Elsewhere we have already proposed ways of identifying the nature of this cognitive doing that is *nonmodalized* and which we called "informative doing."

Chapter 6. The Semiotic Analysis of Legal Discourse: Commercial Laws That Govern Companies and Groups of Companies

1. This study was undertaken in 1970 at the request of the Centre de recherche sur les droits des affaires of the Paris Chamber of Commerce and Industry. The research team was made up of Gérard Bucher, Claude Chabrol, and Paolo Fabbri. Eric Landowski analyzed their results.

2. As a matter of fact, the entire text of Law No. 66–537 of July 24, 1966, contains 509 articles and is 140 pages long. Segments that actually refer to groups of companies are disseminated in some of the articles in question. The final state of the analysis made it impossible for us to restore all the segments constituting the actual corpus of the text. However, to facilitate the reading of the analysis we have translated some, or parts, of the articles we considered to be germane.

3. *Article 1*: "The commercial nature of a company is determined by its form or by its purpose. . . . The form, the duration cannot exceed 99 years; the trade name or the name, the head office, the commercial object, and the amount of capital are determined by the statutes of the company."

4. *Article 5*: "Commercial companies enjoy the right to legal status [in French, *personnalité morale*] from the date of their registration at the Trade Register. The normal transformation of a company does not entail the creation of a new legal status [in French, *personne morale*]. The same holds

with respect to its protraction. Persons having acted on behalf of a company being established before it has acquired the right to legal status [*personnalité morale*] are indefinitely responsible for the acts so accomplished, unless the company after having been regularly constituted and registered assumes the subscribed indentures.''

5. See Chapter 13 of our *On Meaning: Selected Writings in Semiotic Theory*, ''On Evenemential History.''

6. See our article ''Comment définir les indéfinis,'' in *Etudes de linguistique appliquée*, 2 (1963), pp. 110–25.

7. *Article 26*: ''The statutes of a company must contain the following indications:

1. The sum or the value of the contributions of all the joint holders;
2. The share in this sum or this value of each joint holder, whether an active or a sleeping partner;
3. The global shares of the active partners and the shares of each sleeping partner in the distribution of benefits and in the profits due to the winding up of the company.''

8. See *Article 1*, note 3.

9. *Article 35*: ''The capital of this company must be at least 20,000 francs. It must be divided into equal company shares, the sum of which cannot be less than the sum determined by decree.'' *Article 37*: ''All the joint holders of a company must take part in the founding act of the company, either in person or by proxy.''

10. *Articles 423–489* deal with this. *Article 423*: ''Will be punished by a prison term of from two to six months and a fine of from 2,000 to 40,000 francs or one of the above, the joint holders of a limited company who, knowingly in carrying out their duties have made a false declaration regarding the distribution of company shares between the joint holders, the paying up of shares or the deposit of funds, or who have omitted this declaration.''

11. *Article 157*: ''The ordinary general meeting meets at least once a year, six months before the end of the financial year, except when prolongated by legal decision. After reading its report, the Board of Directors or the Director, as is the case, presents to the meeting the general working accounts, the accounts of profits and losses, and the balance sheet. Moreover, the auditors state in their report the carrying out of their duties as defined in Article 228. The meeting deliberates and decides on all questions related to the accounts of the financial year. It exercises the powers attributed to it notably by Articles 90, 94, and 108, or by Articles 134, 137, 140, 145, and 147. It authorizes the issuing of stocks and bonds.''

12. *Article 98*: ''The Board of Directors has the widest of all powers to act on behalf of the company in all circumstances; it exercises these powers within the limits of the company's objectives and subject to those expressly attributed by law to the assembly of shareholders. The disposition of the statutes limiting the powers or the Board of Directors cannot be opposed by third parties.''

13. *Article 358*: ''A share-holding company cannot hold shares in another company if it holds more than 10 percent of the capital of that company. A company that holds more than 10 percent of the capital of another company must inform that company as stated by decree. If there is not agreement between the interested companies to normalize their situation, the company holding the smallest fraction of the capital of the other must divest its investment. If the reciprocal investments are identical, each of the companies must reduce its own so that it does not exceed 10 percent of the other's capital. When a company must divest its shares in another company, the divestment takes place within the time frame determined by decree.''

14. *Article 82*: ''Each subscriber has a number of votes equal to the shares subscribed, without exceeding ten. The authorized representative of a subscriber has the same number of votes under the same conditions.''

15. *Article 354*: ''When a company controls more than half the capital of another company, the latter is considered as a subsidiary of the other.'' *Article 355*: ''When a company controls a fraction

of the capital between 10 and 50 percent of another company, the former is considered as having a share in the other.''

Chapter 7. Toward a Topological Semiotics

1. This is inspired in part by a stimulating text by Alain Renier that appeared in *Sémiotique de l'espace*, published by *l'Institut de l'environment* (Paris, 1974), pp. 23–32.

2. See *Sémiotique de l'espace*.

Chapter 8. The Challenge

1. *Maupassant, The Semiotics of Text* (Amsterdam and Philadelphia: John Benjamins, 1988), p. 182.

2. *Ibid.*, p. 184.

3. ''Toward a Theory of Modalities'' in *On Meaning: Selected Writings in Semiotic Theory*, trans. Paul Perron and Frank Collins (Minneapolis: University of Minnesota Press, 1987), pp. 121–39.

Chapter 9. On Nostalgia: A Study in Lexical Semantics

1. Jacques Fontanille, ''Toward an Anthropomorphic Narrative Topos,'' in *Paris School Semiotics I: Theory*, ed. P. Perron and F. Collins (Amsterdam and Philadelphia: John Benjamins, 1989), pp. 61–87.

Chapter 10. Ten Years Afterward

1. See J.-C. Coquet, *Sémiotique littéraire* (Paris: Mame, 1973).

2. See R. Thom, ''Cyclical Structures in Semiotics,'' in P. Perron and F. H. Collins (eds.), *Paris School Semiotics I: Theory* (Amsterdam and Philadelphia: John Benjamins, 1989), pp. 213–34.

3. See F. Bastide, ''On Demonstration,'' in P. Perron and F. H. Collins (eds.), *Paris School Semiotics II: Practice* (Amsterdam and Philadelphia: John Benjamins, 1989), pp. 109–43.

Index

Index

Compiled by Gitahi Gititi

193

Algirdas Julien Greimas, French semiotician of Lithuanian origin, is professor of general semiotics at the Ecole des Hautes Etudes en Sciences Sociales in Paris, where he has been director of studies since 1965. His other books available in English are *Semiotics and Language: An Analytical Dictionary* (with J. Courtés, Indiana University Press, 1982), *Structural Semantics* (University of Nebraska Press, 1983), *On Meaning: Selected Writings* (Minnesota, 1987), *Maupassant: The Semiotics of Text* (John Benjamins, 1988), and *On Gods and Men* (Indiana University Press, 1989).

Paul Perron is professor of French at the University of Toronto. He is co-author of *Balzac, Sémiotique du personnage romanesque* and editor and translator of Greimas's *Maupassant*. **Frank Collins** is associate professor of French at Toronto and co-translator, with Perron, of Greimas's *On Meaning* (Minnesota, 1987). They both are editors of the forthcoming title *Paris School Semiotics I Theory and II Practice*.

Paolo Fabbri is a professor at the Istituto di Filosofia di Palermo and the Collège International de Philosophie in Paris.